Traveling with Asperger

John Lecher Zapata

Prairie Muse Books
Lincoln, Nebraska

©2025
All rights reserved.
This is an original work based on true characters.
Names, characters, places, and incidents
are the product of the author's experience.
Any resemblance to other persons is entirely coincidental.

No part of this book may be used in another work, with the
exception of critical reviews, may not be copied in whole or in part,
or stored physically or electronically without permission

Prairie Muse Books Inc
Cover by John Lecher Zapata

TRAVELING WITH ASPERGER
Author John Lecher Zapata
ISBN 978-1-952911-77-4

Dedication

This book is the reflection of fifteen years of my heart, a collection of words, memories, and moments gathered from a lifetime of travels across the world. It tells the story not only of the roads I've taken, but of the people who walked beside me, Colleen, Laura, two women whose love and presence helped shape the man I became.

From Colleen, I learned strength, devotion, and the meaning of family. What I learned from her, I carried forward with Laura. Every page carries a piece of those lessons, the laughter, the tears, and the quiet moments that changed me.

My dedication to Colleen is filled with gratitude and reflection, and with my deepest apology for the hurt I caused through my infidelity. Thank you for sharing your life with me. Deep down, I know there were times you wished life would have taken you down a different road. Yet despite it all, your grace, patience, and quiet strength left a lasting imprint on my soul. You will always be part of my story.

To Laura, I dedicate this book to you, my companion, through life's most challenging and tender seasons. Your kindness, care, and unwavering devotion have been my comfort through pain and my joy through uncertainty. Through you, I found peace, purpose, and the will to keep moving forward when I thought I could not. To both of you, your love and your lessons have guided me more than you will ever know. This book reflects that road, and the hearts that gave me the courage to travel it.

With love, respect, and eternal gratitude,

John

Table of Contents

Dedication.............................iii
Table of Contents v
Introduction vii
Asperger 9
My Early Years 11
My Home in Spain...................... 16
Barcelona............................. 20
They Called Me Tiliti.................. 23
The Vrbka's 27
Gordon Ranch 31
Chadron Public Schools
   were not prepared for John.............. 34
The Cave 40
The Navy 42
My First Trip to Europe................ 51
Pampers............................... 63
Business 101 68
Yankton 74
2002 The European Harley Adventure 80
2003 Harley Ride 94
2004 Journey to the Olympic Games....... 104

Jeep Ride Through Europe	119
Jeep to Tbilisi	156
Jeep Trip Through Kazakhstan	166
One Lousy Salmon	196
Hong Kong	207
Bangkok/Phuket	216
Cambodia	226
Singapore	230
2012 Olympics	237
Costa Rica/Belize/Cuba	243
The Age of 77	248
Solitude	250
Last Vacation	253
The love of my life	255
My CHILDREN	284
Milagros	289
If you only knew	293
Laura: Breath of Fresh Air	298
My Stroke	302
Reflecting	305
Obituary of John Lecher Zapata	308

VI

Introduction

EVERY LIFE TELLS A STORY, BUT NOT EVERY STORY IS TOLD. Mine began in a small fishing village in Spain and carried me across the ocean to an unknown place called Nebraska. From the crowded streets of Spain to the wide plains of Nebraska, I have lived a life of contrast, one foot in the past, the other always reaching for what comes next.

I often wonder how a boy born into poverty to a single mother, raised among angler uncles and a gay uncle who cared for me like a father, managed to find his way. My life was never about money but about helping those who needed help. My social skills were not on par with others in my immediate family, and perhaps that question why me, why this path, is what drives me to write. Life has not always been kind to me, but it has been generous in its lessons. Every loss, every heartbreak, every triumph has shaped me into the man I am today: a husband, a father, a builder, a dreamer, and, in these pages, a storyteller.

This book is not just about the places I have seen or the people I have met; it is about how those experiences changed me. It is about survival and reinvention, the fear of not being able to provide for one's family, the courage to keep going. Even after a stroke, when half the body refuses to move, the spirit can still travel freely. Love can arrive late in life and still feel like destiny.

My story is not perfect, life never is, but it is real. I write with the hope that others might find a piece of themselves in these pages: the same fears, the same laughter, the same stubborn will to keep going.

So, this is my introduction, not to who I was, but to who I have become.

1

Asperger

Asperger's, now generally considered part of the autism spectrum, often affects social skills, communication, and the ability to understand unspoken rules. People tend to process the world differently. They may excel in certain structured environments but struggle with relationships, emotional connections, and day-to-day interactions. While many can thrive in specific areas of life, challenges often appear in unexpected ways, particularly in relationships, work, and navigating social cues.

Looking back on my own life, I can now see how Asperger's shaped many of my experiences. In marriage, school, my time in Yankton, in the Navy, and in business, traits of Asperger's — rigid thinking, difficulty with unstructured situations, and a preference for routine — played a role in how I interacted with others. I learned to rely on rules and patterns to make sense of the world, often finding comfort in structure when emotions or social interactions became overwhelming. My business life and personal relationships were both deeply affected by this.

Traveling together with Colleen seemed to be easier than living day-to-day at home. Away from the pressures of kids, responsibilities, and outside influences, I could focus on the present moment. Travel provided enough structure while still allowing me to enjoy the freedom of new experiences. In that setting, I often felt more connected and less weighed down by the constant pressures that Asperger's magnified in everyday family life.

As I grew older, I came to understand that Asperger's influenced not just my career or relationships, but my ability to form deeper friendships as well. My connections with people were often shallow unless someone was willing to put in the effort to really know me. Short-term relationships became easier than long-term commitments. On the road, I could have a conversation with someone new without the pressure of having to maintain a lasting connection. Yet, when I tried to carry that same relationship further, I often stumbled.

It was not until after thirty years of marriage that I finally realized I had Asperger's. By then, many of the struggles in my personal life began to make sense. If my partner and I had known earlier, we could have approached things differently, working through misunderstandings with more awareness and compassion. But at the time, neither of us understood the reasons behind the challenges.

Asperger's also affected friendships, travel, and relationships with colleagues. The tendency to focus on one's own thoughts and routines often meant missing subtle cues from others. While it gave me strength in business and in structured situations, it created distance in more personal aspects of life. Over time, I learned that the same qualities that helped me succeed professionally could create roadblocks in intimacy and understanding.

Today, I can reflect on my journey with clearer eyes. Asperger's is not just a label but a lens through which I can better understand the successes and struggles of my past. It has shaped who I am, influenced every stage of my life, and given me a unique perspective on relationships, work, and the meaning of connection.

2

My Early Years

I was born Juan José Zapata Sucino on March 1, 1954, in the coastal fishing town of Puerto de Santa María, in the province of Cádiz, nestled within the sun-washed region of Andalucía, Spain. My beginning was humble and uncertain. I was the child of a young woman barely eighteen, Milagro Zapata Sucino, whose beauty and quiet strength shaped every part of my early life. My father's identity was never clear. Some whispered it might have been my Uncle Juan Zapata, the lively flamenco dancer whose spirit filled every room, while my mother insisted it was a married taxi driver named Alfredo. My wife Colleen once suggested an even darker possibility, that my mother had been taken advantage of by her own father. Whatever the truth, I carried both my mother's name and her courage.

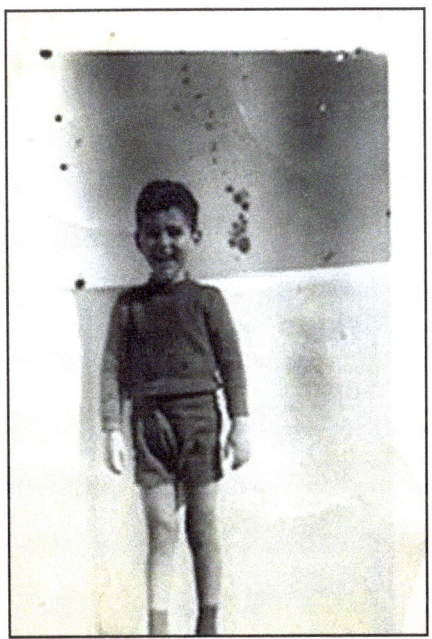

I was baptized in the Iglesia Mayor Prioral, the grand cathedral at the heart of Puerto, just steps from our small home. Fifty years later, I would return to that same cathedral to witness my grandson, Christian Lecher, baptized there, a moment that bridged generations and reminded me how far we had come from those narrow Spanish streets.

We lived in a crowded two-room apartment with my widowed grandfather, my aunt Teresa, and her husband Manolo, their many children, and my uncles Juan and Pepe. At times, fourteen of us shared that space, with no running water and only a communal bathroom at the back of the building. Still, amid hardship there was laughter. The marble-paved courtyard became our playground and gathering place, filled with the sounds of neighbors, who were like an extended family.

My grandfather worked as a mason, proud of his craft but burdened by drink. His temper could be fierce, and more than once he threw my mother and me out into the street. Yet my mother's determination never faltered. She worked long hours cleaning houses in both Puerto de Santa María and nearby Rota, doing whatever she could to feed us. In that perseverance, she gave me the first example of resilience I would ever know.

Over the years, our family grew. My mother had five children — myself, Maria, Millie, and Bobby, though one baby tragically died at birth. She found kindness in people who helped her. Maria was cared for by a woman named Carmen, while Millie stayed with another. I remained always by my mother's side. She used to laugh and say that no one else could keep up with me.

Eventually, the old building began to crumble, and families moved away. My Uncle Pepe stayed behind in our grandfather's room even after the power was shut off. He died young from liver failure, leaving a daughter, Mila Zapata, who remains close to our family to this day.

When I returned with Colleen decades later, we stood before that same building. The marble courtyard was cracked, weeds pushing through the stone, but memories seemed to whisper from every wall. My cousin Jesús removed the heavy metal door knocker as a keepsake. It rests today in Chadron, Nebraska, a small piece of my Spanish childhood preserved across an ocean.

My maternal grandmother, Milagros Sucino Ramírez, had died at thirty-eight during the years of the Spanish Civil War. The official cause was a heart attack, though whispers in the family said otherwise. Even as a child, I felt the sadness her absence left behind.

When I was still small, my mother met Robert Lecher, an American Navy sailor stationed in Rota. He was steady, kind in his way, and offered my mother something she had rarely known, security. Together they would give our family a new beginning. Robert adopted all of us, Maria, Millie, and me, so that we could emigrate with him to the United States.

When my stepfather was transferred to Barcelona, we followed. My Uncle Juan, still dancing and filled with energy, lived there too, and brought joy wherever he went. My stepfather had been reassigned after a disciplinary issue with the Navy, yet my mother stood by him. It was in Barcelona that she and Robert were married, and the adoption papers were finalized.

From there we took the train to Madrid, my Uncle Juan traveling with us. My new name, John Lecher Zapata, had already been written onto the records that would take us to America. Our journey carried us from the salt air of Spain to a place I could scarcely imagine, Chadron, Nebraska.

Chadron was quiet, cold, and endlessly vast. The streets felt empty compared to the busy courtyards of Puerto. We were poor again, but this time surrounded by open land instead of neighbors. My stepfather struggled to find steady work, but his father, Albert Lecher, whom I would come to know and love as Grandpa Albert, offered us a foundation. He became the first man in my life to show me what gentle strength looked like.

Those early years in Nebraska shaped me. I was curious, restless, and often misunderstood. I did not know it then, but I was living with Asperger's Syndrome, a quiet difference that would influence every decision of my life.

I would not hear the word Asperger's until my fifties. It happened by chance in a counseling session I attended with my wife Colleen. As the counselor described its traits, something in me stirred. For the first time,

I saw myself reflected in someone else's words — the focus, intensity, the difficulty connecting in ways others found natural. Suddenly, so many moments from my life began to make sense.

Asperger's is not an illness; it is simply another way of being. It has brought challenges, loneliness, miscommunication, emotional distance, but also gifts: focus, persistence, creativity, and an unyielding will to survive. A former employee once said to me, "Every time you fall, John, you land on your feet." I did not understand then, but he was right. I have always found a way forward, even when the world makes little sense.

That determination carried me through business and through hardship alike. It helped me build a career when no one would hire me, but it also cost me peace at times. I often pushed too hard, misunderstood the emotions of those around me, and mistook stubbornness for strength. It took years and Colleen's patience for me to see the difference.

When she returned to school to study mental health, she began to understand me in ways neither of us ever had. Her compassion, coupled with her knowledge, may have saved our marriage. She no longer saw me as cold or distant but as someone whose mind worked differently. Through her eyes, I learned forgiveness, for myself most of all.

Even now, my thoughts wander constantly, exploring ideas, memories, and possibilities. Yet through every chapter of my life, the one constant has been Colleen. She has given me balance, purpose, and love that endures even when I fail to express it well. My world has always revolved around two pillars, family and work, and she has stood at the center of both.

Asperger's has made me think freely, to see patterns others overlook. I sometimes imagine a thousand computers on an assembly line, each wired the same, except one. That one does not fail; it simply operates differently. That is what Asperger's is. It is not broken, it is unique.

Still, there is a quieter side to it: the loneliness of being misunderstood, the comfort found in solitude. My man cave has become my refuge, a place where I can think freely and find calm.

Once, while sailing on a ferry from Venice to Patra, I noticed a young man speaking softly to himself, carrying on a full conversation with an imaginary friend. His father sat nearby reading, at ease with his son's world. Watching them, I felt a deep compassion, a recognition of difference without judgment. That encounter reminded me how fortunate I was, and it inspired me to finally author my story.

I never saw that young man again, but I will always be thankful for his presence. In a way, he gave me permission to look inward and to speak honestly about what it means to live a life both ordinary and extraordinary.

So, who am I? I am the boy born into poverty in a crumbling Spanish courtyard, the young immigrant who crossed an ocean in search of a future, the man who built his life through trial and stubborn faith, and the husband who learned that love is not always spoken in words. I am John Lecher Zapata, shaped by the roads I have traveled, the people who loved me, and the quiet understanding that, in the end, every life no matter how imperfect, is its own miracle.

3

My Home in Spain

The first home I remember was not a grand house or a quiet neighborhood, but an aging building in Puerto de Santa María, Spain, filled with the sounds of life, crying babies, clattering dishes, and the smell of sea air drifting in from the bay. My earliest memories are of that place, the cracked walls, the narrow stairway that echoed in footsteps, and the neighbors who looked after one another like family. It was there that my story began.

When the building was eventually condemned, the families were scattered throughout the city, and only my Uncle Peppe remained, living in that single room rent-free and using it whenever he needed. For me, that old building became a symbol of everything that would later define my early years — impermanence, resilience, and the constant sense of being caught between two worlds, the old Spain that raised me and the American life that awaited us.

One of the darkest moments in my memory, something I still do not know was a dream or reality, took place during those years. I see myself standing at the end of a train platform on a dark night, holding Tito Juan's hand as we watched my mother pull away on the rear platform of a train, waving as if she were leaving me forever. I asked her about that night many times over the years, but she always claimed no recollection of it. For more than fifty years, that vision has haunted me, and I still do not know if it was a dream or something that truly happened.

By 1958, Mom and I had been living in Rota for a couple of years. My sister Millie was born there that March, while my older sister Maria remained in Puerto with Carmen. When Millie turned two, my mother met my future stepfather, Robert Lecher, a U.S. Navy sailor stationed at Naval Station Rota. I had always believed that Maria and Millie had different fathers. Before my mother met Robert, she had been living with another man, an American sailor whom I thought was Millie's real father.

I remember that man vividly because he once terrified me by holding me over a freshwater tank beneath the apartment floor. Mom remembered the incident too, telling me later that he had always been cruel to me. Although she always insisted that Maria and Millie share the same father, none of us believed her. Many years later, Maria and Millie took DNA tests and confronted her with the results. She broke down crying and finally admitted that they each had separate fathers. That revelation made me question who my own father really was. She claimed it was a man named Alfredo, but I was never entirely convinced.

My mother had a way of keeping certain truths to herself, as if revealing them might unravel the fragile threads holding our family together. I sometimes wondered if my Uncle John, my beloved Tito, could have been my real father. We shared so many traits, not only in looks but in temperament. Colleen once asked my mother directly, without telling me, if it was true, even suggesting the unthinkable, that my grandfather might be my father. It was a disturbing thought, and one I could never fully accept. What I did know for certain was that my father was not theirs. Whether out of pride, fear, or shame, Mom often hid behind half-truths and silence.

Life in Rota improved once Millie was born and Mom began living with Robert. We moved into our own apartment by the sea, its whitewashed walls gleaming in the sun, with a seawall I used to climb to reach the road. I can still hear the distant hum of the waves and the laughter of fishers down by the shore. When Colleen and I returned years later, that part of the city had changed beyond recognition. The cover of my childhood had become a landfill, a beach littered with debris that the tide carried in. What had once been the heart of my youth was now buried beneath the careless progress of time.

My half-brother Bobby was born in that same apartment in 1960 when I was about six years old. He was the second child of Robert and Mom. Their first baby had died at birth while Robert was away at sea, the umbilical cord wrapped around the infant's neck. All of Mom's children were born at home, delivered by a midwife. I remember both births vividly, as if they happened yesterday. Bobby would remain Robert's only child, which felt fitting, as Robert himself had been an only child to Grandpa Albert and Grandma Helen.

Until I returned to Spain years later as a Navy man, Mom always told me that my real father was dead and that I should forget about him. But deep inside, I knew better. I was born illegitimate, the son of a married man, and Mom never wanted to face the gossip or the judgment that came with it.

She and Robert married in Castelldefels, Spain, after he turned twenty-one, against his mother's wishes. Grandma Helen did not want her son marrying a Spanish woman with four children, only one of them his. They had wanted to marry earlier, but without parental consent they were forced to wait until Robert came of age. When they finally did marry, Robert adopted me and my sisters in 1963, and I became John Lecher Zapata.

In 1974, while on Navy leave in Puerto de Santa María, I decided to confront the truth once and for all. I called my parents and asked directly about my biological father. For the first time, Mom admitted what I had long suspected, that he was not dead. She had told my sisters the same lie about their father, and they too had grown to doubt her stories.

My mother was the most caring and generous person I knew, but when it came to her past, she was defensive and evasive. Whenever I asked my stepfather about my father, he would hand the phone to her, as if the question itself carried too much weight. In her thick Spanish accent, she would say the same words she had always used, "Forget about it." Eventually, though, she asked Tito Juan to take me to meet my real father, Alfredo.

Alfredo was a taxi driver for most of his life, eighteen years older than my mother. He was married, with children, when I was conceived. Known as a bit of a flirtation in his younger years, he had fathered other illegitimate children besides me, something my mother knew all too well. He was short, thin, and always smartly dressed in a jacket and tie, a man of quiet pride and few words. I often wondered whether he believed I was his son.

Years later, when my children finally met him, Alfredo was already deep in the grip of Alzheimer's disease. He passed away not long after. I was grateful that my children had met him, but I never fully understood what he felt toward me. Before his illness, whenever I visited Puerto, I would meet him at the bar near his cab stand and share a café con leche. It was our quiet ritual, two men joined by blood but divided by time.

In 2002, I brought my entire family to Spain, and my children wanted to meet him. We planned to visit the same bar where he always sat. When my mother learned of our plans, she hurried there, insisting she needed to be present to tell her side of the story. I stopped her before she reached the bar and asked her to return to my aunt's house. She finally agreed, waiting until later to explain herself to her grandchildren.

At the bar, I introduced my children to Alfredo. We had drinks together, though I did not realize how far his Alzheimer's had progressed. All he managed to say, again, was "¡Qué guapo, qué guapo," "How beautiful, how beautiful." It was a kind Spanish phrase, but it left me uncertain whether he even knew who I was.

In 2003, I visited him again. He invited me into his home, where his wife lay motionless in bed, a victim of a stroke. He showed me photographs of his family, his father, and his hunting trips. I never knew if this was his way of expressing remorse or simply being polite.

In 2004, I rode past his house on my Harley and saw him sitting on the curb. When I stopped greeting him, he seemed more interested in his GPS wristwatch and my motorcycle than in me. For years, he had greeted me with a kiss on the cheek, as was customary in Spain. When that gesture vanished, I knew he no longer remembered who I was.

In his later years, Alfredo suffered the loss of his son to a drug overdose and, not long after, the death of his wife. By then, Alzheimer's had taken everything from him — memory, awareness, even grief. I doubt he understood the meaning of those losses. That was the last time I saw Alfredo.

Whenever I think of him now, I remember that bar in Puerto, the sound of waves rolling against the seawall, and the faint sweetness of café con leche between us, two lives that began together yet barely crossed. Spain will always hold that part of me, the boy who watched his mother's train disappear into the night, still wondering if it was all a dream.

4

Barcelona

My memories of our move from Rota to Barcelona are limited, but a few moments remain vivid, some joyful, others harrowing. One experience I have never shared until now took place on a beach in Barcelona. I was with my Tito Juan and my siblings when I wandered too far into the sea. The water quickly grew deeper than I could manage. I began to panic as the waves pulled me under again. I shouted for my uncle between gulps of salty water, but no one heard me, until someone finally did. A man heard me and rushed into the water and carried me to shore, laying me down in the sand just as my uncle came running toward us. I am certain it was not my time to go; God had sent an angel that day. The man simply walked away, while my uncle, overwhelmed with relief, began to scold me.

Another memory that stands out clearly is the neighborhood we lived in. After a period in Castelldefels, my uncle helped us find a third-floor apartment in the heart of Barcelona, just south of the famed La Rambla. Directly across from our building was a large area filled with ruined, half-demolished structures. I spent hours exploring those crumbling remains. Today, the tallest high-rise in Barcelona stands on the very site where I once played.

I did not fit well with the neighborhood boys. One humiliating incident remains etched in my mind: they surrounded me, teased me, and pulled my pants down in the street. My mother went to the local police, but nothing ever came out of it. Looking back, I realized my difficulty socializing — something I would later understand as a symptom of Asperger's — contributed to my struggles adjusting to an unfamiliar environment.

Despite the challenges, I fell in love with La Rambla. It remains one of my favorite places in all of Spain. The tree-lined boulevard, flanked by one-way streets, is alive with energy — living statues, mimes, street vendors, and people from all social classes. Colleen eventually grew to love it as well, but during our 1980 visit with our four-month-old son Michael, she found it overwhelming and insisted we leave after just one night. The marble walkway has been polished smooth by millions of feet over the centuries, and even the layers of chewing gum have become a strange, permanent feature.

When I was a child, I once joined local boys panhandling sailors on La Rambla. I was nearly caught by one of my stepfather's Navy friends. I could not have been more than six or seven years old.

Near to La Rambla lies the Barri Gòtic, or Gothic Quarter, a maze of narrow streets and medieval buildings just blocks northeast of our apartment. It was a haven for sailors, filled with bars, cafés, clubs, and the women who worked the night. Though dark and gritty, the Gothic Quarter had its own charm, with ancient architecture tucked into quiet plazas.

On the same street where we lived stood one of Antoni Gaudí's most iconic buildings, La Pedrera. Years later, Colleen and I stayed in a hotel directly across from it during two separate visits. Just down the street was an old wall fountain where my mother often sent me to fetch fresh water. The fountain still exists today and still works. I have always called it "John's Fountain," and I make a point to visit it every time I return to Barcelona.

I had always called my stepfather "Bob," until one day, for reasons I still cannot explain, I started calling him "Dad." From that moment on, he became my father. It was easier for my younger sisters to embrace him in that role, but for me, it was a conscious shift. My mother must have loved him deeply, or perhaps she saw in him an opportunity for a better life for herself and her children. She knew he would eventually return to Nebraska, and she believed that following him might offer us a brighter future. I have often wondered if she made the right decision. Would my life have been better had we stayed in Spain?

Not all our days in Barcelona were peaceful. On occasion, my stepfather returned home drunk, sparking loud, violent arguments with my mother, sometimes right in the street. The commotion often drew the attention of neighbors and even the police. I would watch from across the road, hidden among the ruins, as the drama unfolded. My mother was not one to back down. She never tolerated his drinking or infidelity, and she could hold her own in any fight, whether with him or with any woman who crossed the line.

By 1962, plans were in motion for our family to immigrate to the United States. My stepfather still had two years left in the Navy, and the idea was for us to join him once his service ended. But before we could go, my mother reached out to her father in Puerto to bring my sister Maria to Barcelona. Maria had been living with Carmen and her husband for four years and had become like a daughter to them. Carmen did not want to let her go, but my grandfather convinced her it was only a short visit.

With our adoptions finalized and our green cards secured, we were ready. My uncle escorted us by train to Madrid, where we boarded a plane to Bayonne, New Jersey. I remember standing at the foot of the stairs leading to the aircraft, terrified to board. My uncle had to drag me up to the plane.

Originally, my stepfather was supposed to meet us upon discharge from the Navy, and we would travel together to our new home in Chadron, Nebraska. But due to the Cuban Missile Crisis, his ship was diverted to the Caribbean, and his release was delayed. Instead, his mother, Helen Kingston, and her husband, John Kingston, also in the Navy, were called to meet us in Bayonne. They brought us to Arlington, Virginia, where they lived near the Pentagon. We waited for my father there, but eventually, we had to continue the journey to Chadron without him.

None of us spoke English. We did not know what to expect or what the future held. All we knew was that we were leaving one world behind in the hope of finding a better one.

Since leaving Barcelona for the United States, I have returned many times over the years. Without fail, I always make my way back to La Rambla, my favorite place in the city, a street that continues to call me home no matter how far I have wandered.

5

They Called Me Tiliti

I never quite knew where the nickname "Tiliti" came from, but it stuck like glue. Many people in Puerto still remember me by that name and continue to call me Tiliti whenever I return to Spain. In Chadron, though, nobody ever called me that, and maybe that was for the best.

Whenever I went back to Puerto after moving to the United States, the neighbors and friends who had known me as a boy in the old apartment building would recognize me instantly, even if I couldn't place their faces. They'd come rushing up with wide smiles, kisses on both cheeks, and stories from the past, as if I'd never left. They'd laugh, shaking their heads as they reminded me of my mischievous ways. To them, I was still Tiliti, almost like the Shirley Temple of the neighborhood, just with a little more dirt on my knees. I'd smile and play along, pretending I remembered every detail, though in truth I didn't.

Apparently, I'd been quite the handful as a boy. Everyone seemed to have a story about something outrageous I'd done. One tale I heard more than once was about the time I tossed a cat into the well behind our apartment building, the very same well everyone used to draw water. It took a long while, but the neighbors eventually rescued the poor creature with a rope and a bucket. Another time, I tied two cats' tails together and let them run loose through the courtyard. You could say mischief was my calling card, my early form of community entertainment.

When my mother met my stepfather in Rota, where my brother Bobby was born, our lives began to change. My stepfather had been reassigned to a cargo ship stationed in Barcelona, so we moved there, first settling in a beachside village called Castelldefels. Our apartment sat in a complex named Saratoga, just steps from the shore. My uncle, Tito Juan, worked as a flamenco dancer at a nearby nightclub and was always around, twirling through life like he owned the stage. At that time, it was just Bobby, Millie, and me with Mom.

My stepfather's original Navy enlistment was for four years, but he got himself into trouble and spent time in the brig, first in Rota, then later in Portsmouth, Virginia. With his enlistment about to end, he petitioned his mother, Grandma Helen, who was married to a Navy officer at the Pentagon, for help. Thanks to her persistence and powerful connections, he was granted an additional two years in the service, just long enough to return to Spain, marry my mother, and bring all of us to the United States.

I don't remember much about the move from Rota to Barcelona, but a few moments remain vivid. One of the strongest, one I've never told anyone until now, happened on a beach in Barcelona. I had wandered too far into the sea while playing with my siblings and Tito Juan. The water suddenly dropped off beneath me, and I began to sink. Gulping saltwater as I flailed, I remember crying out for Tito between desperate breaths. Someone, I never knew who, realized I was in trouble, pulled me to shore, and walked away without a word. Tito came running, furious and relieved all at once, scolding me as I coughed up seawater. I've always believed an angel saved me that day, and that God must have decided it wasn't my time.

We later moved into the city itself, near the famous La Rambla, our apartment was on the third floor, across from a row of half-destroyed buildings left standing as ruins. I often explored those crumbling walls, never imagining that one day, the tallest high-rise in Barcelona would rise on that very spot.

I wasn't exactly the most popular kid with the neighborhood boys. Once, they teased me and yanked my pants down in public — my first lesson in humility. My mother, fiery as ever, marched straight to the police station to complain, though nothing came of it. Looking back, I think their teasing had more to do with my awkwardness as the new boy from somewhere else, an awkwardness I'd later come to recognize as part of my Asperger's.

Despite everything, I loved La Rambla. It was, and still is, my favorite place in Spain, a wide, tree-lined boulevard buzzing with life, flanked by one-way streets and filled with mimes, living statues, and vendors selling everything from trinkets to lottery tickets. At six or seven years old, I'd go there with other kids to panhandle sailors. One day, I almost got caught by one of my stepfather's Navy buddies, a close call that left me both terrified and oddly proud.

Just a few blocks away was the Barri Gòtic, a maze of narrow streets overflowing with cafés, bars, and everything else sailors could possibly want. Gaudí's masterpiece, La Pedrera, stood right on our street. Years later, Colleen and I would return to Barcelona and stay at a hotel across from it. Twice, in fact. Down the street was an old stone fountain where my mother once sent me to fetch water. It still flows today, and in my heart, it will always be John's Fountain.

At first, I called my stepfather "Bob," but one day, standing in the Barcelona sun, I simply started calling him "Dad." It felt right, and from then on, he was my father. My sisters, being younger, made the change easily. My mother must have loved him deeply, or at least believed that going with him to Nebraska would give us a better life than staying in Spain. I've often wondered whether she was right.

Not all memories of Barcelona were happy. Sometimes Dad came home drunk and fought with Mom in the street, loud enough for the police to show up. I'd hide in one of the nearby ruins and watch, scared but unable to look away. Mom, however, was never one to back down, not from him, and not from any woman who tried to catch his eye. She had fire in her veins, and she knew how to use it.

By 1962, Dad's final two years of service were nearly up, and Mom began preparing for our move to America. She had left my sister Maria in Puerto with Carmen for nearly four years and now called on my grandfather to bring her to Barcelona so we could travel together as a family. Carmen, who had raised Maria as her own, was heartbroken to let her go, but my grandfather promised she would return, though deep down, we all knew she never would.

With the adoption finalized and green cards in hand, we were finally ready, Tito Juan took us by train to Madrid, where we boarded a plane bound for Bayonne, New Jersey. I was terrified of flying. Tito practically had to drag me up the steps of the aircraft while I clung to the railings like a cat at bathtime.

Dad was supposed to meet us in Bayonne after being discharged from the Navy, and from there we were to take a bus to Chadron, Nebraska, our new home. But history had other plans. The Cuban Missile Crisis erupted, and his ship was diverted to the Caribbean.

Instead, Grandma Helen and her husband, John Kingston, a Navy officer stationed at the Pentagon, met us and took us to their home in Arlington, Virginia. None of us spoke a word of English, but we were together, and we were on our way to Nebraska, to a life that seemed a world away from the sea, the sand, and the laughter that had once echoed through the courtyards of Puerto de Santa María.

6

The Vrbka's

FRONTEER AIRLINES: We landed at Chadron Municipal Airport on the cold, dark evening of October 29, 1962. My mother arrived in America with four young children in tow, none of whom spoke a word of English. Likewise, our newly found American relatives didn't speak Spanish. Waiting at the airport to greet us were Grandpa Albert, his wife Ila, her children and grandchildren, the Horse family, as well as Donny Pinkerton and his family.

I did not realize it at the time, but my dad's mother, who was living in Virginia, and my Grandpa Albert were not on speaking terms. My dad eventually told me that his mother had purchased the airplane tickets for us to fly from Virginia to Chadron, and that it was her way of getting rid of us.

Growing up in Chadron, Nebraska, was far more difficult for me than for my younger siblings. It seemed as if every conceivable challenge had been stacked against me from the beginning. The Chadron Public School system was not equipped to manage a child like me, so I was enrolled in Assumption Academy. I didn't speak English. We were poor. I had never attended school before. I was eight years old and started first grade. I was Hispanic, a foreigner, and, though I only understand it now, I had Asperger's. To top it all off, I was now living in what many would call a redneck town.

I couldn't have drawn a more challenging hand in life even if I had tried. Looking back now, I don't know how I managed to survive my childhood and teenage years in Chadron during the 1960s and 1970s. Yes, there were other Hispanic families in town, but they were nothing like us. These families were well-established. They owned homes, spoke fluent English, were native to the area, and their parents held decent jobs. We were different. Quite different.

Despite the challenges, I remember being welcomed warmly by our American relatives. My new grandfather arranged for us to live in an apartment above a restaurant owned by George Gross, who also ran the Chuck Wagon on Highway 20. This apartment was located next to Grandpa Albert's own place above the Buddy Bar. Both of those second-floor apartments have since been removed for reasons unknown to me.

The Vrbka's: It was while I was living in the apartment on Main Street, directly above George Cross's restaurant, who also happened to be our landlord, that I first met Bob Vrbka, his family, and his two brothers, Danny and Randy. They lived just three blocks down the street from us, and I spent a great deal of time at their home. Eventually, they moved to another part of Chadron, settling on South Morehead Street. Although it was a bit farther for me to walk, by the time I started third grade, our family had also moved, this time to South Mears Street, just a half-block away from the Vrbka household.

I never really knew what Mr. Vrbka did for a living, except that he tinkered with TVs and radios in a garage behind their home. I always assumed he received some kind of military disability pension, because I never knew him to hold a steady job. He was a large, intimidating man, harsh in appearance and, unfortunately, abusive toward his family, especially Danny. He had a short fuse and wouldn't hesitate to threaten me with his belt, though he never acted on it. Most of the time, he was drunk, and the tension inside their home was always heavy in the air.

Danny had been held back in third grade, which made him closer to my age, since I was two years older than most of my classmates. He and Bob had both attended Assumption Academy the previous two years, just as I had. On the first day of public school, I stopped by the Vrbka house to walk with Bob to East Ward Elementary. Mrs. Vrbka initially assumed I was still attending Assumption and told me we wouldn't be able to walk together, since the schools were in different parts of town. I remember smiling proudly as I told her that I was now going to East Ward with Bob. Our walk to school was two miles, while Danny and my sister Maria only had to walk a few blocks to West Ward from our house on Mears Street.

Between my third and fourth grade years, our family moved again, this time to Minor Hall Ranch, located just south of Gordon, Nebraska, where my dad worked as a ranch hand for a few months. Living on the ranch and running free near the Snake River left an impression on me. That time of exploration, with its endless fields and wide-open skies, stayed with me.

Years later, those memories inspired me to purchase a ranch of my own near Hay Springs.

After that brief stay, we returned to Chadron and moved into a home on North Morehead Street in the Kenwood neighborhood, the last house I lived in before eventually striking out on my own. Coincidentally, my grandfather Albert also lived in Kenwood, just a block away. Even though we had been gone only a few months, Danny and I picked up our friendship as if no time had passed.

It was through Danny that I met the Schmidt family: his aunt and uncle, his cousin David, and Peggy. We first encountered them at a football game in Valentine, Nebraska.

As the years went by, Danny and I remained inseparable, while Bob and Randy gradually moved in different directions. Bob was about three years older than I was, and Randy a few years younger, so naturally we drifted apart. I had mixed feelings about my relationship with Bob. While Danny and I shared a deep, loyal bond, Bob, on his way to feed his pony north of my house on Morehead Street, would often stop by and ask if I wanted to come along. It was during one of those encounters that Bob made inappropriate sexual advances toward me. I did not fully understand what was happening, but it left me confused and uncomfortable. I instinctively pulled away and began to avoid him after that.

When I attended West Ward Elementary, Maria went to Kenwood Elementary, which was only a few blocks from our home. The best part of going to West Ward was that Danny went there too. Having him by my side meant the world to me, for he understood where I came from and the struggles I faced. Our friendship gave me a sense of safety and belonging during a time when I often felt like an outsider.

We spent countless afternoons exploring the woods behind "C" Hill, just behind Chadron State College. Armed with a can of pork and beans, we would build makeshift cookouts among the trees, talking and laughing for hours. Another favorite spot was a grove of trees northwest of town, near West Ward. A spring runoff trickled through that area, and we used to swing from a rope tied high in a tree, pretending to be Tarzan. Danny often spoke about running away from home. His words carried a sadness I did not fully understand at the time, but I knew his pain was real.

Another treasured hideout was the southwest corner of Wilson Park.

There, dense roadside bushes created a perfect sanctuary for our childhood games. We built forts in the overgrowth and crouched low, aiming our stick guns at passing cars on Maple Street. Those carefree afternoons with Danny remain etched in my heart as some of the happiest moments of my youth.

While Danny and I were in middle school, we both played football for Coach Thompson. One of our games was in Valentine, Nebraska, where I met Danny's aunt and uncle and his cousins, the Schmitz family. Among them was his cousin Peggy, whom I found myself very infatuated with.

The Schmitz family lived on the Rosebud Indian Reservation. Danny and I visited them once during Christmas break, and I remember being fascinated by the reservation and how different life there felt compared to Chadron.

One of the last times I saw Danny was just before I left for the Navy. Neither of us knew it would be our final goodbye. We promised to write letters and stay in touch, but life has a way of interfering with youthful promises. That day never came.

Years later, while I was serving in the Navy, I received a letter from my father that delivered devastating news. Danny Vrbka had been killed in a tragic car accident on the highway between Chadron and Spotted Tail, as he was returning from a party. The news hit me like a hammer to the chest. Danny wasn't just a friend; he had been one of my closest companions, someone with whom I had shared laughter, dreams, and boyhood secrets. I always thought that one day, as grown men, we'd reunite and reminisce about those joyful days in the woods — our forts, our rope swings, and the quiet moments we never told anyone about.

Although Danny was raised Catholic, his parents being deeply devoted, he despised going to church. Years later, he even told me he would never set foot in one again. I wasn't there when he passed, but I was told his funeral was so large that they held the service in the Assumption Academy Arena to accommodate the crowd.

.

7

GORDON RANCH

SOME OF THE MOST CHERISHED MEMORIES of my childhood took root at the Minor Hall Ranch near Gordon, Nebraska. It was the peaceful isolation, free from peer pressures, which made those days so special. While we were still living on Mears Street, my father met some folks through his hobby of showing pigeons. They managed the Minor Hall Ranch, located just south of Gordon, and eventually offered Dad a job. After I finished third grade, we packed up and moved to the ranch. It was south of the Niobrara River, and we lived about a block away from the Snake River which fed into the Niobrara.

The ranch was nestled in a picturesque corner of the Nebraska Sandhills, at the very source of the Snake River. This river began from an artesian well only a couple blocks away from our house, situated in the middle of a lush hay pasture. Beavers were constantly at work, building dams that flooded the fields. One of my daily chores was to break those dams and drain the water so the hay could be harvested.

We were permitted to keep two milk cows, which I had to milk each day, and three horses: Snake, Piccolo, and Trinket. Dad rode Trinket, a particularly mean-spirited horse, while I rode Piccolo. My sisters rode double on Snake. I took every opportunity to explore the surrounding hills and trails on Piccolo. Unfortunately, Piccolo had a habit of rubbing himself against barbed wire fences, with my legs often caught in between. To this day, I carry the scars from those adventures. I once fell forward off Piccolo when he refused to jump a small creek. I wasn't badly hurt in the fall, however Piccolo stepped on my hand, and I had to visit the Gordon hospital.

That fall, we started school, just a mile from our house. Sometimes we rode our horses; other times Mom drove us in the Oldsmobile she had learned to drive while we were living on the ranch, which was the best place to learn to drive without running into another vehicle. It was during this time that I met Rhonda Radcliff, a kind and beautiful ranch girl with whom I would remain penpals for many years after we left.

Our home on the ranch was far from modern. It lacked basic amenities like running water. We had a hand pump on the front porch and filled buckets, letting the sand settle before using the water. Our toilet was an outhouse, and baths were taken in a large metal tub that Mom would refill with hot water. Looking back, that little two-bedroom house on Mears Street was a mansion in my eyes, but the ranch were memories that I always had.

I recall a prank my sister Maria once pulled. She gave me what I thought was chocolate, but it turned out to be Ex-Lax. I didn't find it funny and held a grudge for quite some time. At one point, Dad made me dig a new hole so the outhouse could be moved. That experience may explain my lifelong aversion to portable toilets.

Despite these primitive conditions, I never felt deprived. In fact, I could have happily stayed at the ranch forever. I knew no better and adored the freedom and beauty of that life. When we finally had to return to town, I was heartbroken, and I cried. The brief time I spent in the Sandhills left a permanent longing in my soul to someday own my small retreat out there, just a place to escape and breathe.

Not long after our move to the ranch, Sundance disappeared. He had been gone for a month. Dad later told us that the ranch owner had spotted him from an airplane, running wild across the Sandhills alongside a pack of coyotes. Eventually, Sundance returned, skinny, weathered, but ready to settle back in.

When we moved back into Chadron, to a house on North Morehead Street, Sundance's adventures only continued. You could author an entire book about his escapades. Over the years, he survived being shot multiple times, including once with an arrow, was hit by vehicles so often we lost count, poisoned, beaten, and even detained by the police. Yet every time the vet recommended euthanasia, Dad refused, and somehow Sundance would pull through.

For years, he followed me to school, sometimes several miles, and always found his way back home. He left a trail of mischief in his wake. Occasionally, the police would pick him up and take him to the dog pound near the fairground. The facility was primitive by today's standards, and jailbreaks weren't too difficult. More than once, I helped free Sundance and his companions. Officer Happy Halstead would come by afterward and ask if I knew anything about the dogs getting loose. Of course, I always denied any involvement with a smile.

I was just like Sundance, only wanting to go on a journey. Sundance eventually entered retirement when Mom and Dad moved to an acreage south of Chadron. Age had caught up with him, and he could no longer roam as he once did. He passed away at around 17 years old, and we buried him at the end of a canyon on my parents' land. He was more than just a pet; he was a legend and a beloved member of our family.

This brief time that I spent at the ranch left such a large impression on me that I eventually bought my home seclusion of 1,000 acres on the Niobrara River just eleven miles south of Hay Springs.

8

CHADRON PUBLIC SCHOOLS WERE NOT PREPARED FOR JOHN.

Looking back, I never understood how difficult those early school years were for me, or how different I was from the other students. In some ways, I was grateful to be two years older than my classmates. When kids picked on me, it often ended in a fight, and often, I came out ahead thanks to my age and size advantage. I often wonder how many beatings I might have endured had I been in a class with peers my own age.

My first two years of elementary school were spent at Assumption Academy, the only school in Chadron with a Spanish-speaking teacher at the time. It was there I experienced my first sanctioned boxing match, right in front of the entire first grade class. Nick offered to bring his boxing gloves from home that afternoon. Since Lee Miller and I had gotten into a confrontation earlier on the playground, it was decided that we would box each other. I later learned that Lee was my second cousin. Can you imagine something like that happening in schools today?

That match was only the beginning. Many more fights will follow in the years ahead. I don't remember, or could even begin to count, how many times I got into a fight with Steve Baker. Most of the time, people complained about my age and size, never recognizing that I was just a child trying to defend myself against bullies the only way I knew how. Losing a fight never bothered me, but if I won, the consequences often escalated. Parents would call my house to complain, and sometimes even the police would show up to talk to me. For me, fighting became a weekly routine.

School never came easy, especially when compared to Maria, who was book-smart and never seemed to get into trouble. We were placed in the same first grade class at Assumption Academy, the very school my stepfather had attended years earlier. I hated being in the same class as Maria. She would run home and report every little thing I did wrong while conveniently forgetting anything I did right. Truthfully, it has always been difficult to have a good relationship with her. Even if we weren't siblings, I doubt we would have ever been friends. That feeling, I must admit, still lingers today.

Maria and I clashed from the very beginning. She had grown used to getting her way while living with Carmen. When she came to live with us, she had to learn to share a lesson she never quite mastered. Even now, she remains one of the most selfish people I know. And yet, she was expected to stay with our family in our home, just like the rest of us. After we left Assumption Academy, we were never placed in the same class again. I was always the one sent to the school furthest from our home.

At Assumption, Maria, I, and a handful of other children ate lunch in the kitchen rather than the cafeteria. I never understood why, but I suspect it was because we were so poor. Years later, I overheard that our tuition may have been waived. I also heard that my Grandma Helen paid for my first year, but my dad couldn't afford the second. That's why, by my third year, we transferred to public school.

The first time I was ever kicked out of school was during a school picnic at Finnegan Park. I had been climbing on the roof of the restroom building when a nun warned me to stop. I ignored her and climbed it again. That earned me a trip home. For a long time, I thought that incident was why we didn't return to Assumption. But eventually, I learned the truth — an argument between my stepfather and the school over unpaid tuition was the real reason we didn't go back.

After that, we attended public school. Four years later, Assumption Academy closed its doors, and all its students transferred to the public system.

What can I say about Sundance, that scrappy little mutt who captured our hearts and remained part of our family for seventeen years? He had been run over by cars on multiple occasions, shot with a shotgun, a .22 rifle, and once even had an arrow lodged in his stomach. He also had one of his ears torn in half. Despite all this, my dad kept taking him back to the vet, getting him patched up repeatedly. His resilience was unmatched, and our commitment to him never wavered.

Every day that I attended middle school, about five miles away, Sundance would follow me to school and return home, waiting for me after class. On a few occasions, he was picked up by the dog catcher. He was one of two pups who was born to Ringo on Mears Street when I was about nine years old. At first, my stepfather gave away all the puppies, intending to keep only Ringo. But every time Sundance was given away, he found his way back to us. One owner said he chased sheep, another claimed he killed chickens. Whatever the reason, no one wanted to keep him, but Sundance was determined to stay.

Eventually, when Ringo disappeared and no one else would take Sundance, my dad relented. Years later, my mom told me that Tony Cisnaro killed Ringo and threw him in a garbage can. Sundance had chosen us, and we finally chose him. And after all that, he was my dog, and I was glad to have him.

Some of my fondest childhood memories are from the time we lived at Minor Hall Ranch. It was the isolation that made it feel so special, being free from the judgment of peers and the pressures of school life. Life there was simple, quiet, and peaceful, and through it all, I finally felt like I belonged somewhere.

As we transitioned into middle school and entered the seventh grade, I became involved in sports, while Danny was held back by his father, who insisted he had too many responsibilities at home to participate. Danny, bow-legged, naturally athletic, and always wearing a cowboy hat, had the solid, imposing build of a "brick shithouse." Without question, he was the most gifted athlete in our school, regularly dominating every event he entered. As first-year students, Danny, Steve A. Baker, Doug Jones, and I earned spots on the varsity wrestling team under Coach Bill Kant.

During our first year of football, Danny played fullback. Every time he touched the ball, he scored. I vividly remember a game against Gordon. The final score was 77–7, and Danny was responsible for most of our touchdowns.

Sadly, by that same year, Danny had begun using pills and drinking heavily. By his junior year, he walked away from sports entirely. Coaches visited his home repeatedly to get him back on the team, but he never returned. I've always believed it was his overbearing and abusive father that derailed the path he could have flourished on. If Danny had stayed clean, he might have gone down in history as one of Chadron High's greatest athletes.

Danny was charismatic with women and rarely without a girlfriend, a trait that, over time, contributed to his decline. To this day, I've never had another friend quite like Danny. His home felt like a second one to me. In contrast, I didn't have any girlfriends in high school. If I wanted to date, I would have to go to Hay Springs, Rushville, or Crawford. It was my Asperger's that made casual relationships difficult in my own town. The girls who knew me in Chadron saw me only as a friend, never as a boyfriend.

Most boys experience a crush on a teacher, and mine was Mrs. Franken, my seventh grade social studies teacher. Ironically, she was also the one who sent me out into the hallway more than anyone else. Still, I found myself inexplicably drawn to her.

One Christmas season, a few of us decided to find a tree for Mrs. Franken's classroom. We wandered the hills behind the college in the bitter cold, cut down one that we thought was the perfect tree, and dragged it back. Unfortunately, it looked awful by the time we returned. Disappointed, we bought another from the A&W parking lot and proudly delivered it ourselves.

One of the most remarkable teachers I ever had was Mrs. Irene Wiley, our English teacher. A petite woman with a huge heart, she opened each class by reading Animal Farm and always carried a yardstick, using it to give playful taps to the head when we got out of line. I must've had the hardest head in the class. She broke several yardsticks on me. But what I remember most was her deep kindness. Every year she sends birthday cards to her former students. For many of us, including me, it was the only birthday card we received. She kept this tradition until her sudden death in a car accident. Her legacy lived on in the hearts of students who remembered her fondly every year.

Then there were the Jones boys, the principals. Just when you thought you'd got rid of one, another would appear: Jerry, Wayne, and Rex, none of them related. Jerry was the middle school principal, Wayne the assistant principal, and Rex the high school principal. Each of them had a turn administering corporal punishment to me. Of the three, I liked Rex the most. He was also the football coach and, despite handing out the most detention, was the fairest.

Rex later moved to Lincoln to work with the Nebraska School Activities

Association. I ran into him a few times after Colleen and I relocated there. Wayne eventually became the high school principal and passed away a few years ago. I saw him at a class reunion at the Elks Club. Neither of us said a word. As for Jerry Jones, I never knew what became of him, and frankly, I still harbor resentment.

Looking back more than forty years later, the behavior of the Jones boys was abusive, something that would never be tolerated in today's schools. Not only were they abusive, but most of the teachers lacked the training and understanding to support someone with Asperger's, or someone from another country struggling with language. There was little awareness, no accommodation, and almost no empathy.

At Chadron Middle School, I stood out. I was sixteen, had a driver's license, and owned a car. That didn't sit well with Jerry Jones. He once falsely reported to my insurance agents, Larson & Larson, that I had been "bumper bumping" cars in the school parking lot during lunch. That lie caused my insurance to be canceled and made it difficult to get future coverage.

School was always a challenge, not because I wasn't intelligent, but because many teachers didn't know how to teach someone like me. I had Asperger's, though at the time, no one even knew what it was. My school records didn't reflect my true abilities.

I never followed the traditional academic path. I excelled in Industrial Arts and P.E. but barely scraped by in other subjects. I was a visual, hands-on learner. While others listened to lectures, I learned by doing, keeping my 1953 Plymouth running through trial and error. I could walk into a room, see how something was built, and recreate it. I taught myself how to build without formal training.

My Construction Management degree from the University of Nebraska at Kearney gave me the basics to teach shop class, but not the real-world skills I used later to build a construction company. Honestly, I wouldn't have made a good teacher.

I never dated girls from my class. After seeing them every day for years, they felt more like extended family. While other guys dated girls from nearby grades, I didn't. Once I had a car, I started heading to neighboring towns. One of the Larson twins had a crush on me and waited after football practice. She was older and once asked me for the homecoming dance my first year. My father wouldn't let me go. That was the first time I ran away from home. I ended up staying with the Vrbkas for a few days.

I only had one sexual relationship with a girl from high school, and that didn't happen until college. We stayed friends after graduation. She was beautiful, intelligent, a cheerleader, and admired by everyone. Any guy would've been proud to be with her.

When I was fifteen, Danny Vrbka and I visited his Aunt Laura and Uncle Walleye Robertson near Rosebud, South Dakota. They had a daughter, Peggy, and a son, Sam. On one visit, they introduced me to their neighbor, Kristi Dew. We spent three unforgettable days riding horses, attending a dance, and just being together. Despite the closeness, it never crossed my mind to kiss her, until she surprised me with one as I boarded the bus back to Chadron. That kiss sent my heart racing in a way I'd never felt before. I've often wished I could relive those three days.

Long-term relationships have always been hard for me. Unless someone made a real effort to understand me, it was impossible to form a deep connection. Short-term relationships were easier, especially during my travels, because they didn't require sustained emotional investment. I don't mean to say I didn't enjoy companionship. I had my share of flings before settling down, but living that way was simply easier for me to manage.

9

The Cave

My relationships, particularly with women but also with people in general, have often remained on the surface. Unless someone made a genuine effort to understand me, any chance of forming a deeper connection was slim. Looking back, I realize now how much of that distance came from my Asperger's. I did not always know how to open, how to read the subtleties, or when to trust. During my travels, I found it easy to strike up conversations with strangers, safe in the knowledge that those moments were fleeting. Tomorrow will always bring a new town, a new face, and no expectations.

That does not mean I did not crave connection. I enjoyed the company of women and experienced my fair share of flings before settling down. But intimacy, emotional intimacy, required vulnerability, and I often protected myself by keeping things light, fast, and untethered. It was easier to keep my heart guarded than risk it being misunderstood or broken.

When I was seventeen, I landed a job at the 77 Cave, a bar and grill owned by a strong-willed woman named Eva. I worked in the kitchen, flipping pizzas and making sandwiches. For a teenager, it was thrilling, especially with Go-Go dancers performing during the week. The dancers lived upstairs in the hotel above the bar and dined on the meals I prepared. Part of my job was to get them to sign their meal tickets so Eva could deduct the cost from their wages.

As the weeks went on, the dancers began to flirt, and I soaked it up like dry ground under a spring rain. I was young, curious, and craving affection. Soon, the food tickets stopped getting signed, and I did not press them. I would stay after my shift, hanging out with the girls upstairs, and often, I would spend the night with them. There was something intoxicating about being wanted, physically, intimately, even if it was not love. Of course, I was too naive to realize how obvious it all looked from the outside. Eventually, Eva found out and fired me. I was devastated, but deep down, I knew I had crossed a line.

Around that same time, my life began to unravel. I stayed out drinking, skipped school, and built up more detention hours than anyone in Chadron High history. Most kids got a scolding; I was serving weeks at a time. The school was trying to scare me straight, or maybe they just wanted me gone. I missed wrestling, the one place I felt strong and focused, and without it, I started to feel lost.

One night, overwhelmed by everything, I made a decision that felt both terrifying and necessary. I packed up my car with clothes, old tapes, and a couple of my dad's guns, and I took off. My goal was Pine Ridge, South Dakota, and I followed the gravel roads, hoping to leave my problems behind me in the Nebraska dust. My first stop was White Clay, Nebraska, where the clutch in my car gave out. A guy at a nearby garage took pity on me and allowed me to use his tools and hoist to fix it. I found a replacement clutch locally and, over the course of hours and sweat, got the car back in working order. Over the years, I had learned to do my own mechanical work, and changing a clutch, while physically demanding due to the weight of the transmission, was something I was comfortable handling. That small act of kindness stayed with me, proof that even when you are running, not everyone is trying to stop you. After the repair, I made it to Rosebud, South Dakota, and stayed with the Robertsons, dear friends who had not yet heard I was officially on the run.

Eventually, I found myself in O'Neill, Nebraska, where I picked up ranch work feeding cattle by hand. The job was exhausting and dirty, but it grounded me. For a moment, out there under the vast prairie sky, I felt still. It was the first time in a long time that I could hear my own thoughts and begin to understand what they were trying to tell me.

Close to Mission, South Dakota, I decided to take a chance and visit the Robinsons. But before I could get there, I was stopped on the county road by a local sheriff. After checking my information, they discovered I was listed as a runaway and took me into custody. I spent time in jail before the sheriff contacted my mom. Soon enough, both Mom and Dad made the trip to pick me up. In Nebraska I was still considered a minor.

10

The Navy

At 18 years old, I was in constant trouble during high school. I had set the record for the most hours spent in detention, and I openly disliked the principal. In Nebraska, I was already of legal age to drink alcohol, and while still in high school, I gradually became older than most of my classmates, eventually turning twenty before finishing. I had dropped out for numerous reasons, but my mother insisted that I earn my GED. She even went with me to classes at a church in Kenwood to make sure I attended. I eventually took my final exam at Chadron State College under Dr. De-Selms, the father of my classmate at Chadron High.

I wanted to join the military, and my first choice was the Air Force. The recruiter had originally told me that I could not join without a high school degree or its equivalent, a GED. He even pointed to the line in the brochure that needed it. That ended my chances there.

With my GED in hand, I contacted the Air Force recruiter to let him know I had completed it. He arranged for me to fly to Denver, Colorado, for my physical. That flight from Chadron to Denver was the first time I had been on a plane since coming over from Spain in 1962, about 11 years earlier. Flying had always frightened me, so I prayed and made the sign of the cross before takeoff.

Once I was in Denver, I passed all the elements of my physical except the hearing. I had a loss of high-frequency hearing, which by itself prevented me from joining. It was discouraging to watch all the other Air Force recruits swear in while I had to return home with no future in mind.

While walking through downtown Chadron, I ran into a Navy recruiter I had spoken with earlier in the year. I told him about my disappointing experience with the Air Force. He listened carefully and seemed to understand my frustration. Then he explained that he could get me into the Navy through the United States Navy Reserve out of Cheyenne. He assured me the Navy would accept my GED, teach me a trade, and set me on a better path. Before long, he scheduled my ship date for boot camp, telling me the rest I would learn once I got there. So, I packed a small bag, and he drove me to Cheyenne, Wyoming, where they gave me a short physical without the hearing test. I swore in. Somehow, though I don't remember exactly how, I got to Denver, Colorado, and flew to Chicago O'Hare International Airport.

In boot camp, the recruits were assigned to various companies, and each battalion was made up of many companies. We had our company commander, a first-class petty officer, and a battalion commander, a chief petty officer. Together, they formed the chain of command that oversaw this class of recruits.

The first day at camp, we learned how to line up, left turn, right turn, straight ahead. We marched together in our civilian clothes to the chow hall, where the more seasoned recruits mocked us for being the new guys. There we stood in civilian clothes, with long hair and beards. We stuck out badly; the group was made up of guys from all over the country.

On the second day of boot camp, we were issued our recruit uniforms — clothes, jackets, hats, and gloves, before having our heads shaved and receiving ditty bags filled with hygiene items. The cold outside made those jackets, gloves, and hats essential, and we quickly came to appreciate them. That little ditty bag became a lifeline, and we learned right away how important it was to take good care of it.

Once the formalities were complete, training began. To my surprise, there wasn't as much physical training as I had imagined from television portrayals of drill sergeants yelling at recruits. Instead, the focus was on order, discipline, and uniformity. Throughout basic training, there was never any scheduled PT. It seemed like we learned more about tying knots, how to salute, and how to live in close quarters.

Training during the week ran from Monday through Friday, while Saturdays were reserved for gym activities, basketball games, relay races for company flags, and other competitions. That was the exercise I experienced most during boot camp. Fresh out of high school, I was in excellent shape and had played sports all my life, so whenever we ran races or relays, I often came out ahead. Sundays were considered our day off, usually a time to attend church, but they could also mean extra PT if you messed up during the week, and I did my share along with two other recruits. I was asked by my company commander to volunteer to box as a company representative. He chose the three of us not because he thought we would excel, but because he saw us as troublemakers and wanted us punished by getting our butts kicked.

I was reluctant to box, but I wasn't given a choice. They matched me with a guy who looked like a seasoned weightlifter and an experienced boxer. Everyone seemed eager to see me take a beating. But my opponent had smoked too many cigarettes over the years, and by the end of the first round he was gasping for air. I overwhelmed him so badly that the fight stopped early. All of us who won our matches were rewarded with a ribeye steak at the chow hall, but it was no comparison to a ribeye from my home state of Nebraska.

My social skills and the way I behaved were had not improved any since I left Chadron. I can say now that I did not have many friends or people I associated with. Boot camp had its rough patches; I got into a couple of fights in the laundry room, nothing major but enough to remind me that standing up for yourself was necessary. I volunteered to carry our regimental flag at the graduation ceremony, and it meant everything to me. Carrying the flag symbolized that I had finally become part of something larger than myself and had found a place where I belonged.

Upon graduation from boot camp, I was assigned to Machinist Mate School at the Great Lakes Naval Training Center, only about a mile away. But before we went to school, otherwise known as A-School, we were given a couple of days off, and we made a trip to Kenosha, Wisconsin. We heard it was the whorehouse capital of the United States. Me and another recruit made the trip since it was not very far.

There were recruits all over town, downtown, in the bars, walking on the sidewalks, outside of the hotels, everywhere you went, there were Navy recruits in their dress white uniforms.

After graduating from Boot Camp, I spent the weekend in Kenosha before reporting to my dorm at the Great Lakes Naval Training Center. We found a couple of hookers, and they took us to their motel room. They were black. It was the first time I was ever with a Black woman, and to my recollection, I paid about $15.

My orders were to attend school and train as a machinist's mate, a position responsible for keeping the ship's internal mechanical systems running. The goal was to understand how all the moving parts worked together to power and use a vessel at sea. As machinists' mates, however, our responsibilities focused more on the internal mechanical systems that propelled the ship forward, such as the propellers and the cooling systems that kept everything running smoothly.

School turned out to be anything but easy. I found myself buried in books, wrestling with formulas, and struggling to pass the required tests. No matter how hard I studied, I couldn't seem to get the grades I needed. Eventually, the instructor told me directly that I wasn't going to make it through machinist's mate school. One positive element that came out of A-School was that I met a couple of friends. One was a guy from West Virginia by the name of Rick Whitehead, and the second was Tom Hartong from Baton Rouge, Louisiana. I stayed connected with both after the Navy; they always were decent guys. Rick was a signal operator, a true hillbilly with an accent. He was shipped out to Hawaii to serve on a ship, while Tom and I both got different ships in Norfolk, Virginia. With that, my path changed. I had no choice but to leave school, and before long, I was on my way to the fleet.

I was assigned to work as a machinist's mate. The only difference was that I was only an E-2, performing the same tasks and duties as those who had graduated from school and entered as E-3s. The E-3s had more experience and earned more money, while I carried the lower rank and pay despite doing the same work. While on the ship, the U.S.S. Claude V. Ricketts (DDG-5), a destroyer stationed in Norfolk, Virginia, I continued my duties as a machinist's mate. I was assigned to the engineering department, which was in the guts of the ship, tending to the mechanical systems that kept us moving across the sea.

Life aboard was demanding, with long hours spent in the hull of the ship. Looking back, I saw where my Asperger was clear. I hardly ever got along with my shipmates, even though I was not doing anything wrong. They just simply did not like me. Eventually, I was taken out of the machinist's mate position working on the mechanical systems and reassigned to the dishwashing room, where my new duty was washing dishes for 30 days. This move made me feel singled out and humiliated, as if it were punishment for something I never understood. I don't remember what I did wrong, but I was the first sailor ever assigned to wash dishes. I don't know what it was about me that got me into dishwashing, for a comparable situation had already happened back in boot camp, where I was assigned to the chow hall to wash dishes for ten days. I was the first sailor from the engineering division ever assigned to the kitchen washing dishes, and that only added to the sense of embarrassment and isolation.

After completing my 30 days washing dishes, I was reassigned to the A gang. The A gang managed air conditioning and heating systems, along with various small mechanical jobs and auxiliary equipment such as ovens and dishwashers. It was led by a first-class petty officer named Moe, from Philadelphia, who had only about four months left before retirement. I liked Moe and got along well with my fellow sailors in the A gang. We often went out bar hopping and chasing women in different ports. I really enjoyed working in the A gang, and Moe and I developed a strong respect for each other.

Once I was assigned to the A gang, things started turning around for me. At that time, I wanted to make the Navy my career. I was eventually promoted after passing the test from Fireman Apprentice (E-2) to Fireman (E-3). To my surprise, I was even congratulated by the executive officer of the ship for passing my test and becoming a Fireman.

It was during this first cruise to the Mediterranean that I got the chance to visit my Spanish family in Puerto de Santa María. During this first Mediterranean cruise, we visited Valencia, Rota, Villefranche in France, and Naples. I also served as the ship's interpreter for Spanish whenever needed. On one occasion in Málaga, Spain, we had to pick up something that was needed for the ship in Rota. I went with one of the lieutenants, and together we drove from Málaga, Spain, all the way to Rota, Spain, where another Navy port existed, to retrieve the part.

It was during my visit to my family in Puerto de Santa María that Israel got itself involved in a war with the Arabs. My ship was scheduled to return to Rota, where I would meet it. But instead, the ship was reassigned to go off the coast of Israel to support the Israelis in case anything happened. After some time of not knowing where my ship was, I communicated with the base in Rota, and they told me the ship would be in Villefranche, France. So, I caught a supply plane from Rota to Villefranche to join my ship.

The cruise to the Mediterranean ended, and we returned to Norfolk, Virginia, where the ship was scheduled to go into the shipyard at Portsmouth. This is where the downside of my Navy career began. I met a woman who was also in the Navy, and I really liked her. Her name was Christy. While the ship was in dry dock, I shared an apartment in Ocean View, Virginia Beach with three other sailors. During that time, I lost my Navy ID card and went to get a replacement. By mistake, the new card listed me as a 3rd Class Petty Officer instead of Fireman (E-3). I had nothing to do with this error, but it would eventually set in motion the events that led to my leaving the Navy.

Once I was on the Norfolk Navy base, I decided to go to the Petty Officer's Club, which was a little nicer than the Enlisted Men's Club. The policy was clear, only Petty Officers were allowed, but since I had a Petty Officer ID, I decided to go in. I had heard that the women there were more available and older since their men were still out to sea. On the way into the Petty Officer's Club, I was spotted by another member of the A gang, a second-class Petty Officer named Muff, who asked me what I was doing there. Since I had already shown my ID to security, I decided it was best to leave. Later, I got a new ID that showed my true rank, and I had left the mistaken Petty Officer ID back at my apartment. Somehow that incorrect ID disappeared from my apartment and ended up in the possession of the captain of the ship. I can only assume one of my roommates, Sam or another sailor from Arkansas, whose name I don't recall, was asked by Muff to find it and hand it over. The roommate from Arkansas was later killed in a motorcycle accident, and I suspected he might have been the one who passed the ID along. Eventually, I was written up by the Master-at-Arms and had to go to Captain's Mast, which was like a court on the ship. Although it wasn't my fault, I still technically had possession of a fake ID, so I pled guilty. As a result, I was stripped of my Fireman rank, reduced back to Fireman Apprentice, restricted to the ship, and given a financial penalty.

Since I was restricted to the ship, I could only leave with permission, and then it was just to go to the chow hall. There was always a duty officer posted at the gangway, so the only way off required proper authorization. I soon discovered a hole at the very bottom of the ship with a ladder leading down to the dry dock, and that became my escape route. Using it, I began sneaking out to see Christy in Norfolk. I did this every day. I nearly got caught several times, but somehow, I always managed to make it back without being caught.

One time when I was supposed to be on the ship, I was called to report to the Master-at-Arms, and since I was not on board, I could not report. Eventually, the Master-at-Arms found me after I returned to the ship and decided that he was going to take me to the brig. Stupid me, I decided that

I was not going to go, and I took off running through the Portsmouth shipyard. I hid inside a garbage dumpster long enough for security to leave. Once I saw that the security was not looking for me, I moved on. I was able to get off the base without being discovered by security.

I managed to find my way to Meg's house, who was having an affair with me and a couple other sailors, while her husband was gone to sea. He was a submariner and often gone on six-month cruises. I had bought an old car from Meg, and she was holding it for me while we were in the shipyard. Meg lived in Norfolk, Virginia, next to Ocean View where I lived. The car was not at Meg's house, but she told me where it was, and I continued to hitchhike to find my car. While hitchhiking, I was picked up by the local police department in Norfolk and was ticketed. However, once they ran my name, they found out that I was on the run from the Navy. The Navy asked the local PD to put a hold on me until the MPs, the Military Police, could come and pick me up. The Military Police escorted me directly to the brig, where I was held until I could appear before a summary court-martial. The charges against me were not serious, but they landed me in the brig for 90 days and I was also busted down to E1, which was the same rank that I entered boot camp with.

Once again, my Asperger's set me apart, and many of the other inmates did not care for me at all. I was treated with less respect than a drug dealer or a murderer who was there awaiting sentencing. Once, one of the other inmates threw a metal ashtray up in the air like shooting a basketball and hit me right in the chin, which almost broke my jaw. I was lucky it only needed a few stitches. I don't recall what I did, but I ended up in solitary the last 10 days of my 90-day sentence. I was never a bad guy during my life, but I stood out from everybody else. I kept trying to call Christy whenever I had the chance, to no avail, but one time, Sam and Christy came to visit me while I was in the brig to explain that they had got together as a couple and were going to move on without me. So much for friends and love.

Once I was released from the brig, I was ordered to report to the U.S.S. Iwo Jima, a troop transporter for Marines that was getting ready to go to the shipyard, the last place I wanted to go. So, I asked to be assigned to a ship that was heading to the Mediterranean, and instead I was sent to the U.S.S. Blandy. The Blandy was a smaller destroyer than the U.S.S. Claude V. Ricketts, but nevertheless, it was going to the Mediterranean, which I always enjoyed. The first stop was in Rota, Spain, which was about twenty miles from Puerto de Santa María, where my family lived. So, I was able to visit my family once again. The second port for the Blandy was Barcelona, Spain, a place that I love dearly even to this day.

It was in Barcelona where I first got the travel bug when I met some backpackers who were traveling around Europe on a Euro rail pass. This inspired me to want to do the same thing. I don't recall what happened next, but I ended up packing my bags, selling my bicycle, and leaving the ship, going AWOL. I was not gone for two hours, but I should not have left the ship. When I got caught, I ended up back on the ship in the brig. Whatever it was that pushed me to leave, my plan had been to make my way to Rota, Spain, and turn myself in there.

The executive officer of the ship ended up being my representative before the captain's mast. He explained that if I agreed to leave the Navy under general conditions, I would still receive all my benefits. That sounded like the best way, so I agreed. Soon after, they put me on a supply plane that flew out of the air base to Rota.

From Rota, I waited for a flight back to Norfolk, Virginia, where the Navy would process me out. It was a sobering and humbling end to my time in uniform, one that taught me lessons I would carry with me for the rest of my life.

11

My First Trip to Europe

Mark Pollard and I first crossed paths through the fraternity I joined during my freshman year at Chadron State College. I was fresh out of the Navy, restless, and hungry for adventure. I did not have a lot of money. In fact, I only had $400 to go on such a trip, but I still wanted to take my backpack and go. Backpacking through Europe had been in the back of my mind since the day I stepped off the ship, and when I read, maybe overheard, that you could sometimes work your way across the Atlantic on a cargo vessel, it didn't take much convincing. Mark liked the idea, and soon we were hatching a plan.

Our first leg was a long drive east in my 1966 Chevy Impala, a car I had pieced together the year before. It was not much to look at, but it ran well enough to get us to New Jersey, where one of Mark's friends had agreed to let us park it. From there, New York City awaited.

We must have been a sight — two Nebraska boys tramping around Manhattan with oversized, brightly colored backpacks, standing out like we were searching for a campsite instead of a way to Europe.

At the docks, reality quickly sank in. The romantic notion of working for our passage across the Atlantic was a dead end; even if we could have managed it, the voyage would have eaten up our summer. Disappointed but undeterred, we made our way to Kennedy International Airport to explore other options. That is when we discovered the cheapest ticket to Europe was not from New York at all, but from Newark: a $275 flight to Luxembourg on Air Luxembourg. With little hesitation, we boarded a bus and made our way to Newark. Our trip suddenly became very real.

I had only $400 in my pocket when the trip began, and between the cross-country drive, the airfare, and incidentals, I was already running thin. But at that age, with no ties and no fears, not having money seemed less like a problem and more like part of the adventure.

Luxembourg was our gateway to Europe. After landing, we wandered into the city center, where we toasted our arrival with our first European beer and meal. From there, the goal was simple: to reach Paris, where my uncle John had lived for decades. With no real plan, we walked west out of town, thumbs ready, hoping for a ride. Instead, we nearly walked the entire distance to the French border, dragging our packs along country roads.

Hungry, we ducked into a small roadside restaurant once inside France. The menu seemed cheap, so we splurged, ordering a meal fit for kings. Only when the bill arrived did we realize our mistake. Luxembourg francs traded at twenty to the dollar, while French francs traded at only four to the dollar. The numbers on the menu had tricked us. We managed to scrape together enough to cover the bill, but not without learning our first hard lesson of international travel: always check the exchange rate.

That night, rain drove us to set up our tent in what looked like a grassy, sheltered spot beside a tall stone windbreak. Exhaustion and jet lag knocked us out cold. The next morning, the sounds of children's laughter woke us. To our astonishment, we discovered that our "windbreak" was a marble tombstone, and we had pitched camp on the grave of a decorated French military officer. Mortified, we packed up in record time and moved on.

Eventually, we found our way into Paris. My uncle's apartment was there, but he was off vacationing in Spain. With nowhere else to go, we checked into a modest hotel near Notre Dame and spent our first night roaming the historic district, wide-eyed at the sheer size and beauty of it all.

The next day, once we reached my uncle, he welcomed us to stay in his studio. It was a humble place, on the seventh floor of a walk-up building, with no elevator, bathroom down the hall, and barely big enough for a bed and a sink. He had lived there for twenty-five years, and it became our base for the week. Mark took the floor, while I claimed the bed. By this time, I had grown tired of him; he was arrogant, carried more money than I did, and had expensive tastes. He wanted to go his own way to Italy, while I was already looking south toward Spain.

On the way to Barcelona, Mark and I decided to split up, thinking it might be easier to hitchhike when there was only one of us. While waiting for a ride, I happened to be next to a cherry orchard. I ate more than I should've, for that evening I dearly paid the price for eating so many.

I was already getting tired of Mark and the break felt like a relief after we separated and each of us started hitchhiking alone. I caught a ride first and went about a mile down the road before spotting Mark still standing there with his thumb out. For a moment, I wanted to drive right past and leave him to his own fate, but instead I convinced the driver, who was already heading to Barcelona, to pick Mark up as well. In the end, we arrived together.

For me, Barcelona was more than just another stop. Two years earlier, after leaving the Navy, I had promised myself I would return someday with a backpack. Now, standing on Las Ramblas with one slung over my shoulder, promise fulfilled. Speaking the language made things easier, and it did not take long to find a hostel. That first night, we wandered into a bar where we met three Canadian girls, Connie, Donna, and Deanna, who were celebrating Connie's birthday. They were traveling much like we were, backpacks and all. Connie and I were immediately friendly with each other, but Mark could not get anywhere close to Donna or Deanna, Connie's two friends. His arrogance pushed them away, and before long, it pushed me away too. As the night wore on, Connie and I slipped off together, laughing and talking into the early hours. I wasn't allowed into her hostel upstairs, so we ended up sitting on the cold marble floor of the lobby, sharing stories in hushed voices and enjoying the kind of quiet connection that only seems to happen when you're young, far from home, and living out of a backpack. Over the next few days, we explored Barcelona together, while Mark left for Italy and I began planning my own journey south to Puerto.

I invited the girls to visit Puerto later, and they agreed. To get there, I boarded a commuter train toward Valencia without a ticket, not wanting to spend the little money I had left. I slipped between cars or ducked into bathrooms whenever the conductor came through. After arriving in Valencia, I went to the beach and decided to camp out there. It was raining that night, and by morning I was cold, damp, and restless. With hitchhiking proving unsuccessful, I headed to the train station where I met a young Australian woman traveling in the same direction. We decided to team up, first trying our luck hitchhiking, but not a single car slowed down. Giving in, we boarded a train — she had a ticket, I did not. I bought the cheapest fare to the next town, planning to ride farther, and for miles I managed to dodge the conductor by slipping between train cars or hiding in bathrooms. Eventually, though, the conductor caught me asleep on the train, and I was put off at the next station. Fortunately, I hitched a ride with a man driving from Madrid all the way to Málaga. It was one of the easiest and longest rides of the whole trip. From there, I worked my way down the coast by short rides, sleeping on a beach in Torremolinos before finally reaching Marbella.

In Marbella, I found Charo, someone I had met a year earlier while going to school in Chadron. She was from Spain, and her brother, who worked at Midwest Furniture, also lived in Chadron. Through him, Charo had become a friend of my mother's and, in time, a friend of mine as well. To my surprise, when I saw her again in Spain, she was eight months pregnant by her longtime boyfriend, a man she had dated before her trip to America. After three days, I moved on, determined to reach Puerto. The train ride was long and slow, winding through treacherous mountain passes, but eventually I arrived at my Aunt Teresa's home, where Uncle John was staying.

Not long after I arrived in Puerto, my aunt received a call telling her that Connie and Deanna had arrived and were waiting for me at the train station. Donna had stayed behind in Barcelona with a Spaniard she had met. The three of us together did turn heads with my family in Puerto, myself and two girls alone at Uncle John's villa!

Connie and I traveled south into Morocco with little money between us. My mother wired the last $85 from my savings back home, and Connie lent me dollars to get by. We had dreamed of reaching Marrakech, but after stopping in Tangier, Rabat, and Casablanca, the chaos and poverty wore us down. We turned back, grateful just to be on Spanish soil again.

Back in Marbella, Connie and I endured one miserable night camping on an anthill before finding a hostel. I picked up a small job sanding and painting a sailboat in Puerto Banus, working for a British woman who lived in town. The money was not much, but it was enough to sustain me. Looking back, it's hard to believe how far we had come with little more than backpacks, $400, and youthful nerve. With Connie at my side, that first trip became more than a journey, it was a defining chapter in my life.

Backpackers back then tried to survive on what Frommer's guide called "Europe on $10 a Day," while I managed it for about $2 to $3 a day. On that first trip abroad, every dollar counted, and survival meant stretching every cent.

Eventually Connie left Marbella. She wanted badly for me to go with her, but I stayed around so I could continue to work and save enough money to continue my journey. I eventually hooked up with an older gal from Germany and stayed with her in her hostel, spending nights going to other hostels looking for parties. After I had earned enough money, I decided that I wanted to go to Pamplona, Spain. I wanted to be there for the bulls running which starts on July 7.

Prior to Connie leaving Marbella, I informed her that I would meet her and Deanna in San Sebastian after the running of the bulls. It was time for me to head up towards Pamplona via Madrid. By then I had saved enough money so that I could buy a ticket to Madrid, where I would then catch a different train to Pamplona. It was nice not to have to hide from the conductors on the ride to Madrid. But the train to Pamplona was a different story. It was so jam-packed that people were spending time together at the windows. A conductor could not have even made it through the cars. It seemed like nobody was over thirty years old, and everybody had their backpacks, drinking their wine straight from the bottles. It was hectic, all that drinking and noise. I spent time together with a group of kids about my age from all over Europe. Nobody had any money, nobody had a place to stay. But each day we were able to find shelter and continue partying where we left off early that morning after the run. If we got hungry, we would all go into a small grocery store and steal as much food as we could get away with. We would meet later at a designated area and share what we all got.

After about four days of watching the bulls run, getting into the arena with them and not showering, it was time for me to go north toward San Sebastian to meet Connie and Deanna. My body was sore, my clothes smelled of sweat and wine from the chaos in Pamplona, I was running low on money again, but none of that mattered. The thought of reuniting with the girls gave me a burst of energy. I packed up my things at the campground by the river and set out on the road, eager for whatever came next.

I found the girls exactly at the same hostel they told me to meet them at on a certain date. San Sebastián itself was absolutely one of the most beautiful cities I had ever seen. The waves slammed into the concrete seawall and exploded upward, spraying saltwater mist over everyone walking along the promenade. People laughed, cursed and others ducked for cover, but it did not matter, the place was alive. The city felt raw and restless, full of youth, music, and motion, and I could not help but get swept up in it.

Deanna was on her way to England, with Connie three days behind. Connie stayed behind for couple of days before also leaving to go meet Donna and Deanna in England. I decided to take the train back up to Paris, France, to see if my uncle was there. Getting on an overnight train to Paris was easy; no one bothered you except the immigration officers at the border, and all they wanted was to make sure you had a valid passport. It seemed as if there were no conductors on board, so I let my guard down and made the foolish mistake of slipping into an empty cabin and stretching out on one of the bunks to get needed sleep. Big mistake. Someone shook me awake, and there stood a conductor making his rounds through the cabins. It was early morning, with only about an hour left before we reached Paris. When the train finally pulled into Paris, the conductors escorted me straight to the police stations. Luckily, they only checked me over and then let me go.

From there, things became a blur. I do not even remember exactly how I ended up in Calais, France, but eventually I found myself at the massive seaport where ferries crossed over to England. I drifted among the long lines of lorries, weaving through the smell of diesel and salt air, and struck up conversations with truck drivers. Most waved me off, but finally one agreed to take me along. Before long, I was aboard the ferry, rolling across the Channel inside the cab of his truck. Since I rode with a driver who was legally carrying cargo, I never passed through immigration. At the time, it felt like sheer luck. Only later would I realize how that skipped checkpoint would come back to haunt me, because packed in my bag was a can of pepper spray. To me it was nothing more than a defensive tool, but in England it was treated as a prohibited weapon.

When we rolled off the ferry into London, I felt a mix of relief and unease. Relief, because I had finally crossed the Channel. I was uneasy, because I knew the pepper spray in my pack could spark trouble if anyone decided to check me. The truck driver let me out somewhere near the city, wished me luck, and disappeared into the blur of traffic. London spread out before me, sprawling and electric, its streets alive with people and the rumble of red double-decker buses. I wandered among them with my backpack slung over my shoulder, feeling like both a ghost and an intruder, trying to get my bearings and figure out where I might rest my head that night.

My first stop in London was the American Embassy. I went there hoping they might help me buy a ticket back to the United States. At the entrance, a Marine guard searched my bag and pulled out the can of pepper spray. He explained that it was not legal in England and told me to leave it there before I went any further. Word seemed to spread quickly inside, and soon everyone in the Embassy knew about it. More than once, they asked me to hand it over, but I stood my ground and refused.

When the Embassy denied my request for a ticket, they offered only one form of help: they said they could assist me in placing a call to the United States and ask someone back home to wire money. It was not what I had hoped for, but at least it was something. With no better option, I gathered my things and left the building. As I stepped down the long stone staircase, already thinking about how I might survive the next few days, a Bobby, a London police officer, was waiting at the bottom. He stopped me and asked me to search through my bag. The Embassy had already called him. When he opened it and found the can of pepper spray, his face hardened. Unfortunately, I was now under arrest.

A paddy wagon soon pulled up, and the Bobby loaded me inside. They drove me straight to the courthouse, which also had a jail attached. By then it was clear where I would be spending my first night in London. Strangely enough, I felt a bit relieved because not only did I have a bed for the night, but I also had free food to eat.

The next day, they brought me before a judge who sat high above the courtroom, wearing what looked like a white wig. When my case was called, I pled guilty. The judge told me that I would have to forfeit the pepper spray, and once I did, they would release me.

After my release, I turned my attention back to survival. I had less than twenty dollars to my name, and I knew it would not last long. I searched for options and found a tourist map that showed campgrounds scattered around London, some for camper vans, others where tents were allowed. I followed the directions on the Metro out to one of them, checked in, and pitched my small tent. The campground was massive, like a canvas city, with showers for travelers and a sea of brightly colored tents belonging to people from all over the world. It was overwhelming but comforting too. I was not alone in being a wanderer.

Still, I needed money. While riding the Metro one day, an idea struck me. If I could not find work, I could appeal directly to the generosity of strangers. I stopped at a print shop and bought a large white piece of cardboard, about two feet by three feet. On the left side, I authored my story: how I had lost my wallet and was raising enough money for a plane ticket back to the United States. On the right side, I drew a barometer with a $300 goal, coloring it bit by bit as I gathered donations.

Armed with my sign, I began approaching tourists, explaining my situation, and asking for small contributions. Each coin or bill filled in a little more of the barometer, and while progress was slow, every bit gave me a glimmer of hope that I might raise enough to find my way home.

While going sightseeing at various tourist areas, I held up my sign and asked for donations from passersby. To my surprise, most people were kind and generous. In just two or three days, the coins and bills added up quickly, and before long I had collected $2,000, more than enough to cover my return trip to the United States.

Once I had the money in hand, I wasted no time. I went out and bought myself a ticket from London to New York, with a stopover in Shannon, Ireland. Holding that ticket felt like a lifeline, proof that I was finally on my way back home.

However, before leaving on my flight, I had three days to fill. I decided to take a train north of London to a town where Donna was planning to attend nursing school and where Connie and Deanna were going to spend a week with her. On the train, I met a friendly kid who struck up a conversation with me. Since we arrived late that evening, he generously offered to let me stay the night at his home with his parents. The next day, he promised he would take me to where the nursing school was.

The following day, we set out for the nursing school and went to the dorm where Donna was supposed to be living. But when we got there, there was no sign of her, Connie, or Deanna. With no one around, we turned back toward the young guy's house. As we walked up the street, we suddenly saw Donna, Connie, and Deanna coming toward us with a couple of other girls by their side. The timing could not have been better.

That night, we all went to a local pub and had a good old time. After spending a couple of days with the girls, I headed back to London to catch my flight to New York. The flight was long, but eventually I touched down in New York and then caught a bus over to New Jersey, where my car had been parked. The battery was dead, so instead of buying a new one, we gave it a push, popped the clutch, and got it running. From there, I drove home. My first trip to Europe was over, and I returned with more money than I had when I first set out.

12

Pampers

It was 1981, Colleen and I had been married for about three years, and we had a six-month-old baby named Michael, who could not yet walk. I was eager to show Colleen the world, and I wanted to start early. Together we began talking about going to Europe, backpacking, exploring, and taking little Michael along with us in a baby stroller. That would become our very first trip together as a family.

At the time, we were living at the Overton house just outside of Lexington, the old homestead that Colleen had discovered years earlier. It was a quiet, comforting place surrounded by open fields and endless Nebraska skies, a perfect home for new beginnings and big dreams.

So we bought a couple of backpacks, one sturdy pack filled with Pampers, and the other stuffed with the essentials that Colleen and I would need for the journey. We purchased two plane tickets, since Michael could fly for free, and began preparing for what felt like a grand adventure. In the spring of 1981, we boarded our flight bound for Shannon, Ireland.

Our first stop was to visit Father Patrick O'Byrne, who had retired and returned home to Ireland after years of service. He had promised to meet us at Shannon Airport, and the thought of seeing a familiar face waiting there gave our journey a sense of comfort and purpose.

We departed from Omaha, Nebraska, first flying to Chicago, then on to New York, where we would catch our international flight to Shannon, Ireland. Upon arriving in New York, we learned that Michael would also need a ticket to fly. We explained to the ticket agent that we believed children his age could fly for free, and she replied, "Yes, domestically, but not internationally."

Funds were tight, but we scraped together enough money to buy Michael a ticket. Leaving him behind was never an option. Once in the air, the stewardess was exceptionally kind, making sure Michael was comfortable, He sat peacefully in his baby stroller, sleeping between Colleen and me, while we gazed out over the Atlantic toward the new adventure that awaited us.

When we finally arrived in Shannon, Colleen and I were completely exhausted. Father Pat was waiting for us at the airport with his sister and brother-in-law. They drove us to his sister's home, where Colleen and I collapsed into bed and slept for ten hours, trying to adjust to the time difference. During that time, Father Pat's sister kindly cared for Michael, giving us a much-needed chance to recover from the long journey across the Atlantic.

Once we were rested, we enjoyed a warm breakfast before setting out with Father Pat to see the place where he had grown up, his family home, a three-story stone house that had stood for centuries. The thick stone walls held the damp chill of Ireland, and the only warmth came from the old fireplaces scattered throughout the house. The air was cold until you stood close enough to feel the glow of the flames against your skin.

Father Pat, being who he was, never truly retired. Instead, he returned home and started volunteering at a local church and coaching the men's rugby club. His energy, good humor, and devotion were as strong as ever, Seeing him back in his homeland, still serving, still leading, was both inspiring and heartwarming.

After a few days of exploring the countryside near Father Pat's home, visiting the local pubs, and sampling the Irish food, it was time for us to continue our journey. We caught a train to Dublin, where we boarded a ferry across the Irish Sea to England. From there, another train carried us into London, where we spent several days exploring the city and its famous sights.

Colleen had brought along my handwritten journal from my first backpacking trip through Europe and read from it as we toured certain areas I had once described. It was like reliving those early adventures, but this time as a husband and father. After spending a couple of nights in London, we caught another train to the English Channel coast and boarded a ferry bound for France. From there, we continued by train into Paris, where we were welcomed by my Tito Juan, who helped us find a small local hotel that cost us one hundred dollars a night, a considerable sum for us at the time.

I had been in Paris before, but my Tito Juan was a wonderful guide. He took us all over the city, showing us places that cost little or nothing to see. He knew every corner of Paris, having lived there for more than twenty years as both an entertainer and a chef. He was a marvelous cook. One day he bought avocados, tomatoes, and onions, then invited us up to his little suite apartment four stories high, where he made us a simple but delicious salad.

Another day, we decided to visit the Eiffel Tower. We left Michael in the care of a friend of my uncle who lived in the same building, trusting that he would be well looked after. But when we returned later that afternoon, Michael was nowhere to be found. The woman was frantic, running through the streets, crying, and fearing the worst. My uncle tried to calm her, insisting that everything would be all right, that they had only gone for a short walk.

Moments later, Colleen spotted Michael being pushed in his stroller toward the building by a neighbor. She ran to him, scooped him up, and hugged him tightly, tears of relief streaming down her face. She kissed him over and over, so thankful and shaken by how close we had come to a moment of terror in the middle of Paris.

After about three nights in Paris, I bought a ticket for my Uncle Juan to meet us in Puerto de Santa María, and we set out for Spain. Our next destination was Barcelona, though I can't quite remember whether we traveled there by train or by rented car. One way or another, we made our way south toward the Mediterranean, filled with anticipation and excitement for the next chapter of our journey.

Once in Barcelona, we found a small hostel that fits within our budget, though Colleen wasn't especially pleased with it. Still, it provided us with a place to rest and regroup. I showed her where I had once lived and the plaza with the fountain directly across from my old apartment, the very spot where I had often played with Dad and my sisters years earlier.

We visited the Barcelona Zoo, which was as beautiful as I had remembered, full of color, gardens, and the lively sounds of animals and families. At that point, I distinctly remember renting a car in Barcelona and driving south toward Valencia, one of the cities where I had once been stationed during my first European backpacking trip. From Valencia, we continued down the coast to Marbella, Spain, where I managed to reach Charo and her new boyfriend. The four of us went out together for dinner, sharing food, laughter, and stories that bridged old memories with new experiences.

After spending a couple of days in Marbella, we continued our drive southward, eventually rounding the great curve of the Rock of Gibraltar before turning back north toward Puerto de Santa María, our final destination in Spain. My Uncle Juan was flying in from Paris to meet us there, and we could hardly wait to see him.

When we finally arrived in Puerto, we stayed at my aunt's house, where all of her children came by to greet us and to meet Colleen and Michael for the first time. It was a wonderful feeling, one of those deeply emotional moments that stays with you forever, to finally have my beautiful wife and my newborn son meet the rest of my family in Spain.

Once we settled in Puerto de Santa María, we planned to stay for several days. I took Colleen to see our old house and showed her how time had changed it. The once lively home where I had been born now stood in sad disrepair. The bedroom where my grandfather had lived, and where my Uncle Pepe often stayed after having too much to drink, was nearly unrecognizable.

The floors were warped and buckling, weeds pushed up through the cracks, and the wooden timbers of the balcony were sagging dangerously. What had once been a warm family home was now a shadow of its past. Standing there with Colleen and Michael, I felt both sorrow and gratitude, sorrow for what was lost, and gratitude for the life we had built that allowed me to return, eighteen years later, to show them where it had all begun.

During our stay, I showed Colleen the church where I had been baptized in front of the Chapel of Saint John the Baptist. We ate all the seafood we could find in downtown Puerto and took Michael to the beach. I was so happy to have my family there that it nearly brought tears to my eyes.

While we still had the rental car, we decided to drive over to the Navy base in Rota. I showed Colleen the old apartment where my family once lived. The entire area had changed. Now there was a wide walkway along the waterfront wall that I used to climb as a boy to reach the beach below. Looking down, I realized the drop wasn't nearly as far as it had seemed back then, but as a child it had felt like a tremendous climb.

We drove through Rota, and I pointed out some of the places I used to spend time whenever my ship was in port. After the tour, we returned to Puerto for a couple more days before deciding to make one last trip, to Tangier, Morocco, for what would be the second time in my life.

My cousin Manolo and my Tito Juan accompanied us — Colleen, Michael, and me — down to Tarifa, where we caught the ferry across the Strait of Gibraltar to Tangier. Once there, we stayed at the Holiday Inn on the waterfront. We walked along the broad promenade between the road and the ocean, where I noticed a huge excavation site to our left. Five hundred men were working with shovels and picks, digging out the foundation for a new hotel. When I asked why they didn't use heavy machinery, someone explained that machines were too expensive and labor was cheap.

After touring the Medina and spending a couple of days exploring, Colleen grew uncomfortable with the environment. We had a small disagreement and decided it was best to cut the trip short. From Tangier, we caught a flight directly to Madrid, where we then boarded our plane back home. Just as quickly as it had begun, our two-week adventure ended, a journey that marked the beginning of a lifetime of travel together.

13

Business 101

I first started out with Lecher Construction Company in Overton, Nebraska. The business had its roots in an earlier venture that did not even have an official name. People just called it Kearney Roofing. I began that while I was still attending college in Kearney, Nebraska. I did not have much work, just determination and a sense that I could make something out of nothing. Back then, I would call Doug Treptow. Sometimes we would work together. Other times a couple other guys would do a roof while I went out looking for work. Together we made a surprisingly good team. While I was in it for the long-haul, Doug was a premedical student who eventually became a doctor. If I recollect, even Colleen helped us with the roof.

At first, it was simple — a few tools, an orange and white Ford pickup truck that I put a ladder rack on, and a willingness to work harder than anyone else. I was young, strong, and ready to take on the world. Roofing led to remodeling, remodeling led to concrete, and concrete led to full-scale construction. That is when I decided to change the name to Lecher Construction Company.

Big mistake! Looking back, that decision marked a turning point. I thought I was expanding, reaching higher, doing more, becoming something bigger. I was stepping into a world that would bring me both my greatest successes and my deepest regrets. First, one should never name a company after their own surname, because when the business goes bad, your reputation goes right down with it. A company can rise and fall, but a name, your name, carries the weight of every failure, longer than any business.

Lecher Construction Company was incorporated in 1979, the year after Colleen and I were married. At the time, we were still doing roofing work in the Overton and Lexington areas, and I had started bidding on small commercial jobs. I met Johnny Kealey, Colleen's uncle from Hastings, Nebraska, and that meeting would change everything for me. I also started building my own shop and office on the same property that our farmhouse was on.

Our first commercial building was the Windmill State Park Maintenance Building near Gibbon, Nebraska, just off the interstate. You can still see it from the road today. We subcontracted the concrete and hired a framing crew for the structure. I worked side by side with the local tradesmen, doing whatever it took to get it built. The project totaled about $35,000, not much by today's standards, but to me, it was a huge step forward.

Johnny Kealey co-signed my first bond for that job as a favor to Colleen. I paid him $1,500 for doing so. Gene Lilly, of Gene Lilly Bonding in Lincoln, Nebraska, provided my first official bond, a milestone, and a large hurdle that I had to overcome to get into commercial contracting. Little did Johnny Kealey know when he cosigned that bond, soon I would be competing against his own company and taking projects way from. That moment marked my transition from small-town roofer to legitimate contractor. I still remember holding that bond in my hands, feeling like I had finally joined the big leagues.

After that, I bounced around in the SBA bond programs before reconnecting with Gene Lilly Surety. By then, Gene Lilly had passed away, he died suddenly at an AGC convention, and Bob Cerone had taken over. Working with Bob was different, but he believed in me, and that belief kept me in the game. As the years went on, I started bidding against Johnny Kealy's own company.

Bob Cerone was only an agent who connected me with Merchants Bonding Company out of Des Moines, Iowa, the kindest, most professional people I ever met. Through that relationship, I began building housing projects across Nebraska, first an eight-unit complex in Trenton, then twelve units in Beaver City, and twenty-four in Gothenburg. Each job grew bigger and more complex. Then came the forty-eight-unit complex in McCook, my biggest job yet, built for the elderly. I wanted to prove myself, but it turned out to be too much, too soon. It broke me.

At the same time, I was also building maintenance buildings for the State of Nebraska and Super 8 Motels along Interstate 80. My estimating was not as sharp as it should have been, and neither were my social skills, which I now understand were shaped by Asperger's. It made it hard for me to have a good relationship with project owners or managers, forcing me to focus only on public works projects where bids always went to the lowest bidder. Every job felt like a tug-of-war. I worked hard with little profit margin, sometimes with none to cover the bills. Had I been a better communicator, I would have been a better negotiator and would not have had to bid on every single project just to stay alive.

By then we were approaching the five-year mark, but my business was financially sliding into a deep hole. I had always dreamed of moving to Colorado. I loved to ski and imagined building a new life there. But instead, my short-lived business career was collapsing. Merchants Bonding Company eventually had to step in and start paying my company's bills. That was a hard pill to swallow.

That is when I got involved with the SBA 8(a) Program, a federal initiative designed to help minority-owned businesses get government work. I threw myself into it, determined to rebuild. But there was only so much federal work in Nebraska, and two other contractors were already active in the same program. So, I made a bold decision, I moved my company and family to California, where there were more opportunities and more risks.

I remember going out to California and meeting with all the SBA representatives. They assured me there would be work if I made the move. So, I found a condominium for my family, went back to Nebraska, and said, "We're moving to California." And just like that, we did. I drove a semi-truck loaded with everything we owned — back then you did not need a CDL — while Colleen followed in the van with our three kids. It was quite a trip, filled with equal parts hope and fear.

My first job under the 8(a) program was for the Bureau of Reclamation out of Sacramento, building a new wooden bridge across the Fresno River Bridge near Madera, California. It was a huge leap from the kind of projects I had done in Nebraska, and for the first time, I felt like I was truly part of something bigger.

I opened a small office above an antique store in downtown Clovis and worked there until I could afford a proper space. My family adjusted well to the area, and before long, we were an institution at Mountain View Preschool, where all the kids attended before elementary school at Cathedral of the Rising Christ, a small Catholic school. I had to get my California contractor's license, though I did not realize how critical that was until later. In the meantime, I completed a couple of jobs without a valid license, something that could have landed me in jail. But back then, I was still learning, still hustling, still trying to make it all work.

Through it all, Merchants Bonding Company continued to stand by me. I will never forget that. I told myself that if I could ever get back on my feet, I would pay them back in full. It was not just a financial debt; it was a debt of honor.

By then, I had become a good-sized contractor in Fresno. I bought a new home for my family and made a large down payment. On the outside, it looked like success, but inside, I was still wrestling with the same demons, the inability to connect, the frustration that came with being misunderstood. The only people I had a good relationship with were the ones who worked for me, the ones who followed direction without question.

Merchants Bonding was trying to distance their relationship from me, though they convinced Jack Gethman of Gethman Construction, another client of theirs, to enter a silent partnership with me. The only problem with this was since I was in the 8a program it did not allow to have large businesses or nonminority involved in the management of the company. Jack made things worse. He began cutting corners, even canceling the office coffee service, and that told me all I needed to know about his priorities.

When Jack filed a lawsuit against me, I had no choice but to file for bankruptcy just to get him out of my life. Soon after, the SBA discovered my prior involvement with Jack and removed me from the 8(a) program. Everything I had built, the company, the California move, the new life, fell apart.

I struggled for the next couple of years, doing things I knew I should not have done just to survive. Desperation makes you take shortcuts, and those shortcuts come back to haunt you. Around the ten-year mark in California, I was indicted for mail fraud. It was a hard fall; one I brought entirely on myself.

Just because you leave a state does not mean the mistakes stay behind. I learned that the hard way. After moving my family back to Lexington, Nebraska, I made the decision to return to California, plead guilty, and face the consequences. The judge sentenced me to fifteen months at the Yankton Federal Prison Camp. Walking through those gates was one of the hardest things I had ever done, but it was also the start of something new, honesty.

Although Asperger's has often been a challenge, especially when it comes to connecting with people, it has also been a hidden strength. It gave me the focus and persistence to keep going, even when everything fell apart.

When I was released from Yankton, I made myself one promise: I would never again cut corners or lie to get ahead. I would never again rely on needing a bond or becoming a general contractor, because I did not have the temperament or desire to go through that ordeal again. I wanted my wife Colleen and children to be proud of me for I had brought bad karma upon them.

I bought my old 1977 Chevy back in 1979 from a dealer in Lexington, Nebraska. It belonged to another construction company called Weaver Construction, now known as Sampson Construction. It was a blue crew cab, and from that point on, every truck I bought in the Lexington and Overton area was blue. When my company finally broke into Nebraska, I drove that same truck back to California. Later, I had it painted white, and every truck I bought afterward was white as well.

One day, after a court hearing in California, I came out to find that my truck had been towed. I did not have the $300 in cash to get it out. The old truck, half-restored and missing all windows, sat at my house on Santa Ana until the bank foreclosed the property.

Yes, I drove that truck all the way back to Nebraska without windows, wearing only a motorcycle helmet and face shield. Whenever I needed gas, I would fill the tank, move the truck to the side of the station, and go inside for a cup of coffee. After paying for the coffee, I would quietly drive away. It was a strange kind of survival, but it got me home.

After being released from the Bureau of Prisons thirty years ago, I promised myself and my family that I would never do anything again that would make them ashamed of me. While in Yankton, I had already begun planning a new business, one that would do demolition work, projects that did not require bonds. I called it Midwest Demolition and I have a fleet of red trucks.

We repainted the old Chevy red, bought small tools, and within three months of my release, I started Midwest Demolition Company. Colleen may be gone now, and the old truck may be retired, parked behind my shop alongside others, but it's still there, still red, a reminder of where I came from and what I rebuilt from nothing, and Midwest Demolition bonding company is no one else but Bob Cerone with Gene Lilly Surety. The first 15 years of my business career turned out to be disastrous, but after Yankton I made the promise that never again when I put my wife and children in harm's way. It has been 30 years and Midwest Demolition and has been thriving with one hundred employees.

14

YANKTON

AFTER I PLED GUILTY IN FRESNO, CALIFORNIA, to one count of mail fraud, the judge sentenced me to fifteen months. I asked to serve my time at Yankton, South Dakota's Federal Prison Camp (FPC), otherwise known among inmates as Yankton College. Rumor had it that Dan Rather had once attended Yankton College. There was no security fence and only a few cameras scattered across the grounds. The atmosphere was not at all what most people imagined when they thought of prison. We could walk across the street to the dining hall and gymnasium, carefully waiting for cars to pass first. The entire facility looked and felt more like an old college campus than a penitentiary.

In 1984, the Bureau of Prisons purchased Yankton College after the school closed that December for $3.1 million, following approval by the bankruptcy court. It was converted into a federal prison camp and officially opened in 1988. Yankton College had been the first college established in the Dakota Territory, and by the look of its aging buildings and classic architecture, it was not hard to tell how far back its history went.

Megan and Colleen drove me up to Yankton, and we tried to make the most of the time we had together. Along the way, we passed a cornfield that had already been harvested. To our surprise, it was filled with pheasants, more than I had ever seen in my life. I used to hunt them and could never find one, but that day they were everywhere. It felt like some kind of sign, though I could not say what it meant.

That night, Megan, Colleen, and I stayed in a small motel near the prison. We went out for supper, talking and laughing a little, trying to keep things light even though we all knew what was coming. The next morning, they drove me to the camp where I was to begin serving my sentence. Saying goodbye was one of the hardest moments of my life. Watching them drive away hit harder than the sentence itself.

I learned quickly that a person in prison with Asperger's was not going to get along with many people. Even in prison, you still needed social skills. The drug dealers and smokers had their own tight little clique, and if you did not smoke or have cigarettes to trade, you were automatically on the outside. For someone like me, living with Asperger's meant seeing the world in black and white, rules and structure, right and wrong, and prison was anything but structured or fair. The constant complaining, the lack of personal space, and the unpredictable behavior of others could drive a man to the edge. To survive, you had to learn how to read people fast, when to speak, and when to disappear into the background. It might have been a minimum-security camp, but for someone with Asperger's, every day was a minefield of misunderstandings waiting to happen. The invisible barriers between groups were as solid as any wall. I survived by keeping to myself, sticking to a routine, and observing everything before making a move.

I was a good person, but I was not a good prisoner. If someone did something to me, they always seemed to get away with it. But if I did something to somebody else, no matter how small, I always seemed to get caught. I was not smart enough to hide it, or the staff just watched me more closely. Either way, the rules never seemed to work in my favor.

When new inmates arrived, they were given an orientation with everyone who came in that week. It did not take long for rumors to start. If a guy came in with a reputation for being a rat, the first thing he would do was try to pin that label on someone else to deflect attention. That is exactly what happened with Dan Marino, who checked into the prison the same day I did. He had helped send his own father-in-law to prison for life, yet he ended up in a minimum-security camp because he had cooperated with the government.

Marino was a convicted drug dealer and a pain in the ass from day one, but I found a way to get under his skin. I knew he was taking GED classes while I was finishing my college degree through the camp's business program. Whenever there was a crowd of guys around, I would call out, "Hey, Marino, how do you spell GED?" He hated that. Eventually, he dropped out of the class altogether. The truth was, he was too embarrassed for anyone to know he had never finished high school. As far as I was concerned, Marino was a real loser.

The hatred between Marino and me only grew worse as time went on. With just two months left before I was set to go home, things reached a boiling point. Marino somehow made a deal with a big, burly inmate to put human waste in my pillowcase. When I found out, I nearly had a nervous breakdown. The cruelty and humiliation hit me harder than anything else during my sentence. From that point on, I kept my distance from him completely. The hatred between us ran deep — and it was mutual.

Even though I loved to play softball, I was not well-liked enough to be invited to play on a team. I always walked to the chow hall and the gym alone. When I sat down at a table with other inmates to have a bite to eat, they would stand up, grab their trays, and move to another table. For whatever reason, they did not want to be associated with me.

As a footnote, a couple of years later, after I started Midwest Demolition, I hired some of these same men from the halfway house in Omaha to work for me. It did not seem like I ever had any friends in that place, nor did I really want any.

Once, I found a walking partner on the track, and one night while we were walking, I decided to take a piss just off the track onto the grass. My partner stopped and did the same. As we were peeing, another inmate walked by. The next day, I was called in to talk to the lieutenant about what we had done. The lieutenant lied when he said he could see us on camera, when in fact there were no cameras in that area. The truth was the inmate who walked by us while we were peeing snitched me out but did not snitch on the other guy who was with me. Like a fool, I told the lieutenant who the other guy was, and the two of us ended up doing extra duty at night. Either way, we were guilty, and we should never have taken a leak on the grass directly across the street from people's houses.

About two months before my scheduled release, the administration decided they had had enough of me. I had been filing BP-8s left and right, raising hell over everything from case handling to inmate treatment. I was supposed to be released to a halfway house, but instead, they sent me to FCI Waseca. It was a tougher, more hard-nosed facility that housed cartel members and major drug traffickers, guys doing money laundering and big federal cases. Compared to Yankton, it was a different world: structured, intense, and with far less tolerance for someone like me.

In the federal prison system, there is a method for filing grievances with the administration known as the BP-8 through BP-11 process. It starts with an informal complaint (BP-8) and can move all the way up to the Bureau of Prisons' Central Office in Washington, D.C. Each step requires a different staff member to review your complaint and respond within a set time. Inmates called these written requests "kites." Filing one was often the only official way to make your voice heard, though responses were usually slow and worded to protect the system rather than fix the problem.

I raised so much hell with the administration after that incident with Marino that they finally decided to move me. They took me to a cell at the county jail, where I spent the remainder of my time in Yankton. At least there, I was away from Marino and the constant tension.

Being who I was, I filed a record number of BP forms during my time there. I knew how to use the system, and I was not afraid to make noise when something was not right. The staff, in return, found their own way to get back at me. Whenever one of my complaints was scheduled for review, they would have a guard from the midnight shift call me out of bed to "hear the case" at three in the morning. It became their little game, but I did not back down. If anything, it only made me more determined to make my point.

I was simply smarter than most of the guards who worked at Yankton FPC. But that did not matter. In prison, intelligence counted for little when you were up against authority. The guards, referred to by inmates as "HACK," short for Horses Ass Carrying Keys, the overwhelming power to direct me, to control what I did and when I did it, and to remind me that no matter how smart I thought I was, I was still the one wearing khaki.

Two weeks later, I was transferred to FCI Waseca, a low-security federal correctional institution in southern Minnesota. At that time, Waseca was still a men's prison before it was converted into a women's facility years later. Life there was simpler. Instead of one big dorm, the prison had smaller rooms with three or four inmates, giving us a little more privacy and making it easier to keep to ourselves.

The FCI counselor assigned to me could not understand why I had been transferred from Yankton with only two months left to serve, but after meeting me, she figured it out quickly — I was a pain in the ass. Even so, she treated me fairly and seemed to respect the fact that I stood up for myself, even when it caused me trouble.

Getting transferred to an FCI did not bother me as much as knowing that, for the next two months, I would not be able to see my family because it was too far for them to drive. Colleen did visit me once at the county jail while I awaited transfer. Once I arrived at FCI Waseca and went through orientation, I recognized a familiar face from Yankton. He was there for disciplinary reasons. I, on the other hand, was there simply because I was a pain in the ass.

I was able to find a job in the prison system working in the architectural department, where they drew plans for improvements to the facility. Because I had prior experience in construction and business, the position came naturally to me. It gave me a sense of purpose and a way to use my skills, even if it did not make life any easier outside that office. It was a decent job that gave me an opportunity to refresh my own past architectural experience.

However, one thing I could not have a good relationship with was stupid inmates, and every prison has several of them. In the architectural office, there was one inmate in particular who did not know a thing but could talk up a storm, always trying to make himself look tough. Eventually, I got into it with him. He attacked me, but by the time the guard walked in, he was the one on the floor.

I was kicking his butt because I used my takedown move from my old wrestling days. We were both sent to solitary, which consisted of two medical rooms with a concrete bed. We were both held there for about three days before the unit manager had to come in and give us our sentence. Myself, I requested further advanced disciplinary unit where several members from the administration would be present. This required them to move me to a higher facility where there was solitary confinement. And that was a request which I was entitled to as one of my rights. However, with only a few days left of my sentence, they decided not to honor my rights and left me in solitary confinement for another four days until I was released.

And just like that I was a free man. I took a bus to Des Moines, Iowa on my day of release, the 24th of December, where Colleen was waiting for me and we went home together.

15

2002
THE EUROPEAN
HARLEY ADVENTURE

ONE OF MY MOST MEMORABLE ADVENTURES took place in 2002, when Colleen and I shipped our 2000 Harley-Davidson Road King to Paris, France, with plans to ride south through France and across the border into Spain, finishing our journey in Puerto de Santa María. The trip was carefully timed so that we could meet our four children and my grandson, Christian, in Madrid. It was a dream we had talked about for years, combining our love of travel, family, and the open road.

Our biggest decision wasn't whether to go but how to get the kids there safely. Should we send all four on the same flight or divide them into two different planes? Colleen knew how anxious I was about flying, and when I asked her opinion, she said she'd leave that decision to me, and that told me everything I needed to know. If anything happened to the kids, she'd never forgive me, so after thinking it through, I decided to put Michael, Samantha, and Christian together on one plane, and Katie and Megan on another. It felt like the safer bet, even if it meant doubling the nerves.

The Harley had already been crated and shipped overseas a week earlier, and once the freight company confirmed its arrival, Colleen and I booked separate flights to Paris. I landed first and waited at the gate for her so we could go through immigration together. Stepping into Charles de Gaulle Airport brought that unmistakable feeling of excitement, the beginning of a new adventure, the hum of foreign languages, and the smell of espresso drifting through the terminal.

After collecting our luggage, we took a taxi to the freight depot where our Harley awaited us. When I finally spotted the wooden crate marked with our name, it was like finding buried treasure. But getting it open was another story. I borrowed a crowbar and began prying off the boards one nail at a time until the bike stood free. The relief didn't last long, because when I hit the starter, Harley refused to turn over. After all that effort, it wouldn't start.

The freight handlers helped me locate a local Harley-Davidson shop, and within thirty minutes, a young man who looked like a weightlifter arrived with a flatbed tow truck. He barely spoke English but knew exactly what to do when he saw the Harley. With a confident nod, he secured the bike with heavy straps, then motioned for Colleen and me to climb into the cab beside him. As we rode through the outskirts of Paris, I could tell by his grin that he took pride in helping fellow riders, even if we couldn't share more than a few words.

He drove us straight to a Harley-Davidson shop on the edge of the city where the mechanics immediately went to work. You could tell Colleen was eyeing the well-built driver while she grinned at me. While the mechanics worked on the bike, Colleen and I crossed the street to a small café and ordered two cups of coffee. It was a clear, cool morning that made Paris look like a painting, with cobblestone streets, old iron balconies, and the soft sound of scooters echoing between the buildings. Within an hour, the mechanic waved from the doorway and gave us a thumb-up. The problem turned out to be nothing more than a loose cable in the throttle switch, and the total bill came to less than two hundred dollars. We both laughed in relief, knowing our adventure could finally begin.

As we rode into the city, it took us a while to locate our hotel, but once we did, we were truly relieved. Then came our next challenge: parking. The clerk explained that if we left the motorcycle in the street, it would certainly get towed. To my surprise, he suggested we park it on the sidewalk directly across from the entrance, so that's exactly what we did. Every night, I'd glance out the window just to make sure it was still there, gleaming under the streetlight.

Colleen, Michael, and I had been to Paris once before, years earlier, when my Uncle John had taken us around the city. He was a wonderful guide, full of energy and good humor, leading us from Notre-Dame to the Eiffel Tower, to the Arc de Triomphe, and along the Seine. That earlier trip gave us a taste of the city's charm, but this time it felt different, because this time, we were beginning an adventure entirely on our own.

Over the next few days, we prepared for the long ride ahead. I double-checked the Harley, organized our gear, and studied the map that would take us south through France's countryside toward Bordeaux, across the Pyrenees, and into Spain. There was a feeling of anticipation in the air, one that only comes when you're about to set out on the open road, unsure of exactly what you'll find but certain it will be unforgettable.

We spent three days in Paris, visiting the Eiffel Tower, the Louvre, and Notre-Dame, and dined several times in the Saint-Michel district of downtown Paris. The French food was wonderful, and the atmosphere was thrilling, romantic, lively, and full of that unmistakable Parisian flair.

Once we decided to leave, our plan was to head toward Geneva, Switzerland. After finding our way out of Paris, we began driving through some of the most scenic countryside I had ever seen. We avoided the interstates and took the side roads through small villages, winding through the mountains toward the Swiss border.

After arriving in Geneva and checking into our hotel, I asked the English-speaking desk clerk for advice on parking the Harley. He directed me to a large underground garage, and I managed to find it without trouble. It was massive, single-level, well-lit, and secure.

That evening, Colleen and I went out for supper near Lake Geneva. We ordered a large platter filled with every kind of shellfish imaginable, and afterward, we walked along the lake, admiring the lights reflecting on the water. I decided to leave the Harley in the garage while we explored the city. We took local transportation, enjoying the change of pace.

When our time in Geneva ended, we rode south toward the French Riviera and the town of Nice. We didn't ride fast, preferring to stay under the speed limit and follow the quiet country roads, taking in the beautiful scenery at our own pace. Other motorcyclists sped past us on sport bikes, crouched low against the wind, while Colleen and I rode upright and comfortably on our Harley, enjoying every mile.

After two days of travel, we arrived at our destination, Villefranche-sur-Mer, the same port where my Navy ship had anchored years earlier. In those days, the little village had been a fishing community, but now it was a charming tourist destination.

We found a clean, comfortable hotel, though the bathroom was down the hallway, a bit unusual for us. The kind lady who owned the hotel allowed us to park the Harley in a secure yard behind the building for the duration of our stay.

From there, we set out on foot whenever we wanted to explore. I wanted to show Colleen everything, every street, every bar, every place I had once visited. But time had changed the town. Where there had once been sailor bars, there were now boutiques and cafés, and Colleen enjoyed those boutiques just as much as I had enjoyed the bars years earlier.

Near our hotel ran a light rail train that stretched the length of the French Riviera. One day, we decided to take it to Monaco and visit the famous Monte Carlo Casino. When we arrived, we found the train station built into the mountain, requiring several escalators to reach the streets below. The yachts in the harbor were enormous floating palaces owned by people whose wealth was beyond imagination. The casino itself was elegant and historic, and though we were on a budget, we couldn't resist stepping inside for a quick look.

Another day, we took the train in the opposite direction to Nice, a much larger and livelier city. We wandered through the outdoor markets, filled with colors, scents, and foods that could make anyone gain ten pounds just by looking at them. Every afternoon during our travels, Colleen and I made it a habit to take a short nap, and in Nice, we found a grassy hill where we lay down together under the sun.

Later, we visited a department store where Colleen wanted to browse. Somehow, we became separated, and for over an hour, I searched in panic, imagining the worst. Finally, I decided to return to the train station, hoping she would do the same, and sure enough, when I arrived back at our small platform in Villefranche, Colleen stepped off the next train, not looking particularly amused.

After a few days, it was time to head toward Spain. We followed the coastal highway, spending one night in Marseille before continuing. As we neared the border, we decided to stop for one final night in France, in a small seaside town called Banyuls-sur-Mer. We found a tiny family-run hotel, the smallest we had ever stayed in, but it was warm and welcoming. Too tired to go out, we ate dinner there and took a quiet evening walk along the beach before turning in.

The next morning, we crossed into Spain. There were no grand gates or fanfare, just a small shed no larger than a portable booth and a sign reading "España," but to me, it meant everything. I was home again, heading toward my beloved Barcelona, where I longed to walk La Rambla and savor every kind of tapas imaginable.

The drive through Catalonia was stunning, with fields of sunflowers, rolling hills, and bursts of tulips in every color. As we neared Barcelona, traffic thickened. We eventually found a hotel with an underground garage so steep it felt like a 60-degree angle going in and out. After settling in, we dropped off the laundry and headed out on foot to explore.

Barcelona was as vibrant as ever, with music, laughter, and food everywhere. We strolled through the Gothic Quarter, down to the Columbus Monument, and indulged in tapas until we could eat no more. It happened to be the 2002 World Cup, and Brazil had just won. The entire city exploded with joy. Colleen and I joined the celebration, buying bright yellow Brazil soccer shirts and dancing down La Rambla with the crowds.

When it came time to head to Madrid, we decided to take the overnight train and have the Harley shipped on the same route. I delivered the bike to the station a day early so it could be loaded and secured properly. Colleen and I booked a sleeper car, giving us a chance to rest as the train rolled through the Spanish countryside.

By morning, we arrived in Madrid. I collected the Harley from the cargo section, then met Colleen out in front of the train station with our bags. From there, we rode to the airport to meet our children. While waiting for the second flight, I decided to rest my eyes. I must have fallen asleep, because when someone tried to wake me, I shot up yelling, "¡No me Toca! ¡No, me Toca!", Spanish for "Don't touch me!", only to find it was Katie trying to wake me.

Once everyone had arrived and we gathered all the luggage, we loaded into the car and began the long drive south to Puerto de Santa María. It was a full day's journey, especially with a baby, but Colleen and I had done it before when Michael was young. I led the way on the Harley, with the family following behind in the car. We spent one night in a roadside motel before continuing.

By the following afternoon, we arrived at my aunt's house, where my mother and my uncle Tito Juan were waiting. Tito Juan had recently retired from Paris and moved back home, living near my aunt's place. We all stayed together in a modest three-bedroom apartment filled with the aroma of incredible home-cooked meals.

While in Puerto, we decided to take a guided day trip to Tangier, Morocco, via the Spanish enclave of Ceuta. We crossed the Strait of Gibraltar by ferry and boarded a bus into Tangier for a quick tour of the Medina. Midway there, the bus had to stop so Katie could get off and be sick, as she had always been prone to motion sickness unless she was the one driving. My cousin Miguel and his wife Rosie joined us for the day, and it turned into one of those short but unforgettable journeys.

Days later, I received a message from my office asking me to call home immediately. When I reached Colleen's mother, she broke the sad news that Grandma Berriger had passed away. I took Colleen aside, held her tight, and gave her the heartbreaking news. She was close to her grandmother, and though we were far from home, we grieved together.

Colleen called her mother, and they discussed the situation at hand before deciding that Colleen should continue her vacation with the family. The conversation brought her peace of mind, and by evening, her laughter had returned. After a day or two, we decided to take a day trip to Marbella. Colleen and I had been there a few times before, but we wanted the kids to experience its beauty, the sea breeze, the bright Andalusian sun, and the rhythm of life that makes the Costa del Sol feel like paradise.

My cousin Lola agreed to watch baby Christian while we were gone. After a couple of days of planning and enjoying the calm pace of our vacation in Puerto, we packed our things and headed south toward Gibraltar before turning north toward Marbella. The drive was scenic, the road winding along the coast with the blue Mediterranean glimmering to our right. We stopped at a small gas station to grab some snacks and stretch our legs. Michael, being Michael, stayed in the back of the small station wagon we had rented, half-listening to music. Suddenly, the song "The Ketchup Song" by Las Ketchup came blasting from the radio. The girls instantly recognized it and jumped into an impromptu dance, laughing and moving in perfect rhythm to the beat that had become a sensation all over Spain. Their carefree dancing filled the air with joy, though it absolutely drove Michael crazy.

Once back on the road, we stopped briefly at the yacht club in Puerto Banús, a glamorous marina lined with luxury yachts and seaside cafés. Colleen wanted to buy flowers to throw into the Mediterranean Sea in honor of her grandmother. The girls walked down near the edge of the pier, the salty air brushing their faces as they gently tossed the flowers into the water, watching them drift and swirl with the waves. It was a quiet and beautiful moment, filled with love, remembrance, and the peaceful sound of the sea.

From there, we continued into Marbella to show the kids this charming coastal town, a place that had always felt special to me. Marbella, with its narrow cobblestone streets, whitewashed houses, and lively plazas, has a way of capturing the heart of anyone who visits. As we walked through the old quarter, the scent of fresh bread and blooming jasmine filled the air. I had been there several times over the years, and each visit brought a new appreciation for the simple beauty of Spanish life.

By late afternoon, Samantha began to grow restless and wanted to return to Puerto to see baby Christian. We made our way back along the same scenic road, the sunset reflecting on the sea like a path of gold. When we reached Puerto de Santa María, we stopped by Lola's house to pick up the baby. The moment Samantha saw him, her whole face lit up with joy. We headed home afterward, exhausted but happy, and went straight to bed after a long, beautiful day on the coast.

Before leaving Lincoln for Spain, we had arranged for baby Christian to be baptized in the same church where I had been baptized as a child, a place filled with family history and memories. The entire family attended, along with our Spanish relatives. Michael proudly served as the godfather, and Kathy Mack as the godmother. I stood beside Sammy, watching as the priest poured holy water over Christian's head. Afterward, he unlocked a small gate behind the statue of the Virgin Mary, revealing the Virgin's great cape that hung in sweeping folds above the altar. He invited Sammy and the baby to walk beneath it, a traditional Spanish blessing said to bring divine protection. Rosa quickly took the baby from my cousin Miguel and followed, eager to share in the moment.

Following Spanish custom, we hosted a dinner in Christian's honor at a local restaurant just outside of town. The tables were filled with family and friends, laughter, and the sound of clinking glasses. Traditional dishes of paella, seafood, and tapas filled the air with wonderful aromas. It was a perfect evening of joy and gratitude, a celebration not only of Christian's baptism but also of the family bonds that tied us across continents.

As our trip neared its end, the girls made the most of their final days on the beaches and at the lively flea markets, where vendors sold colorful scarves, handmade jewelry, and trinkets of all kinds. Colleen and I spent our evenings in the old quarter, enjoying seafood dinners by the waterfront and reminiscing about how far our lives had brought us, from the plains of Nebraska to the shores of southern Spain.

Before we left there was one final thing that I had to get accomplished. My children were pestering me that they wanted to meet my dad. So, I took them all down to the little bar right down the road from his home. And sure enough, there he was drinking little shots of wine and talking to his friends. I didn't know whether he recognized me, for I had not seen him for years. He was getting old and was starting to get Alzheimers. I found out that my mother was on the way down to that bar only to defend herself, but I cut her off down the street. I saw her charging like a bull toward the bar when I stopped her and told her to go and that she could tell her side of the story to the grandchildren later when they got home. She turned around and went back to the apartment while my children sat in the bar with their grandfather.

On our final day in Spain, we drove to Madrid, spent the night at a nearby hotel, and returned the rental car the next morning. As our plane lifted off the runway, I looked down at the land that had given me so many memories over my lifetime — childhood, family, love, and renewal. We were heading home to Lincoln, Nebraska, ready for a well-deserved rest after one of the most memorable family trips of our lives.

16

2003
Harley Ride

In 2003, we decided to ride our Harley-Davidson motorcycle to Tangier, Morocco, to see how far we could travel down the coast of Africa. We began our journey along the southern coast of Spain, leaving from Puerto de Santa María and following the road toward Tarifa, a small port city known for its ferry that crosses the Strait of Gibraltar. Once there, we carefully loaded the Harley onto the ferry and set out across the water toward Tangier.

Starting in Cádiz, the coastline was alive with charming seaside communities and wide sandy beaches. The sparkling blue of the Atlantic merged with the Mediterranean breeze, creating a landscape that was nothing short of breathtaking. The ferry ride itself was brief but meaningful, crossing one of the narrowest points between Europe and Africa, only nine miles of water separating two continents that had exchanged people, goods, and culture for centuries.

When we arrived in Tangier, the scene was instantly hectic. After getting our passports stamped and unloading the motorcycle, we rode through the city's winding streets. Tangier pulsed with energy, the sound of car horns, the calls of street vendors, and the chatter of people moving quickly through their daily routines. Narrow alleys overflowed with colorful fabrics, spices, and trinkets, while the scent of freshly baked bread mingled with the salty sea air. It was chaotic yet full of life, every turn revealing another layer of its vibrant culture. Tangier had long been a crossroads between Africa and Europe, once a haven for writers, spies, and wanderers in the mid-20th century. Even in 2003, it still carried the mystique of its international past.

We made reservations that day at the El Minzah Hotel, located near the Medina in downtown Tangier. The hotel itself was elegant, with traditional Moorish architecture, arched doorways, and tiled courtyards filled with the scent of orange blossoms. Built in the 1930s by the British aristocrat Lord Bute, El Minzah had once hosted celebrities, diplomats, and authors like Paul Bowles and Tennessee Williams. From our room, we could see the bustling streets below and the distant shimmer of the harbor. It wanted to step back in time, blending old-world charm with a quiet sense of luxury.

When we arrived at the hotel, I went inside to check in with the clerks while Colleen waited outside, sitting on the motorcycle as if she were guarding the Harley from being stolen. She wore short pants and a white tank top, and her fair skin and long blonde hair made her stand out to everyone passing by. When I finished checking in, I walked back outside and was immediately met by Colleen's frustration. She was upset that I had left her out there alone, feeling exposed and embarrassed. People had been staring, and she told me she felt as though every passerby had mistaken her for something she was not. That moment reminded me how different our worlds could feel, even when we were standing side by side.

After a couple of days of sightseeing in Tangier, we headed along the coastline toward Rabat. The road south followed the Atlantic, bordered by dusty hills and ocean views that stretched endlessly. Along the way, we stopped at a roadside goat barbecue stand and tried the local food, which was rich in spices and smoke. Rabat, Morocco's capital, was far quieter than

Tangier, with broad boulevards, palm-lined avenues, and colonial architecture left over from the French protectorate. But after one night, we realized we didn't care much for its formality, and the pull of the open road drew us back north toward Tangier. The next morning, we caught the first ferry back to Spain.

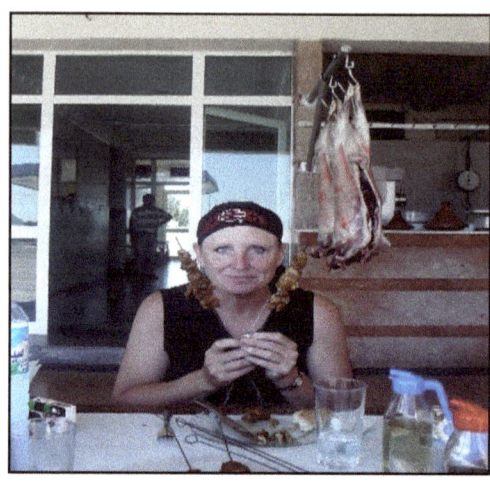

Once across, we rode along the coast to Marbella, stopping overnight at the Rock of Gibraltar. The towering limestone formation, rising more than 1,300 feet above the sea, marked one of the most famous natural landmarks in Europe, a reminder of the centuries of naval history that passed through the Strait. From there, we continued to Marbella, a resort town known for its beaches and Mediterranean charm, where we rested for a couple of days. Marbella has always been one of my favorite places to go and relax. From the very first European trip to my very last, I have always stopped and visited Marbella. Marbella has always been the hometown of Charo and her family.

Marbella has always been a magnet to backpackers because it hosts hostels for them to have a place to stay without paying too much. From Marbella, Colleen and I rode up to Ronda, Spain, one of the most breathtaking places we had ever seen. Perched high in the Andalusian mountains, Ronda was built around a deep gorge called El Tajo, which split the city into two. The famous Puente Nuevo bridge spans the gorge, a stone marvel dating back to the 18th century. From its edges, we could see rolling hills dotted with olive groves and whitewashed villages shimmering in the distance. The air was crisp and cool, and every curve of the mountain road offered another postcard view. From there, we descended two hundred miles back to Puerto de Santa María, completing a journey that had taken us through the most beautiful corners of Spain and North Africa.

Once back in Puerto, we decided to rent a car and head west to Lisbon, Portugal. Lisbon was a city of hills and light, where trams rattled through narrow streets lined with tiled facades. We spent days wandering the Alfama district, listening to the mournful sound of Fado music drifting from small taverns, and tasting the famous custard tarts known as pastéis de nata. The city carried a quiet grandeur shaped by centuries of exploration and discovery; it was from these very shores that ships had once sailed to chart the unknown world.

From Lisbon, we made our way to Pamplona, Spain, for the famous Running of the Bulls. This time, instead of sleeping in a tent in the park as we had in our younger days, we stayed in a hotel of the three Kings, at an astonishing $500 a night, even back then. It was a reminder of how much had changed over the years, but the excitement of being part of that tradition was as strong as ever.

We were there only to watch, not to run, but the atmosphere was electric. The festival of San Fermín dated back to the 13th century and had become world-renowned, partly thanks to Ernest Hemingway's novel *The Sun Also Rises*. The narrow cobblestone streets of Pamplona were lined with red and white scarves, shirts, banners, all blending into a sea of tradition and danger. While trying to enter the bullfighting arena among thousands of people, I suddenly felt a small hand in my pocket. When I looked down, I caught a boy no older than ten trying to pickpocket me, while an adult nearby tried to pull him away. It all happened in an instant.

Once inside the arena, chaos reigned. From the stands, we looked down at the arena floor where hundreds of runners darted in every direction, bulls charging after them in a mix of bravery, fear, and sheer madness. Watching them, I couldn't help but remember my first trip to Europe when I was twenty-two, running on that same arena floor like a young fool with a VCR camera in one hand, trying to record my own daring. Now, standing beside Colleen, I felt the same thrill, but from the safety of the stands.

Every morning in Pamplona, we woke up early, enjoying a king-sized bed and a magnificent breakfast buffet at the hotel. If you weren't at the arena by five in the morning, you'd never have a seat. Watching the event each day brought back memories of youth, courage, and the hunger for adventure. It was one of the most valuable experiences I ever had. I would return to Pamplona two more times in my life, each visit different but equally unforgettable.

Our 2003 Harley journey ended in Madrid, where we dropped off the rental car and caught our flight home. The trip took us across continents and cultures, through dusty roads and glittering coastlines, through laughter, exhaustion, and reflection. It was a reminder that adventure is as much about the road ahead as it is about the one that leads you back home.

17

2004
Journey to the Olympic Games

It was the summer of 2004, our third consecutive year riding motorcycles through Europe, most of our time spent in Spain. That year felt special from the very beginning. The rhythm of travel had become second nature to Colleen and me. Every road, every port, carried a sense of familiarity and adventure. Our daughter Megan, her friend Megan Schultz, and Courtney joined us for the summer, eager to experience Europe the way Colleen and I had come to love it — freely, one town at a time.

We decided to rent a house in the heart of Puerto de Santa María, a lively coastal town along Spain's southern edge. The city, steeped in centuries of maritime history, was once one of the great ports of Andalusia during the Age of Discovery. Its streets are lined with cafés, seafood markets, and narrow cobbled alleys that opened suddenly into sunlit plazas filled with laughter and music. Our rented apartment was modest but perfect, close enough to the beach that we could hear the faint crash of waves at night and the calls of vendors drifting up from the plaza below.

We also rented a small car from the airport in Jerez, though I can't quite recall what it was after all these years. The girls spent their days basking on the beach and their evenings at the open-air flea market, where lights, music, and laughter filled the warm night air. They explored stalls filled with handmade jewelry, colorful scarves, and the sweet scent of churros and roasted nuts. There was always something to do and somewhere new to discover.

One day, the girls wanted to visit Tangier, Morocco, so we drove down to Tarifa to catch the ferry across the Strait of Gibraltar without Colleen. I felt not only like a guide but also a bodyguard. We took the ferry over for a day trip before they returned home to the States. The time Megan and her friends spent in Spain went by quickly, filled with shopping for trinkets, beach days, and boy-watching. In any case, they were having a wonderful time, and both Colleen and I were happy for them.

That summer, Colleen and I made a bold plan to travel to Athens, Greece, for the 2004 Olympic Games. It was an ambitious idea, but we were determined. Getting tickets wasn't easy, especially for foreigners, so we used my uncle's name and address in Spain to qualify as Spanish residents. The plan worked perfectly. When the tickets finally arrived by FedEx at his home, we had everything we needed for what promised to be a once-in-a-lifetime experience.

When the time came, my cousin Raffaele took the girls to Madrid to catch their flight home to the United States, while Colleen and I packed up for the next leg of our journey — our ride to Athens. The plan was to follow the Mediterranean coastal road all the way to Rome, savoring the seaside towns, vineyards, and winding roads that connected one country to the next. From Rome, we would board a train across Italy to the port city of Bari and then take a ferry across the Adriatic Sea to Greece.

Before leaving for the Games, I arranged with the local Harley-Davidson shop in Spain to ship my Road King motorcycle back to the United States. The cost was $900, a lot at the time, but worth it to ensure the bike's safe return to Lincoln, Nebraska. Once we knew the Harley was on its way home, we were free to travel without worry.

We started our drive south toward Gibraltar, where the legendary Rock rises 1,400 feet above the sea, marking the entrance to the Mediterranean. The ancient Greeks once believed this was one of the Pillars of Hercules, the edge of the known world. From there, we turned north along the coast toward Marbella. Having visited before, we didn't linger long. Instead, we pressed on to Málaga, where we spent the night in a small hotel near the center of town. The next morning, we walked through the old city, its streets shaded by colorful awnings and lined with bougainvillea. We ate our continental breakfast at a café surrounded by locals and their well-behaved dogs, a charming detail of Spanish life.

Continuing north, we reached Granada and toured the Alhambra Palace, the magnificent Moorish fortress dating to the 13th century. Its intricate carvings, flowing fountains, and breathtaking views of the Sierra Nevada mountains made it feel as though time itself had paused.

Our next stop was Alicante, where we browsed a modern flea market before moving on to Valencia. I remembered Valencia from my Navy days, the lively port, the beautiful women, and my first taste of Bacardi and Coke. It was also the birthplace of paella, Spain's national dish, and we made sure to enjoy it where it was first perfected, rich with saffron, seafood, and Mediterranean flavor. We visited the Oceanographic, Europe's largest aquarium, an architectural wonder filled with marine life from across the globe.

From there, we drove to Barcelona, my favorite city in the world, while stopping at several beaches on the way. The drive itself was unforgettable, the sun shimmering off turquoise waters, the scent of the sea mixing with olive groves and vineyards. Once in the city, we stayed at the same hotel as during my 2002 Harley ride. We ate tapas near La Rambla, the city's most famous boulevard, alive with street performers, artists, and souvenir stands. We took a sightseeing bus to explore the works of Antoni Gaudí, including the breathtaking Sagrada Família, still under construction more than a century after it began. Colleen's favorite stop was the Olympic Stadium, where the famous flaming arrow lit the cauldron during the 1992 Games. Standing there, I could almost feel the magic of that moment.

We walked all the way back to our hotel from the far end of La Rambla, stopping at every shop along the way. I'd rest my feet at cafés while Colleen explored. From Barcelona to Nice, France, we retraced much of the same coastal road we had taken on the Harley in 2002, the views as spectacular as ever.

Our route carried us along the French Riviera, through Marseilles, a port founded by the Greeks in 600 BC, and then to Cannes, where we spent the night in a room with a breathtaking oceanfront view. That evening, we ate the best pizza of our lives, just fifty feet from the hotel, simply because we were that hungry. The next day, we visited the Palais des Festivals, home of the Cannes Film Festival, and walked across the same red carpet once graced by the world's greatest movie stars. I was so in love with Colleen. I could always tell her that, but I did not know how to express it.

After a few nights of rest, we continued toward Villefranche-sur-Mer, where my Navy ship had once docked. Standing there again brought back powerful memories, the sound of the sea against the harbor walls and the faces of the men I had served with. From Villefranche, we drove along the coast to Monte Carlo, crossing briefly into Monaco to visit its legendary casino and stroll the glittering streets lined with Rolls-Royces and yachts.

All of the sudden after crossing into Italy the landscape everywhere you could see turned into the most beautiful field of every variety of flowers you could imagine. Our days had settled into a rhythm of early drives, afternoon naps, and late dinners under the stars. Once across the border, we headed straight toward Venice. I noticed the tiny Mini Coopers everywhere and immediately took an interest all the sudden in them. We didn't realize we'd have to park in a massive lot and carry our luggage to a taxi, since in Venice, the streets are canals.

The confusion between the parking lot and our hotel made for a rough start, but once we figured things out, the city revealed its magic. One evening, we found the only casino in town. I wasn't properly dressed, but they had a closet full of jackets for guests. Even so, luck wasn't on our side.

The next day, we stopped at St. Mark's Square to rest and listen to a live band under the colonnades. Everyone else stood outside the café, so Colleen and I decided to sit down for a beer and a Coke. When the bill came, thirty-eight dollars, we quickly understood why everyone else was standing. "Stupid tourists," I joked.

We took gondola rides, water taxis, and even visited a glass factory on Murano Island, where artisans crafted the most beautiful glass we had ever seen. We bought red vases and decorative plates. I then shipped them home — items that still sit proudly in my home in Mexico today.

Our next stop was Florence, the birthplace of the Renaissance. Though neither of us were museum enthusiasts, we admired the city's art and architecture, especially Ponte Vecchio, the medieval bridge lined with gold shops glittering in the sunlight. The food in Florence was some of the best of our journey, rich with flavor and history.

From Florence, we made the three-and-a-half-hour drive down to Rome, where Katie had arranged a hotel for us. Rome was a feast for the senses — the Colosseum, the Roman Forum, and the grandeur of the Vatican left lasting impressions. I returned the rental car only to find out there was a hefty fee for dropping it off in another country. I paid without complaint; another lesson learned on the road.

Our next leg would take us to Athens for the Olympic Games. From Rome, we boarded a train to Bari, then caught a ferry across the Adriatic Sea to Patras, Greece, about two hours from Athens.

Traveling was no longer easy. We had no car, and we had to haul our luggage ourselves from train to ferry and beyond.

Onboard the ferry, dozens of backpackers camped out on deck, unrolling sleeping bags and turning benches into makeshift beds. It reminded me of my younger days, traveling light and free.

Though Colleen and I had a small private cabin, our age and comfort demanded it, I couldn't help but envy their spirit.

Finding a taxi to Athens was a challenge, but eventually, we made it. The drive through the Greek countryside was beautiful, rolling hills, olive trees, and whitewashed villages gleaming under the sun.

Colleen was ready for the Games, dressed in red, white, and blue, and waving her handmade signs. We arrived at the house we had rented for two weeks, $5,000 for a comfortable home near a Metro line that connected to every Olympic venue. Athens, transformed for the Games, had new highways, modern trains, and freshly painted buildings. The city pulsed with excitement and pride. I got so tired that I had no choice but to lie down and take a short nap so I could make it through the evening. I took it right there on the lush grass under the overhead of the Olympic stadium, we were about four hours too early, but then, it was better than being too late.

We attended the Opening Ceremony, basketball, track and field, boxing, and gymnastics events. The energy inside the stadium was electric, an ocean of flags, cheers, and anticipation. Watching the athletes march in, I felt immense pride just to be there, witnessing history.

When we were not at events, Colleen and I explored Athens, walking hand in hand through Olympic Park, climbing the steps to the Acropolis, and relaxing in cafés over strong Greek coffee and pastries. At night, the ruins glowed softly against the dark sky, a perfect blend of past and present.

That trip to the 2004 Olympic Games was one of the most memorable experiences of our lives. It was a journey that combined everything we loved — travel, culture, history, and the joy of discovery. Looking back, I realize it was also one of the last great adventures we shared before life began to slow down. The memories of that summer, of Colleen, the open road, and the Mediterranean sun, remain etched in my heart forever.

As we prepared to head to the airport, I realized I still had two tickets for the Closing Ceremony. I handed them to our generous host, along with directions to the nearest Metro station, hoping she would enjoy what we could not.

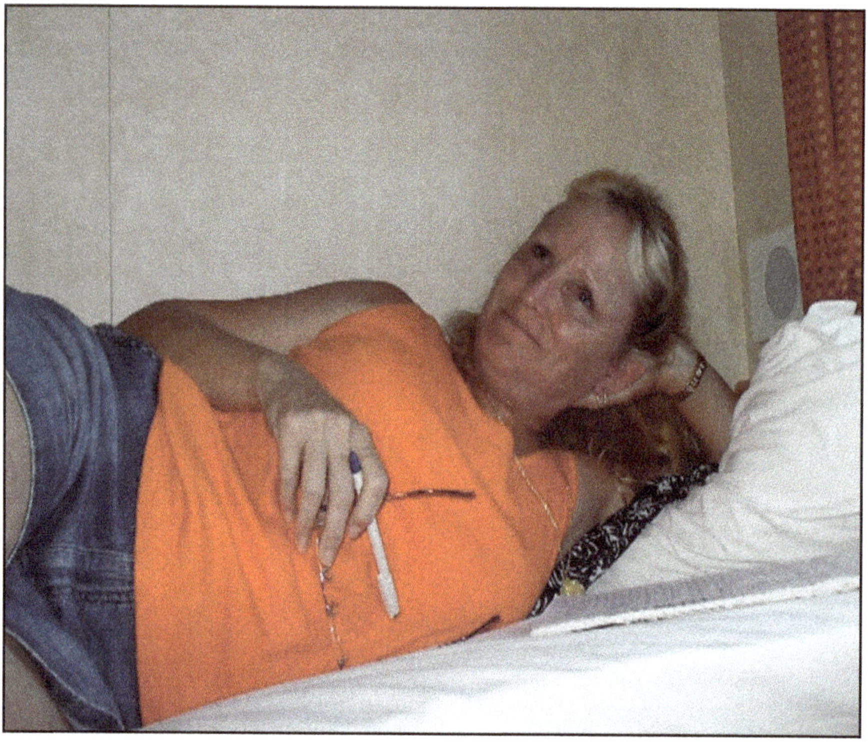

HI
LINCOLN
NEBRASKA
USA

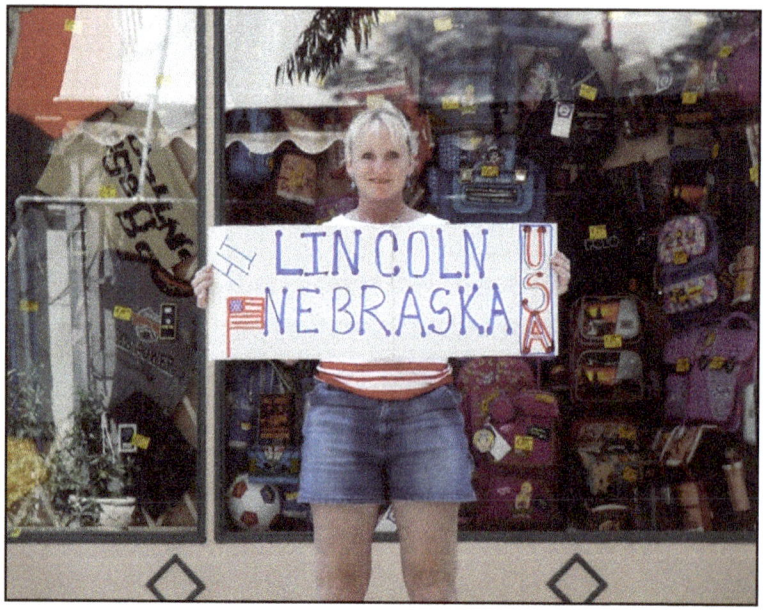

And so, our 2004 journey to the Olympic Games ended for us, another chapter in our book of life, written in miles, laughter, and love beneath the Mediterranean sky.

18

JEEP RIDE THROUGH EUROPE

WHY WOULD ANYONE IN THEIR RIGHT MIND want to drive around the world, especially when flying or a cruise ship would be so much easier! It can only be full of hardship; long days, nights; and putting one's own life on the line if I wasn't careful as to where I went and not to mention the cost of the trip itself. I have always traveled in ways that someone else wouldn't even think of doing or would even want to attempt.

I started planning my trip about a year ago by renovating a 1952 Jeep Willy Trailer that I purchased online from the government. I wanted the trailer paint to match the Jeep in color and made a few changes to accommodate for weight, my ability to accomplish certain things while on the road considering my age and physical condition. I put hydraulic lifts inside the trailer to lift the top so that when I needed to open the trailer with the cargo on top of the trailer, it would not be so difficult.

I changed the axle on the trailer so that all the tires, both on the trailer and Jeep, were interchangeable with each other. I installed a couple of Jersey cans on the rear of the trailers and wired the entire trailer, so it worked as one unit rather than two separate components. In theory, the Jeep alternator was wired to charge the battery to the hydraulic lift, while the generator would also charge the battery on the Jeep if needed. Inside the trailer, I built in a couple of propane cookers, installed a wash basin, added containers, and wired in a refrigerator.

Well, it's time to start thinking about the trip. The jeep and trailer are on their way to Amsterdam on a ship and will arrive there on June 17th ready to start my journey. I am starting to get into that travel mode.

Amsterdam: First day in Amsterdam and what a day it was! However, before I fill you in on today's happenings, let me bring you up to date. Both Colleen and I arrived in Amsterdam on Wednesday. I arrived around 12:00 A.M. from Chicago and she came in from Ireland about 11:00 P.M. after last minute changes due to a mess up with British Air. Thursday of this week we did a bit of sightseeing and ended up checking out both China town and the famous "Red Light District." Never in my life have I seen so many beautiful women in such a low, degrading job behind glass doors attempting to lure you in. These women do not like to be videotaped (ask Colleen) and on top of that, it was illegal. It was posted in obvious locations that there was no photography. When I looked over my shoulder, one of the gals suddenly popped out of her glass cage and started pounding on Colleen.

It was a very hectic day for me. I spent most of the day making a trip to Rosendall to pick up my Jeep and Trailer. I took a train from Amsterdam Central to Rosendall, NL. It was supposed to take 1.30 hrs. but got delayed on the track for about 45 minutes. When I got to the train station, it was my intention to take a taxi to the location where I was supposed pick up my Jeep. Not a taxi in sight and I was already running late. I finally realized that Holland and Brazil were having their World Cup match today and no one was going to get those taxis. Finally, after begging everyone for a lift, a taxi showed up. I quickly got into it and he took me 4 blocks to where my Jeep was awaiting me.

I was impressed with the many garden houses that people had alongside some canals. Many of these garden houses might have been retirement resorts where people enjoyed weekends in their 6' by 8' huts with a beautiful garden surrounding these well-maintained, high-end huts.

Also, while driving back to Amsterdam, I noticed hundreds of boats in a row in the middle of what looked like an alfalfa field. Finally, when I got a better look, I realized that there were canals everywhere, and where there is a canal, there are boats of all sorts, sizes, and types. Getting back to Central Amsterdam was a chore since Holland beat Brazil 2-1; the town exploded with excitement. Just imagine driving in from Memorial Stadium after Nebraska has beaten Oklahoma.

To get from Amsterdam to Luxembourg should have taken about four hours, but it took Colleen and I about seven hours following maps that we could not read. Once we figured out how our GPS worked, it was no problem getting around.

The City of Luxembourg is located within the Country of Luxembourg. The country itself is not big. Bordered by Belgium, France, and Germany, it's a very green and lush country where hotels do not need air conditioning. On my first trip to Europe with Mark Pallard we landed in Luxembourg and slept on the outskirts of the cemetery. Thank goodness it was not this cemetery. Luxembourg was liberated by Patton's Third Army in 1944-45. In fact, he is buried here in Luxembourg at the American Military Cemetery alongside 5,000 American troops who were killed during the War.

I visited the cemetery this morning. It was unbelievably beautiful and well maintained. It had a 20ft hedge all around it in the cemetery. The grave markers are arranged in a pie shaped formation with Gen. Patton at the small end of the pie, appearing as if he is addressing his troops. Gen. Patton died in an automobile accident just across the border in Germany.

We stayed at the Grand Hotel Cravat for about 140 Euros per night, which was Gen. Omar Bradley's headquarters during WWII. Gen. Patton's 3rd Army Headquarters was down the road at the International Hotel. A decent sit-down meal in Luxembourg cost about 60 Euros for two.

July 4th, Independence Day: While driving around in the Merzig, Germany area in search of an old cemetery in a village, (where Colleen located on the Internet her 8th great-grandfather was born sometime in the 1600s), we came across a very small downtown area (one bar). There we met people who were hanging around under a tent outside the bar. With the men (wearing identical T-shirts) drinking beer, we came to find out that these guys were part of a club in the village and were having their annual crowning of their new King and Queen. It appeared though that they were mostly having a good old time laughing, joking, and drinking beer. All were nice.

It was here where we met Dominique who quickly became a friend who showed us not only the old abandoned cemetery, but also introduced us to Cristina and Joseph, two of the local historians who knew a lot of the information that Colleen was searching for regarding her ancestors, and found one of them.

For the next six hours Colleen and Joseph sat down and went over hundreds of pages of records that Joseph himself has acquired over the years. All of this was going on while at the same time everyone was drinking beer and plenty of schnapps till late into the night. These people were nice to us and treated us like family. The information that we acquired from these new friends led us to a city called Trier.

Saarland: The River Saar meanders through the small German federal state of Saarland. Its capital Saarbrucken has a population of just over a million. The state once was an important coal mining center. Since coal is imported nowadays, the Saarland has undergone many changes which have included the growing of grapes for wine, tourism, and porcelain manufacturing. The Saarland borders France and Luxembourg and you can experience French lifestyle in Saarland including the French cuisine. Most people are bilingual and are known for their love of life, their outgoing spirits, being very open-minded, and drinking beer of course.

The Saarland is among the most densely wooded areas in Germany, with beautiful rolling hills, winding river valleys, and plenty of opportunity for biking along the river or taking a boat ride (no casino boats here) or as in many other areas, shopping.

We spent the night in a bed and breakfast in Mettlach, a village located on the Saar River and known for its Porcelain china, not as pricey as it is in the United States. We sent five boxes back to Lincoln for the kids. Katie is going to love that FedEx bill.

Our second night in Saarland was spent in Trier where Colleen spent a considerable amount of time researching her ancestors. Surprisingly, she was able to find out quite a bit of information. She further discovered that her family could have originally been from Beurig, Saarland, and that is how they came about with their own name (Beiriger).

Trier is considered one of the oldest cities in Germany, with old Roman

Empire influences in their extremely old structures. After one last drive through the Merzig area and more pictures, we were off to Frankfurt to spend the night. Tomorrow…Berlin. Here in the USA, one should not complain about our gas prices. It's costing me about 115 Euro to fill up my gas tank, or about $138 after the exchange rate. Guess I will have to quit eating.

Buchenwald Concentration Camp: You always hear of the horrific events and sites in history, but unless you have been there to see for yourself, you will never know the true meaning of what "The Holocaust" means. Colleen and I got there after it was officially closed, but we had the run of the place. The camp is located about seven miles uphill from the City of Weirmar, Germany, which was the birthplace of the Nazi Youth Movement. We drove along a handmade (by the Jews) road referred to as Blood Road. There was also a railroad that was built in the same place. While Colleen was reading the history markers near the long-gone railroad, I stumbled upon a set of railroad spikes and a steel plate that the weather had recently exposed. I will be hanging on to one of the spikes I found.

As you enter the camp area, a large, tall monument has been built next to 30 or 40 mass grave sites about 50 to 60 yards long. Further into the camp, there still existed numerous buildings that were used by the Nazis for numerous reasons such as barracks, work areas, storage and most notable to me was the crematorium. For reasons unknown to me, the Nazis had built and established a zoo at this location also, with various kinds of animals including bears.

Inside the barbed wire fence, there were foundations of the actual barracks where the detainees were held and slept. I refer to them as detainees because not all were Jews. There were Polish citizens, political prisoners, and at one time after the war between 1945 and 1950 when the Russians controlled the camp (referred to as Special Camp #2) there were over twenty thousand German Soldiers plus Nazis and anyone else that the Russians wanted to have disappear. Eight thousand people died in this camp after the camp itself was liberated and the Russians took over the camp. The Russians simply replaced them with the Nazis in their misdeeds.

Berlin at Night: Seems that Berlin like many other large cities is divided into burrows of communities. We, in Lincoln, refer to them as "subdivisions." However, burrows here are communities within a community with their own shopping, restaurant areas, tourist attractions, and other creatures of the night.

Colleen and I decided to go to the Haskesher Market area on the recommendation of our hotel concierge. It was a 12-Euro-cab ride from the hotel to Haskesher. I gave the cabby 15 Euros and he returned 2 Euros. The way I figured it, he kept what I was going to give as a tip.

We wanted to have sushi for dinner and proceeded to find a restaurant that served it. The first Sushi restaurant we went to also sold pizzas, so we walked around the corner and ate sushi at a more traditional Sushi Restaurant. Sushi prices here are comparable to those in Nebraska, but the Maki rolls are about half the size of those in Lincoln. Although we ate sushi inside the restaurant, most of the restaurants are on the sidewalks, packed with patrons enjoying dinner, drinks, and their cigarettes.

Along with the street vendors and musicians, there were also the street hookers. Now, these girls were not your typical street walkers that you see many places. Each one of these girls could have been in a Victoria Secret catalog. All decked out in corsets, tall with platform high heels, stockings, boots, and a fanny pack with a can of pepper spray hanging from it. Also, for some reason, they all had long straight blond hair. None of them approached me, but Colleen was holding on tightly to my hand so I would not get any crazy ideas.

According to what the female cabby on the way back to our hotel told us, "These girls are all good German girls." She said it as if she was proud of them and that their prices usually range from one hundred Euros and up. She then proceeded to talk about the girls that were coming in from the

Eastern European countries, (Bulgaria, Romania, etc., etc.), and that they charged from 5 Euros on up.

People here in Germany and the Netherlands talked about the Eastern European immigrants like Americans talk about the Mexican people in the United States. They all say the same thing. "They are taking good jobs away from the Germans girls."

Berlin, Olympic Stadium, Brandenburg Gate: In the 1936 Olympic Games held here in Berlin, Jesse Owens stood before Adolf Hitler and refused to bow to him, ('attaway Jesse). Today, Jesse Owens' name remains engraved on the granite walls of the stadium, while Hitler's name has been removed. The "Fuhrer Box" where Hitler sat and watched Jesse Owens compete was also removed. Jesse showed the world that people of assorted colors and cultures were no different than those of Hitler's own race.

I do not believe that the German people should have removed Hitler's name and many of his comrades' names from the walls of the Stadium. Good or bad, history was made, and no one should erase history. It should stand as is and let it serve as a reminder to all of us of the past, so that we may apply what has occurred in the past, to eliminate evil in the future.

Since this is my first time in Berlin, I was surprised to see that all reminders of the Nazis or Hitler ever existing have been removed or destroyed. My favorite site we visited was Brandenburg Gate while I am sure that the Stadium was Colleen's favorite. Brandenburg Gate is famous for many events in history, including Nazi troops doing their high step marching through the gate and plaza area. But my favorite event that took place here was when President Reagan stood here and said, "Mr. Gorbachev, tear down this Wall!" Also, note that the American Embassy is built adjacent to the Gate.

As Colleen and I were driving through East Berlin after the Wall came down, we were both reminded how East Germany needed to be reunited with West Germany. We seemed to notice that many of the buildings in the East Berlin sector were three to four stories tall and were older. West Berlin has newer, taller high-rise buildings with lots of glass as compared to those in the East sector of Berlin.

"**Spain 1-Holland 0:**" It was not as exciting as I'm sure it was in Amsterdam and Spain, but nevertheless, on a strip of asphalt between Victory Tower and Brandenburg Gate, there was what the Germans refer to as a "Public Viewing." An area strictly set-up for watching the World Cup with beer and bratwurst, there were stands lining both sides of the parkway for about a mile.

There were a few locations along the way that provided seating for some of the estimated twenty thousand people; that was where Colleen and I were fortunate enough to find a couple of those seats. Otherwise, everyone was on their feet throughout the entire match, including two overtimes.

After the game, we walked back to our jeep and headed for the hotel where a nice soft bed was waiting for us. The Public Viewing was set up in anticipation that the Germans had an opportunity to be in the Final Match. With an estimated 300,000 people hopefully coming to the Public Viewing, it had at least eight large screen TVs. Oh well, VIVA ESPANA!

Jeep and Trailer: To my surprise, the Jeep and Trailer are running well (Good job, Walt), on the Autobahn. We chug along about 65 to 75 miles per hour while the rest of the traffic goes about 120-140 miles per hour. They sure are moving.

I did have one major issue, though. When I first picked up the trailer, I plugged the refrigerator into the trailer plug and left it overnight. The next morning, I came to find that both batteries were completely dead. They would not take charge, so I had to replace both batteries with new ones at Hila (like Wal-Mart). I kept the bad batteries in hopes of getting them recharged and will keep them as a spare set for issues down the road. I am sure I will need them. Other than that issue, everything works well.

Prague, (Praha) Czech Republic: We left Berlin and headed for Poland where we wanted to visit the Auschwitz Death Camp. Driving on German roads is an experience. All drivers wanting higher speed limits in the United States should come to Germany and drive on their roads for an adventure or go to Indy where I am sure it is a lot safer. We made it to Prague safely and spent the night at Hotel Imperial.

Prague is a beautiful, old city with some of the most amazing architectural designs I have seen in all my travels. How architects and construction workers manage to build some of these buildings that are over five hundred years old never ceases to amaze me. We had drinks on a terrace right next to the Vltava River with an amazing view. The Charles Bridge crosses the Vltava River. Colleen and I went for a walk across the old bridge which was being renovated with new stones on the walkway with a method of stone laying that I have never seen before.

Among all the tourists and construction work were several street vendors either selling their goods or attempting to entertain you in one form or another. Then at the end of the day, we got our jeep out of the parking garage and headed out for Poland.

Behind The Iron Curtain: Many of you were too young to remember the Iron Curtain and some of you did not even care about it.

The Iron Curtain, as referred to during the Cold War, is an imaginary line that started in Northern Germany and divided Germany into West and East. This line extended south on the western border of the Czech Republic, Slovakia, Hungary, and the old Yugoslavia. It was an ideological barrier between the old Soviet Bloc and Western Europe between 1945-1990, a barrier that prevented free exchange of information and ideas.

Fast forwarding to today, the curtain is gone, and you can travel between all European countries without the border checkpoints, visas, or soldiers carrying machine guns asking you for your papers. The curtain today between East and West is mostly an economic barrier. As Colleen and I traveled from Germany to Poland via the Czech Republic (Prague), we started to notice that the buildings were older and in need of repairs in more abundance than those in Western Europe.

People outside of the City of Prague barely spoke any English in comparison to other countries. Nowhere, at least along the roadway that we traveled, were there any single dwelling homes (except for farmers and villagers). Although gas prices have remained the same, our cost of staying in four-to-five-star hotels has drastically gone down. Here in Bielsko-Biala, we got a five-star hotel for $105 that included parking, breakfast, a nice supper, and wireless internet. The community was not a tourist attraction, but it was close to a couple of locations we wanted to visit.

Czech Republic still has not converted to Euros as its main currency, but I am sure that it will be forthcoming. It's hard to understand how much you're paying for something unless you have a calculator in your back pocket. We have been using the heck out of our visas credit card for any major shopping. I would hope the banks would be able to figure out the exchange rate. As I continue driving east, I am sure that my basic, everyday needs will get even lower and I am looking forward to that.

Auschwitz: You never know the magnitude of an event in life until you've been there to see it for yourself. All over the world, Auschwitz has become a symbol of terror (genocide and the Holocaust.) It was established by the Germans in 1940 in the suburbs of Oswiecim, Poland, a city that was taken over by the Nazis.

Originally, the camp was set up for mass arrests of Poles, but in 1942 it quickly changed its role from death by incarceration to death by gas for the Jews. Auschwitz was to be yet another concentration camp that the Nazis had been setting up since the early 1930s. It functioned in this role throughout its existence. Beginning in 1942, it also became the largest of the death camps. The Nazis had over twenty thousand camps and sub-camps through Europe. Schindler's List was a sub-concentration camp for labor. For those of you who have seen Schindler's List, you'll remember that the only train to have left Auschwitz with live people in them was Schindler's when he bought Jews from the Nazis.

The mere size of the camp itself was overwhelming. Never have we seen an area with so many barracks, foundations of barracks that are no longer there, and old chimneys standing alone where the barracks once were. It looked like a dead forest of chimneys with no leaves. Buildings that once held fifty-two horses were converted to houses for up to one thousand detainees with only one coal-burning stove in each building and no toilet facilities. The horses they once held fared much better than the human beings these barracks later held.

The concentration camp that Colleen and I visited earlier (Buchenwald) was microscopically small in comparison to Auschwitz. The day we were there was extremely hot (98 degrees). I am not sure if there was still an undesirable, horrific smell in the area or if it was just our imagination, but it sure gave us a woozy feeling about the area. Pictures of our visit are in "Where I've Been." Also, you should check out their web page at http:\\ www.Auschwitz.org.

Wieliczka Salt Mine near Krakow, Poland: The Wieliczka Salt Mine is no place for anyone with a heart condition since tourists wanting to see the mines must walk down the stairs built inside an old mining shaft. In all, we had to walk downwards eight hundred steps before we were able to walk horizontally again. Thank goodness for the elevator, referred to as a "lift" here in Europe, that was available for us to exit the mine once the tour was over. No way would I have been able to climb those steps in the shape that I am in. Once down below, the horizontal shaft was extremely easy to walk in, while at the same time there was a constant breeze in your face from the blowing of fresh air through the salt mine. We were told that if the ventilation system became inoperable, we would have about fifteen minutes of air.

Back then, the mine was fully operational for nine hundred years. It used to be one of the world's biggest and most profitable industrial establishments when common salt was commercially a medieval equivalent of today's OIL. At one time, the mine employed 12,000 privileged employees, and it was a privilege during that time to work in the mine. This was an honor that was handed down from one generation to the next. Nowadays, the mine is used as a tourist attraction located on the outskirts of Krakow, Poland.

Today, visitors walk underground for about 2,000 meters (about a mile and a half) in the oldest part of the salt mine and see its subterranean museum which takes three hours for the tour. We only visited 1% of the mine and only three levels of a total of nineteen.

I never realized how beautiful it was down in the shafts of a mine. I was expecting dusty, grimy, and dirty, hard to walk in areas. Instead, there were multiple chapels and altars (14 in all) with huge religious statues carved out of salt over hundreds of years. Most of us think of salt as this white powder that pours out of a shaker onto our food. Although that is the final refined product, in its rough form it's as hard as marble.

Occasionally, concerts and other events take place in the Wieliczka mine's biggest chambers. There is a sanatorium for those having asthma and allergies situated 135 meters deep. As in any other tourist attraction, there were gift shops and restaurants available for those who wanted to spend some extra cash. Boy was I happy I didn't need to walk back up to the top!

Four Countries in 7 hours: Poland, Czech Republic, Slovakia, and Hungary: When we were ready to leave Poland, we asked someone how far it was to Budapest, Hungary. She indicated to us that it was about a 6-hour drive. We put Budapest into our GPS and off we went. The GPS told us it was 186 miles from our location in Poland to Budapest. That is about the distance between Lincoln and our cabin at Johnson Lake (about a 2½ hour drive.)

Immediately after starting our journey, we came upon a traffic jam due to road construction. After waiting for about an hour, I decided that I would pass the stopped trucks, and I proceeded to go about a hundred yards to a Y intersection. I now know why no one else was doing exactly what I was doing. I followed my GPS only to be taken down roads which went through people's backyards no wider than a bike trail. At first, I thought I wasn't even on a road, but when another vehicle was heading in my direction, I knew I was on a road. This road was so skinny that the oncoming car had to back up far enough to allow us to go by without driving into the ditch.

Once back on the main road and past the detour, we once again entered Czech Republic and on to Slovakia where we saw some of the most beautiful scenery one could ever come across. Just imagine driving through western Montana and you would picture what we were seeing.

This whole entire part of Europe is extremely green and vegetated. It is some of the most beautiful countryside that Colleen and I have seen. At least I saw it; Colleen was in the back sleeping. After our 7-hour drive, we safely arrived in Budapest and found our hotel, the Kempinski Hotel Corvinus.

I need to thank my daughter, Katie, for being our travel agent. Once we decide to spend the evening in a certain location, we give her a call on my cell phone, and she locates a hotel online. Then, she would send an e-mail to my Blackberry with an address which we then put into our GPS and bingo, we're there.

Free Advice: Just some free advice for those of you who someday may travel to Europe:

1) Do not let the hotel do your laundry.
2) Do not use the mini bar.
3) Do not add breakfast to your room charges.

With hotel competition on the rise, many top end hotels are giving out rooms for a fair price, while at the same time they make up the difference when they charge you for "extras," like laundry, mini bars, and breakfast.

For example, while staying at the Hotel Grand in Berlin, we were only charged 94 Euros per night for our accommodation (including breakfast). When we inquired with the hotel on getting our laundry done somewhere, they offered to do it themselves. WOW! What a shocker on the charges of 98 Euros ($120) for less than ½ of a machine load. They charge by the piece, and some of their charges for pieces of clothing exceeded the price of buying a new one.

We had gotten addicted to using the mini bar in the room, which is also a big mistake. The prices for the small items in the mini bar are about five times more than the bar down in the lobby. I guess we're paying for "convenience" and not the products themselves.

Breakfast sometimes is automatically included with the price of your room. If it is not, they often offer to add it as part of your room charge. Say "No!" You always have the option of charging breakfast to your room if you do decide to get up early enough to go downstairs and have breakfast. If you do not go to the early breakfast, the restaurants may be close by and you're out the additional charge.

Besides, after having breakfast at these hotels a few times, all the food starts to look the same and does not appeal to the stomach. Most breakfasts include cold scrambled eggs, various cheeses with different slices of meat, fruit, bread, and coffee. Come on, where's the pancakes and French toast or even biscuits and gravy?

Right Back Where I Started: It saddens me that Colleen had to leave Sunday morning to go back home. I will miss her dearly for many reasons that I will not share on this blog. While editing this book 15 years after our trip, we would still be married, had she not left me alone to roam free. In addition to her being in my life, she has the patience that I lack. She could find anything we needed on the GPS, from our hotel to the nearest gas station when we were on empty, and to restaurants when we were hungry.

It was my plan to stay one more night at the Kempinski Hotel in Budapest after Colleen left, but I decided that I wanted to get a mile closer to Türkiye before the end of the day. I checked out of the hotel, got into the Jeep, set the GPS for Belgrade, Serbia and headed out. I drove for about two hours. When approaching the Serbian Border, I came across a line of cars that delayed me three hours before I even got to the border itself.

When I finally got to the border, I was informed that Serbia itself was not part of the European Community. It is an enclave surrounded by European Community Countries and that it required a passport to go through Serbia rather than just an identification card, like in most of the remaining European countries.

Some of you are now wondering "where is my passport?" It is in Washington, D.C. with a visa company getting the remaining visas that I need to complete my trip. I could not get them all before I left, so I sent it back to the U.S.A. once I arrived in Europe. I figured that it would take two weeks at the minimum before I would need my passport when I crossed into Türkiye. The reason I did not get all my visas prior to leaving on this trip was that I left that responsibility on Antonio Taylor, my so-called adopted son by way of Colleen.

Well, "smarty me" thought that I would just go around Serbia by going east through Romania and then south through Bulgaria. It was only an hour to the Romania border, so I decided to stop and have dinner, in which I ordered goulash. After ordering goulash a couple of other times, I came to realize that goulash over here means "beef stew." No more goulash! You must remember back in 2010 there was no iPhone, GPS, or Internet as they exist today.

Once I got to the Romanian border, I encountered a different reason I could not enter this country. The "Schengen Treaty" is a treaty which many of the countries within the European Countries are signatory to.

This treaty opens the border to the citizens of most of the countries in Europe (including the USA) to pass through their borders without a passport or visa, carrying only an identification card of some sort. However, there is a provision in this treaty that excludes — you guessed it — Romania and Bulgaria.

Like in the USA, the Europeans do not want these two country's citizens openly migrating into Western Europe, fearing the Romanians and Bulgarians may take away all the low paying jobs that no one else wants to do.

I spent the night in a small motel along the road back to Budapest and checked in once again into the Kempinski Hotel this morning, right back where I started. Tomorrow is a new day, and I will head west to Austria this time and go south around Serbia from that direction.

Budapest at Night: Wow, on my second stay at the Kempinski Hotel after Colleen left (Monday), I took long nap only to wake up hungry as a horse and dark outside. Rather than eating at the hotel, I chose to go down a couple of blocks from the hotel where Colleen and had had gone shopping on several occasions. This area was the central heart of Budapest tourist shopping, with fine restaurants and numerous stores for tourists to spend their vacations funds on.

Most of the restaurants and all the stores were closed, however I did manage to find a so-called Italian restaurant. I ordered the worst calzone that I have ever eaten (where's the beef), paid my bill, and headed back to the hotel. The difference between these streets in the day versus the streets at night is shocking at the least. With the stores and restaurant closing for the evening, the bars and strip club were opening.

I was amazed as to what people will do or say simply to get you into one of these clubs. Without Colleen around to protect me from the hustlers, I was approached by three separate groups of young girls, working in pairs of two, asking me if I wanted to have a beer. These where normal looking girls in their early twenties. They did not appear or were dressed like hookers, but rather like somebody's young daughter, harmless appearing. Digging deep into my years of experience as a sailor, I realized what was going on.

These girls would use their youth to lure you to a nearby club, drop you off after they collected their finder fees and leave you in the hands of a more seasoned professional whose job would be to get you to buy her a watered downed bottle of champagne for about $300 to $400. No thank you I said, at which time I proceed to head back to the Kempinski only to be approached two additional times by similar groups of young girls wanting to have a beer. Once at the hotel I once again felt safe, and I still had all my cash and credit cards on me except for the cost of that lousy calzone that was not setting to well on my stomach.

Once in the lobby of the hotel, I struck up a conversation with the bellman, sharing with him my recent experience out in the streets only to be shocked once again. He proceeded to point out two incredibly attractive women in the hotel lobby who were approved by the hotels to work in the hotel as hookers. He also indicated that he had a photo album that included other women that were pre-approved by the hotel. I was shocked and did not expect that type of service at this hotel. I quickly headed to the room where I watched Larry King Live and went to sleep (alone).

Budapest to Venice: It was Tuesday morning, and I was ready to start the day off early. I was ready to leave Budapest for the second time and was not going to let anything or anyone slow me down this time. When I checked into Kempinski the day before, they charged me about 40 Euros more than the original stay. I was not in a good mood on Tuesday since I hate getting robbed, so I chose not to add breakfast to keep the cost down.

Now the problem began as I simply chose to have coffee and some toast in the morning. After I had one refill, I proceeded to check out of the hotel and head out for Italy. Remember that I was already upset at the hotel with their additional room charge. Well, I really got upset when they tried to charge me $22, or 17 Euros, for the toast and coffee. I told them that it was ridiculous and that I could have had the entire buffet with all the coffee I wanted for an additional 5 Euros. All they could say to me was, "Sorry sir, those are our prices," as if they could not find any other words to say. I refused to pay that much for the coffee so when they handed me the bill, I changed the price of the coffee to 8 Euros and told them that was all I was going to pay. They accepted my offer, and I handed them my bank card.

At that time, I proceeded to the parking garage only to find out that the battery in my jeep was dead since I left the refrigerator plugged into the cigarette lighter all night. I was able to talk the parking attendant into giving me a jump, for which I donated the 8 Euros I refused to pay to the hotel to the parking attendant's retirement fund. So, as you can see, the day didn't start off so well. Hopefully, it will get better on my way to Venice, Italy, and the Jolly Village Camp.

Venice to Patra: I had done this once before in 2004 when Colleen and I took the ferry from Bari (south of Rome) to Patra on the way to Athens for the 2004 Olympics. Back then, I did not have a Jeep to drive off the ferry, but instead, several non-rolling suitcases and not a taxi to be found. It should be easier this time.

I guess I should back up a bit and cover the period after I arrive in Venice from Budapest. I figured since I am dragging this trailer fully loaded with camping supplies, (except my Lazy Boy) I should try camping. Megan found the Jolly Village Campground on the internet and after emailing the address to me, I was able to locate it without difficulty (lol).

I was anxious to see how this new endeavor would go since I have not been camping since my days as a Boy Scout. I already had one strike going against me since I did not have my propane tanks on the trailer. They were still in Amsterdam waiting to be picked up and forwarded to me. I am sure that by the time they catch up with me, my trip will more than likely be completed. Nevertheless, as a true former Boy Scout, I came prepared with additional small propane cylinders and a small screw-on burner. My first camp cooked meal consisted of fried potatoes, slices of ham, and a couple of fried eggs (or was that breakfast?) I even did the dishes.

After a couple of days of camping, reorganizing the trailer, seeing what I needed for future camp outings, and a quick visit into the old city, in addition to making a trip to the Panorama (Wal-Mart), I was ready to break camp and head to Greece where my passport and I would once again be reunited. After that, I was off to Western Asia where I am sure things will get more interesting.

This morning, I headed to the Ferry about 9:30 AM and got in line to load on board for the approximate 40-hour trip to Patra. We left Venice on schedule and as we were leaving, I saw some of the most beautiful yachts one has ever seen. Along with the City of Venice, I also saw the St. Marco Square. What a beautiful site to remember when leaving Italy behind.

On the Ferry to Patra: One forgets too quickly that when you cross the Adriatic Sea, the young adults and some not so young take over all the hallways, passageways, closets, and crevices including the outside tables and chairs. They are not shy about setting up a tent or rolling out an air mattress on every square inch of the decks. It amazes me how much of their home they can unpack from those knapsacks that they are carrying.

Many of them bring enough food along to feed an army of travelers. Personally, I enjoy the privacy of my cabin, bed, and air conditioning where it is quiet, calm, and relaxing. I can understand why many of them bring their own picnic baskets based on what a meal costs on board. About $30 got me a not so good fish dinner with rice and a salad. Cost of a cup of coffee is around $5.

The seas are very calm and if it were not for glancing out the window on occasions, watching the sea go by, one would never realize that we were even out on the sea. I don't remember being this calm when I was in the Navy.

Arriving in Athens: After arriving in Patra, I quickly found the road for Athens. I then managed to unload the jeep without getting too many Greeks pissed off at me. There was one Greek who happened to park directly behind me and happened to be the last one down to the garage.

It was a two-hour drive from Patra to Athens, and I managed to get there without the use of my GPS. I wanted to go to this certain part of Athens where Colleen and I went and watched our 2004 USA Men's Basketball teams get themselves beaten by a Puerto Rico team. I knew that if I kept going south and kept the ocean to my right side, I would eventually find the general area and did just that around 2:30 in the morning. The street parallel to the beach was absolutely jammed with Saturday night party-goers for about a 10-to-15-mile stretch. The street was lined with clubs, street food vendors, and plenty of people. Due to my late arrival in Athens and the fact that I practically slept across the entire Adriatic Sea, I chose to wait a few more hours before I would go hotel shopping.

It's 5:30 in the morning and here I sit next to the beach, typing away while jamming Carlos Santana. All the people have left, and you can see that the sun will soon be upon us once again. What more could a person ask for at this time? A bottle of Ouzo would be nice.

Where's the Dog Catcher: Wow, I have never seen so many loose dogs in all my Doggon years. I mean, all over the place in packs from three to seven. Like pimps and drug dealers, these dogs spend time together at the intersection of the streets as if they were waiting for something to happen. Will somebody please call the dog catcher?

Get Me Out Of Here: During the 2004 Olympics, Colleen and I visited a city that was clean, jubilant, and exciting. We spent a considerable amount of time in the Omonia Plaza area where today it is downright depressing just to be there. All the buildings, and I mean <u>all</u> the buildings have graffiti on them. The streets are extremely dirty, and unemployment must be at the highest in the country that once was proud of its work ethic. I have never seen so many large groups of men hanging around street corners doing absolutely nothing other than waiting for something to happen.

I do not know why I even bothered to come to Athens. It was the good memories of been here with Colleen and the Olympics that made me want to be here again. Had I known what I was going to experience on this trip, I would have taken a different route once I got to Greece and completely bypassed Athens. Athens has become a rat hole for many things to ferment in.

I wanted to stay near the Omonia Plaza because I had fond memories of our last trip here. Back then, we spent time eating, shopping, and going to the nearby internet café in the area. It was a central location that we went through to get to all the different Olympics venues for the games. Back then magazine stands sold souvenirs, flags, hats, and Olympic memories; today they sell gay porn magazines.

I checked into the Classical Hotel which had the five stars under its name. I think somebody has forgotten to remove some of those stars as the years have passed the hotel by. I would not give it a three-star rating, nor did I want to spend more than one night there. Omonia Plaza is the major hub for all the metros running though Athens. The metro itself had a major facelift for the Olympics, but you could not tell that today due to all the graffiti.

Omonia Plaza is in central Athens among all the government buildings. What once was a hard-working city with its jubilant citizens has now become a police state with both police officers and the Army carrying machine guns and riot gear on every corner of the plaza!

Greece is having its first recession in over sixteen years which has put Greece in a dire financial situation among the European Community. The IMF is wanting Greece to reform parts of their economy policies to continue to borrow funds from the IMF, while at the same time the citizens of Greece do not want to give up concessions and are now rebelling with strikes and protests. The current fuel tanker strike that went into effect the day after I arrived in Greece affected me since there was no gas being delivered by the truckers to the local gas stations.

The first night of the strike I used up an eighth of a tank driving from gas station to gas station hoping to luck out and find one that was open and had fuel. No such luck. I was starting to get a bit scared as I was driving in parts of Athens which I was not remarkably familiar with, and the fuel light had been on for a while. Not wanting to run out of gas in an area which I was not familiar with, I managed to find my way back to the safe underground car park near the hotel where I had been parking the jeep and trailer. At least there, the jeep was safe and in a protected area while waiting for the fuel crisis to get over.

First thing Monday morning, I hired a taxi and drove around until we found a gas station that had enough fuel to give me time to retrieve my jeep and get into the thirty-minute gas line awaiting my turn to fill up. Not till the tanks were filled up, could I breathe again. I could have cared less that it cost me 166 Euro or about $210 to fill up my jeep and the two Jerry cans on the trailer. Never again will I get caught with my Jerry cans being empty. With gas in my tank and my stomach full of Athens, I quickly checked out of the ATHENS and headed north not knowing where I was headed, so long as it was out of town.

Karmena Vourla and the Galini Spa and Resort: After leaving Athens I decided to take my time driving north while I was waiting to be reunited with my passport. After dealing with the gas shortage in Athens, I made sure that my fuel tank was never less than three quarters full. The trip to Athens was a waste of my time.

I decided to drive along the eastern shoreline of Greece on the coastal road nearest the beach. In some of the areas the road was the beach itself. I was looking for a place where I could spend time for a couple of days and catch up with my typing that I neglected while I was in Athens looking for gasoline.

After driving for a couple of hours, I came across a small town called Karmena Vourla. It is a small beach town that caters mostly to Greeks. The town itself mostly runs parallel to the beach. Only a small road separates the shops and restaurants from the restaurant tables on the opposite side of the road and directly on the beach itself, all with large umbrellas covering all the tables.

After driving through town, I noticed a pretty nice hotel on the west side of the road, so I flipped a U-turn and found my way to the Galini Spa and Resort where I got to admit is the best deal of all the five star hotels that I have stayed in during my month of driving through Europe.

For about 90 Euros ($115), I received a room with a sea view of the Mediterranean Sea while at the same time overlooking the beautiful swimming pool and garden area. You will have to check out these photos because it is quite the sight. In addition to the gorgeous sea view room, it included the internet, free parking (a rare item in the city), breakfast and dinner. The food that was included with my stay was extremely delicious with quite a few choices.

One of the most important things that I look for in a hotel is whether there is a Sushi Bar in the hotel or nearby, and there was. I just might have to stay an additional night and catch up on my sushi eating that I have missed. If you get lucky as I did, the general manager will invite you to have a glass of wine. This place is genuinely nice, clean, and very relaxing and after being in Athens for a few days, it's like having a vacation from your vacation.

Thessaloniki, Greece, with only a Half of Tank of Gas: After two nights at the Galini, it was time to move northwards toward my eventual crossing into Türkiye.

It appears that the fuel crisis here in Greece is not nearing an end, for I was only able to find one gas station on the way to Thessaloniki with about a 20-minute line. Wanting to keep my tank as full as possible, I only needed to put in about a quarter of a tank of gas. That was the only gas station on the 120-mile stretch that had no gas, although there were two other stations that still had diesel for sale. I almost contemplated the idea of mixing diesel in with my gas so that I would still be able to continue to move forward but decided not to for fear of causing a more severe problem with the Jeep. Guess desperate people think of desperate things. Thank goodness I am not there yet.

It appears as the settlement talks between the Greek government and the Truckers Union Drivers is not going well, as myself and several million Greeks were hoping. The government now has threatened to throw truck drivers into jail if they do not return to work within the next 24 hours and the drivers are planning to stay fast. This is going to be interesting, and I am glad that I am nowhere near Athens when these two groups start butting heads. It would not surprise me to see the Army driving trucks soon and fulfilling the basic needs of this country. According to the news, it is not only the fuel that has not been delivered but the grocery store is starting to run out of certain goods on their shelves.

The lines of trucks parked on the shoulder of the highway seem to be getting longer and in more locations. I am also seeing less traffic on the roads and cars with people putting fuel into them from a gas can. There will be total chaos if this problem is not resolved soon.

Personally, I do not think that one organization should be able to cripple an entire country as the Truck Drivers are doing to Greece. I guess when the citizens of Greece start going without their basic life needs, which will be soon, then perhaps something will get done.

In the 80s, and the Federal Air Traffic Controllers Union went on strike, Ronald Reagan fired them all and there has not been another government strike since then.

Only 20 Euros: Not wanting to go too far from the hotel with my car today, I asked the receptionist what there was in the area to see. I explained to her my gas dilemma at which time she proceeded to inform me where I could get some gas. She indicated that Shell gas stations were not affected by the truckers strike since they had their own delivery trucks. I quickly asked for directions, and I got on the road in search of this gas station. I must have passed by twelve closed gas stations before I was able to locate the end of the gas line for a Shell station.

It was only about 30 to 45 minutes before it was my time to fuel up. Each pump had its own pumping attendant pumping in the fuel and collecting the money. I removed the gas cap, and he inserted the nozzle. Fifteen seconds later he removed the nozzle, which made me wonder what was going on. I looked at the pump and saw that he had only put 20 Euros worth of gasoline into the tank. I quickly told him that I wanted the tank full and he quickly told me only "20 Euros". In my quiet, collective tone of voice, I mentioned to the attendant that I spent more than 20 Euros waiting in line. Of course, I had my air conditioner on since it was 90 degrees outside… and once again he said, "20 Euros".

I collected my thoughts and decided I'd best be moving on before things got out of hand. As I was pulling away from the station, I noticed a Shell tanker truck pulling onto the major roadway leading into town. I remembered what the receptionist told me earlier in the day about Shell having their own fuel tankers. I proceeded to follow the tanker truck in hopes of him leading me to the next gas oasis and the opportunity to fill up the tank. BINGO. After 20 minutes, he pulled into a Shell station that was closed, and I was on his tail.

The station attendant stopped me from pulling up to the pump and told me to wait a couple of minutes for the tanker to empty his load. By now, everyone realized that a tanker truck was unloading so they immediately got into the gas line behind me, for I was the first in line.

With a full tank of gas and a smile on my face, I decided to take the receptionist's advice and go south of Thessaloniki to a peninsula with beautiful beaches that were about thirty miles away. I headed south where I got lost on occasion but was eventually able to find my way. I stopped at a beach, took pictures, ate lunch, and proceeded to head back since it was starting to get late. I arrived back at the Mediterranean Palace about 7:30 P.M. after spending the day sightseeing. I parked my jeep and looked at my fuel gauge that still showed I had half of a tank left. Oh Well!!!!

Thessaloniki, Greece, Day 2: Thessaloniki, (also known as Salonika or Saloniki,) has of the most beautiful beaches in northern Greece. Thessaloniki is a vastly different city from Athens in better ways. More relaxing place and the central plaza is clean and enjoyable where one does not have to feel guarded all the time. The influence of the east is more pronounced here, not just in the food, but in the relaxed lifestyle. Thessaloniki is the second biggest city in Greece. The nightlife in Thessaloniki is exceptionally great with the bars and restaurant being open air.

Thessaloniki is a modern city bustling with life and movement. This is also the city that we had purchased, not knowing, soccer tickets for the 2004 Olympic Games. Once we realized that we would have to have flown here for the match, we quickly disposed of the ticket for about half the face value.

The main avenue is extremely crowded and full of cars with both sides of the avenue lined with high-end shops and restaurants. Colleen would have had a heyday shopping here. The ice cream and pasty shops here are impressive at the least and hard to stay away from. The main squares are Platia Elefterias and Platia Aristotelous, both on the waterfront, alive with cafes, restaurants, children playing and people just strolling by. This is the place to be in the summer at sunset if you enjoy people watching and walking along the boardwalk near the sea. The old port area appears as if it is getting a facelift with not too many boats there.

Today I walked about two miles along the sea wall to an area where there was a White Tower which is the symbol of the city. The White Tower itself is also a museum of art and history. It was built in the 15th Century and was at one time a prison for insubordinate Janisaries, the soldiers of the sultan who had been taken from their Christian parents as children and molded into his elite storm troopers.

While sitting there, the strangest thing happened to me. A man well dressed, in his late thirties came up and sat down about four feet away. He proceeded to ask me if I was a doctor. I said no, but he then started to tell me about a growth on the side of you know what and it was the about the size of a quarter as he demonstrated that by making a circle with his thumb and finger. I quickly mentioned to the man that it was getting hot and I best be going on.

Above the city is the world of the Epimenidou or Kastra, an area of old neighborhoods with narrow streets where I will not be driving my Jeep through. This is the old Turkish quarter of the city and is the remains of 19th century Thessaloniki and the walls that surrounded the city are still standing.

I still have that same half tank of gas as I had when I first arrived here and it will remain that way until I am certain the gas turmoil is over, or I know I can make it to Turkey with what I currently have in the Jeep and the Jerry cans.

My Man Bag: Go ahead and laugh all you want, but it is a necessity if you travel a lot and do not want to be hauling around a backpack that requires you to take it off and dig through every time you want to get something out of it. The man bag is a lot more convenient and easier to get into. In my observation doing my travels, most men use them here in Europe. Having been pickpocketed on numerous occasions, the man bag has become a necessity doing my travels.

When I came over here for this trip, I brought along my old over the shoulder canvass side bag with one compartment where I threw everything into. It was a complete disaster trying to find anything in that bag. I felt as if I was losing everything that I needed when I needed it.

Finally, after two weeks of total disorganization, I went on the prowl for that special bag that would organize my life while on my travels. One that would not add any additional confusion to my life than I already had. Finally on the ferry ride from Venice to Patra, while window shopping in one of their duty-free shops, I found it. After my inspection and paying close to $50 for it, it was mine. It has seven different compartments with each compartment having a separate zipper securing and separating the items from the other items in the bag.

In the front compartment I have my credit cards and driver's license since I use them the most. On the back side of the bag, I carry my cash in that compartment; with my small digital camera in the exterior compartment on one the end of the bag, with my MP3 player on the opposite end of the bag. Inside the main part of the bag, there are two additional compartments, in which I carry my small buck knife and miscellaneous items. In the main compartment I carry my small water bottle and anything small that I purchased along the way, and finally the most important and used compartment is in the flap where I have easy access to my Black Berry without going inside of the bag every time it rings.

Thessaloniki, Greece, Day 5/Hole in the wall: Well, the strike is over, and the gas stations are once again pumping gas with no lines. My passport will be here in the morning.

Greece to Türkiye: It's early in the morning, and I'll soon be heading out after spending five nights at the Mediterranean Palace. Over the past couple of days, I've been venturing farther from the city center, doing a little exploration. The narrow streets were challenging, but manageable for the Jeep and trailer, and I only ended up on a dead-end road once, which required me to back up a full block. I'm getting good at that. One afternoon, I stopped at a small restaurant tucked away behind the old city. I stepped inside and asked for a menu, but the woman behind the counter just shook her head, she didn't have one. Another patron overheard me speaking English and quickly jumped up to translate for the woman, who seemed to be a one-person operation, host, server, cook, dishwasher, cashier, and owner all rolled into one. She showed me two pans, one with fish and another with some kind of meat. I know what fish looks like, so I took the safe choice and passed on the mystery meat. There are lots of dogs in Greece, and one must be careful about their choices. Just teasing.

Along with the fish I ordered a Coke and a small salad. Having eaten at quite a few restaurants across Greece, I've gotten a good sense of what things usually cost. To my surprise, this hole-in-the-wall turned out to be the most expensive meal I'd had in Thessaloniki — fifteen euros — about eighteen dollars. I've eaten in far nicer places for half that price. This little joint had no overhead, no menu, and no class. She just saw a sucker walking through the door.

Goats galore: After leaving Thessaloniki, I began heading east toward Istanbul, Türkiye. With my earlier gas problem behind me and about ten thousand miles still ahead, boredom was starting to set in. Then, suddenly, to my left, I couldn't believe my eyes, goats, thousands of them, marching in perfect formation like an army going into battle. This reminded me so much of my own goat business back in Nebraska. I owned about five hundred goats with no profit to be made. I wasn't about to miss this photo opportunity.

I drove about five miles to the next exit, turned around, and came back. Watching them reminded me of my old goat business and my nanny goat, Chessy, who used to look me right in the eyes as if she could read my thoughts. She was a good old girl. As the herd came over the hill, I grabbed my camera and waited beside the Jeep. The herder must have been taking them to a new pasture; they knew exactly what to do. Only the bucks turned their heads to give me a look, as if to make sure I wasn't trying to steal from one of their girlfriends.

There must have been at least ten thousand goats in that herd, along with a dozen dogs wearing steel-studded collars, to protect them from fights or predators. None of them paid me any attention as they kept pace beside the herd. Further down the road I spotted several goat corrals built along the mountainside that paralleled the highway. It was an incredible sight that broke up my boredom.

Istanbul firefighters: Upon arriving in Istanbul, I spent my first morning looking for the Azerbaijan Consulate to apply for a transit visa into their country. After that, I decided to tackle another issue, picking up a FedEx package that had been sent to me. Instead of the package, I received a letter at the hotel instructing me to go to the FedEx office to clear up some customs problems.

I plugged the address from the letter into my handheld Garmin and followed GPS, which seemed determined to guide me through every back alley in the city. Three hours later, I had traveled only five miles when the Garmin proudly announced that I had arrived at the Istanbul Itfayesi Fire Department.

Within seconds, ten or fifteen firefighters surrounded me. Once they realized my situation, they jumped into action, pulling out maps, others looked up addresses, others began making phone calls to find the right location. They asked me to park the Jeep off to the side and invited me to sit in their outdoor gazebo, where they offered me tea. While I continued calling around, I chatted with the others as best I could despite the language barrier.

Eventually, they concluded that the address on my letter was wrong and that my GPS would never find the real FedEx office. Finally, one of the firefighters offered to escort me there in his personal car. I have to say, these were the nicest guys I met on the entire trip, and without their help, I would've had to hire a taxi escort just to find the place. To the firefighters of the Istanbul Itfayesi Fire Department, thank you for your kindness and hospitality.

$12 gas cap: You haven't experienced bureaucracy until you've dealt with the Turkish Customs Service, and I couldn't believe how many documents and stamps it took to retrieve one small package, just two gas caps for my generator and one GPS unit.

It started when I got the letter from FedEx instead of the actual package, and after finally locating the FedEx office, thanks to the firefighters, I walked in frustrated that I had to be there at all. The manager, sensing my mood, invited me into his office and offered me tea. Turkish hospitality never fails. He explained that FedEx wasn't the problem, it was Customs, and he then outlined the process for getting my package, which sounded so complicated that I gladly accepted his help.

First, we gathered all the original shipping documents, plus several new forms they created on the spot. Then we went next door to meet the Customs Inspector, a classic movie character type, the kind of heavy set, non-English-speaking official who gets right in your face. I wisely kept my mouth shut and let the FedEx manager handle the talking, figuring that if I said the wrong thing, he'd double the tax just to make a point.

The inspector stamped every page like it was the most important document he'd ever seen. Then it was back to the FedEx office, where even more paperwork was added to the growing pile. The manager called a friend, a customs broker, who had connections to speed things up.

We got into Jeep and drove for about thirty minutes to another part of town near the airport. The broker took the stack of documents and led us inside a government building. We rode the elevator to the fifth floor, got off, and immediately walked down a flight of stairs to the fourth. None of it made any sense, but I followed along anyway. Once inside a small office, another official added even more papers to the pile and stamped everything again with her personal seal.

From there, we went to yet another office where a young man reviewed the entire stack and asked for payment of the customs duty. I handed over the equivalent of twelve U.S. dollars and received my official release form. At last, the prized gas caps were legally mine. When the clerk handed them over, I couldn't help but laugh. After an entire day, three buildings, and a mountain of stamped paperwork, I finally held two small plastic gas caps that together weren't worth five dollars. Bureaucracy at its finest.

On the drive back to my hotel, I couldn't help thinking about how patient and helpful the FedEx manager had been through the entire ordeal. I made sure to thank him properly and even offered to buy him dinner, which he politely declined. As frustrating as the whole experience was, I ended the day feeling a strange sense of satisfaction. In its own way, it was just another adventure, one that added another layer to the story of this long road trip across continents.

The first night I arrived in Istanbul from Thessaloniki, I was using my GPS, which led me directly to the Holiday Inn, where I had a reservation for the following night — not the night I arrived. I was hoping they would have a room available that evening so I wouldn't have to find another hotel and then return the next day. When trying to get a room at 10:00 p.m., they told me they only had one left and that the rate was $340 rather than the $109 per night I had booked for the remainder of the week. Once I pointed out the cost of my upcoming stay, they were quick to say it was "the last room available," and that's why it was priced higher. I'd heard that gimmick before and wasn't buying it.

I contacted Katie, who quickly found me another room down by the water. Getting there, however, became a scene. I spent the next four hours trying to locate the hotel. We were both so frustrated that Chris had to get on the phone with his calmer, more level-headed demeanor to assist. Still having no luck, I finally hired a taxi to escort me to the hotel, realizing I'd never find it on GPS alone, especially since several addresses had similar names.

By sheer luck, while driving down a small, dark street with no streetlights or traffic, I finally spotted the hotel, a 150-year-old building that had once been a conference center before being converted into a five-star hotel. It was beautiful inside, featuring the largest corner suit in which I had ever stayed.

Once settled and awaiting my visa for Azerbaijan, I began exploring central Istanbul. I soon realized the west side of the city was divided into two sections by a transit rail system fenced on both sides, forcing taxis and cars to take long detours. I later learned the government did this intentionally to encourage people to ride the train instead of paying higher taxi fares.

I visited the Grand Bazaar, where both sides of the main alley were lined with carpet and jewelry shops. While window shopping, I met a man and his wife from Rome. We talked for a while, and I learned he had bought his wife's engagement ring there the previous year. They were now returning to Istanbul for another visit. I later received an email from them, which I still need to reply to. I tried my first-ever Turkish taco, and I must say, it was surprisingly good.

The next day I hired what I thought was an English-speaking guide for about 250 Turkish euros ($150 USD). Her English wasn't as good as expected, and when I asked her to tell the taxi driver to take me to the "Big Market," he drove half an hour in the wrong direction and dropped me off at a shopping mall, not what I wanted to see. That mistake cost me another $80 round trip, and I never even got out of the taxi.

Istanbul was also the first city where I really noticed women wearing veils. I asked my guide about it, and she explained that Turkish law does not require women to cover up, unlike in other Muslim countries. Those fully covered in black, showing only their eyes, were Arabic Muslim women, not Turkish.

Leaving Europe: On Tuesday, after picking up my passport with the Azerbaijan visa, I left Europe behind and crossed into Asia. It was here that I truly felt my journey had begun. I felt a deep sadness leaving Istanbul, not just because I was leaving the city, but because I was leaving Europe for the last time. Other than a future trip to London for the 2012 Olympics, I had no desire to return to mainland Europe or Spain.

Colleen and I had visited Spain again in 2009 to see my Uncle John, who was then in a nursing home and not doing well. After his passing and my mother's decision to sell his home, there was no longer a reason or desire to go back. I had always planned our family trips around visiting my uncle whenever anyone was in Europe.

We had seen all the places we wanted to see — and did it our way, not as part of a pre-packaged tour. From my first trip in 1975 to this current journey, I will always remember the adventures my family and I shared. I hitchhiked, used Eurail passes, been a stowaway on trains, rented cars, ridden my Harley, and finally drove my Jeep across the length of Europe, but never once joined a tour group. That just wasn't me.

19

Jeep to Tbilisi

On the Road to Tbilisi: with the Azerbaijan visa finally in hand at 5:00 p.m. on Tuesday, I wasted no time heading east toward Tbilisi, Georgia. I wanted to get a few miles behind me before dark, so I followed the main highway northeast out of Istanbul. I was careful not to make the same mistake the three young Americans made when they accidentally crossed into Iran and ended up imprisoned. Constantly checking my GPS and maps, I made sure I was heading northeast, not southeast.

I drove through the night, taking short naps, until I reached the Black Sea by morning. I followed the coastal road with the sea to my left and Iran far to my right, separated by a hundred miles of Turkish countryside. Eventually, I reached Batumi, Georgia, and managed to cross the border without no difficulty, unlike the truck drivers lined up for miles, waiting their turn.

Thinking I might camp that night, I bought a couple of fish from a roadside vendor near the sea. Once across the Georgian border, I was stunned to see hundreds of cows roaming freely through the streets as if they owned the town. At first, I thought they were sacred animals but soon realized it was simply open range. The cattle did not care who was driving; if they wanted to walk on the road, they did so without hesitation.

Not long after, I found myself in what looked like spring break for the entire country. Thousands of young adults packed into a coastal resort town, causing a 20-mile traffic jam along a dirt road that took three hours to get through. That turned out to be just the beginning. Along the way, I saw groups of boys bathing in irrigation canals beside the road, shirtless, laughing, and cooling off in the 90-degree heat.

The 280-mile drive to Tbilisi, which my GPS estimated would take five hours, ended up taking eighteen. The route was mountainous, with hairpin turns on the worst roads I have ever driven. Every time I tried to pass another vehicle, it felt like gambling with my life.

I had two GPS units with me, but only one worked, and even that only showed the main highway with no detailed roads. I had to stop repeatedly and ask for directions using hand gestures. I had booked a room at the Marriott Tbilisi, but there was no way I would make it that night, so I ended up sleeping in my reclined seat behind the Jeep's steering wheel.

The next day, I stopped at a roadside restaurant frequented by truckers and had them cook the fish I had purchased earlier. When I asked to use the restroom, I made a big mistake. Many third-world countries still use the old squat-style toilets with a bucket of water beside them for flushing. I now avoid those whenever possible. When I finally arrived at the Marriott in Tbilisi, I was sore from all the bouncing on the road and mentally drained from the drive. That night I decided I would get myself a massage since they had an on-staff masseur.

Still needing my Chinese visa, I went to their embassy only to find a sign stating that they accepted applications on Monday, Wednesday, and Friday. So, back to the hotel I went to rest. After catching up on my sleep, I explored Tbilisi but was not impressed. Georgia had separated from the USSR in the early 1990s, and from what I could see, it should not have. The old Russian influence was still visible everywhere, and people continued to speak Russian.

While there were independent shop owners, the free-enterprise energy seen in Türkiye was missing. It was inexpensive, yes, but the locals were barely surviving on about $600 per month.

Why the gas station only sold gas, I will never know. It seemed to me that if they had a pop machine or snacks, it would not only help the business prosper but also serve the customer better. In addition to not carrying anything else, the gas stations seemed overstaffed, with attendants always waiting to serve customers who were rare.

When the day came that I need to go back to the Chinese consulate to get a visa to China, my bad lack continued, they simply told me that they do not issue visas from Georgia, they said in a mean old communist fashion. So off to Azerbaijan. I left.

The shops were barely stocked and sold only limited items instead of a wider variety. Some sold five-gallon buckets of cooking oil and nothing else, while others carried only chemicals but no brushes. As in many places along the road, if you decide to eat at one of the local restaurants, you had better make sure you do not want anything requiring refrigeration. Many of them did not have it. If this were the way communism worked, I could now understand firsthand why it failed.

Crossing the Azerbaijan Border: The Wily Azeri border police were notorious for extorting money from travelers crossing into the country, and I had hoped the stories I read online were wrong.

I sat in my Jeep with the air conditioner running. It was pushing one hundred degrees outside the Azerbaijan side of the border between Georgia and Azerbaijan, waiting my turn to cross into a fenced area guarded by two young soldiers with machine guns. They were managing all the immigration and customs paperwork needed to enter the country.

The young immigration officer, who looked like a miniature Saddam Hussein, had his hands full with men jumping in and out of his unairconditioned office, yelling and begging him to sign their documents before others. It was absolute chaos, with men waiting for hours in the blazing sun just to get their paperwork processed.

When my turn finally came, the officer went out for a smoke break, delaying things even further. I waited patiently, not wanting to lose my place in line. This man had been doing things the wrong way for so long that I felt I could have gone in there myself and reorganized the process to make it twice as efficient.

First, he reviewed each document and then handwrote everything on a form using carbon paper. Aligning the carbon paper alone took over a minute. Every few moments, he would stop to wipe the sweat from his face. Making photocopies was another ordeal. He would stand up, grab a single sheet of paper from his desk drawer, insert it into the copier, sit back down, place the document on the copier, and then press "Start." Why he stood up every single time was beyond me.

Stamping documents was another comedy. The stamp was attached to a twelve-inch chain, and rather than removing the chain, he would wrap it around his palm to keep it from getting in the way. It was one of many mysteries I encountered that day.

The ordeal took two hours. Tempers flared outside in the heat, and for a moment, I thought there might be a riot. But I kept quiet; this was their country, and the last place I wanted to end up in was their jail.

Thinking I was about to leave after paying the official road tax of $21, the officer suddenly held out his hand. I acted dumb until someone whispered, "Give him money." Frustrated and eager to move along, I reached into my pocket and pulled out a twenty and a ten in Georgian currency, money I no longer needed. I handed him the twenty, and he quickly took the ten as well. When I asked, "Finished?" he nodded, "Finished."

After minor inspections by customs and police, I finally drove out of the dusty, dirt-infested border checkpoint and continued toward Baku.

On the Road to Baku: Paying Bribes to Azerbaijani Police. In Azerbaijan, you are the car you drive. Most people drove old Soviet Ladas: overheated, unreliable, and struggling to make it up the next hill. I, on the other hand, was driving a powerful Jeep with Nebraska license plates, which made me look like a wealthy American.

Everywhere I went, people stared at my Jeep and trailer. When they saw the plates, they would ask, "Is Nebraska near New York or San Francisco?" No one seemed to know where Nebraska was. After failed attempts to explain it, I finally started saying, "It's near Chicago," and then they understood.

Just like at the border, the highway police were just as corrupt. Along the road between the border and Baku, there were periodic police checkpoints. My first encounter did not take long, and perhaps, at least this time, there was a small reason for the stopping.

After driving through a small village and getting about five miles beyond it, a police car signaled me to pull over. A young officer, with an older one watching from the car, approached and asked for my papers, which I handed over. Realizing I did not speak Azeri, he handed me his cellphone. On the other end was an older man who spoke broken English and claimed to be the young officer's boss.

The man on the phone told me I had been speeding through the village and needed to pay $100 to the officer. He said they even had a picture. I asked them to see it, assuming it was in their patrol car. The younger officer motioned for me to follow him back into the village, where another man sat in a Russian Lada with a laptop showing a photo of my trailer's license plate.

Sure enough, I had been going five miles per hour over the limit, just enough for them to demand $100. I handed it over and was on my way, though I did get helpful sign language advice from the young officer about "bad policemen ahead."

At the next checkpoint, an older officer wearing a large Russian-style cap saluted me and introduced himself in broken English. He did not ask for any documents; instead, he peered inside the Jeep and asked where I was going, where I was from, and how much the Jeep and trailer cost. His friends gathered around, curious. Then he said, smiling, "John, you give $20, and you go." I nearly laughed aloud but handed him the $20 and moved on.

I managed to pass more checkpoints by tailing closely behind semi-trucks so they could not see me. But eventually, I was stopped again by an officer who insisted I was missing documentation. He wanted $100 and pretended to write something official on a pad.

Fed up with these extortion attempts, I pulled out my phone and pretended to call the American Embassy. As I waited "on hold," he suddenly said, "You go," and waved me on. That is when I realized they did not want any involvement with the U.S. Embassy. From then on, whenever I was stopped, I told the police I was on my way to visit my son at the American Embassy in Baku. I stopped ten more times over two days, but not one of them asked for money again.

First Impressions of Baku: Azerbaijan, shaped like a fierce bird dipping its beak into the Caspian Sea, sits between Russia to the north and Iran to the south, hardly the place one imagines for a thriving democracy. Its people, highly educated in Soviet times, were kind and friendly but often driven by tough circumstances into corruption.

The oil industry poured money into the pockets of politicians and global companies like British Petroleum and Royal Dutch Shell. It was said that "the black economy of Azerbaijan is equal to that of Nigeria," meaning that sixty percent of its gross national product was off the books.

In contrast to Georgia, Azerbaijan was a Muslim country, but religion seemed moderately practiced. Women walked the waterfront in tank tops and Daisy Duke shorts, where men wore collared shirts and sweltering gray trousers, never jeans, held up by stiff cardboard-like belts.

The harbor pulsed with Turkish disco music, and oil derricks shimmered beneath the afternoon sun. The Maiden's Tower, guarding the waterfront, was the most famous site in Baku. I visited the Old Town at dusk. Though most shops were closed, it was impressively clean and well maintained, with charming restaurants tucked among ancient walls.

After a short nap, I set out looking for a sushi bar but had to settle for a Chinese restaurant, which turned out to be surprisingly good. After dinner, I walked around the central district, lined with high end boutiques reminiscent of Rodeo Drive. You could tell the city had money to burn luxury, though little of it trickled down to the poor.

Eventually, I found my way to a bar called "Blackjack," where I ordered a Bacardi and Coke. Two half-drunk Scottish men stumbled in, speaking English, and soon struck up a conversation. After a few laughs, they invited me to another place down the street.

We walked a couple of blocks to a bar where there were ten girls for every man. I knew right away what kind of place it was, and the last thing I wanted was to walk out of there penniless. I had left my man bag at the hotel and kept my cash in my right pocket.

Jim, one of the Scots, bought me a drink and warned me not to buy drinks for the girls. Within a minute, a Russian girl approached, asking me to buy her a "Red Bull and Vodka," the most expensive drink in the bar. Her asking and my saying "no" went on for fifteen minutes.

One of my most favorable memories of Tbilisi and Bacau was the mutton (lamb) restaurants. There were several along the way, but my favorite was just before I crossed the border, when I pulled off to the side of the road where several semi-trucks were parked. As I pulled up, there stood a boy no older than fourteen beside a butcher who was cutting the throat of a lamb, bleeding it while it hung from a pipe. Talk about fresh meat. By the time I finished my own mutton, only about a third of the lamb remained. The meat had already been cooked as shish kebab while drivers stopped to pick up a few pounds to take home. You must look at these pictures. I spent the night in my Jeep's lazy boy, because there was not a hotel within a hundred miles.

On the Boat to Kazakhstan, 8/15/10. I had read about it on the internet, and I couldn't believe how accurate some of the information was from another blogger, including the $4 per night, mosquito-infested, old, broken-down ferry that sat off to one side of the port.

It took me a while to find the port, but it was there, hidden behind an old fence with only a dirt road as an entrance. One would have thought they were approaching an abandoned landfill from years past. Nevertheless, it was the only port to Kazakhstan, and I had to go through it. It was a long, dirty, broken road lined with semi-trucks on the right and rail cars on the left.

Not knowing the ferry schedule, since there was not one, I went in to find out when the next ferry to Aktay, Kazakhstan was. After entering the port, I was directed to the customs office, where, to my surprise, they were expecting me. My Jeep could only remain in Bacau for three days before I would be penalized by customs for exceeding my allotted time, even though I personally could stay for up to thirty days. It did not make sense to me, but I did not want to risk being put into a predicament where customs officials could extort more than their usual fees.

It was 11:00 a.m. on Sunday, August 15, and I was not finished sightseeing in Bacau when customs told me I had to be on the ferry that loaded that day at 3:00 p.m. for Aktay. I quickly returned to the hotel, gathered my things, and checked out. The receptionist was saddened that I was leaving so early, because I had given her one of my business cards and she had been reading my blog. She put in a plug for her city, and I checked out of the Hyatt.

Once back at the port, I went to the customs office, where they informed me, I could no longer drive the Jeep because it had already been checked in. They sent me back to the ticket office on foot, and it had to be over a hundred degrees outside. There, the ticket agent said I had to pay $485. I asked for the ticket first and offered to pay by Visa, but he said no, dollars only, as he sat in his crusty little office. It seemed pricey for a 24-hour boat ride compared to the two-day Patra trip, which cost about $300. I knew he was taking advantage of me, but I had no choice. He made out the bill of lading in Azeri money and handed it to me. Not surprisingly, it came to 321 Azeri dollars, and after number crunching, I figured he took me for about $80.

After reviewing the documentation, the older customs inspector told the girl interpreting that I did not have a road tax receipt for the trailer, even though I had one for the Jeep. I calmly argued that it was all they had given me when I crossed into Azerbaijan. The inspector said he would register the trailer that day if I paid a $20 road tax (sure, I said to myself), otherwise I would be charged a $50 penalty for not having the receipt. Fine, I told them, the cheapest way works for me. All these extortionists apply reasoning to their crooked methods. I went outside and took a nap in my Jeep with the air-conditioning running, burning up half a tank of gas while waiting in the hot sun for four hours before loading.

As we were loading, the old inspector waved at me to follow him into a broken-down trailer. There, he rubbed his thumb and forefinger together where no one else could see him, wanting the $20, which I handed over. I should have asked for a receipt, but maybe not. Once aboard, all the drivers were cussing and flipping off the port; it was clear they had endured the same ordeal, and the Georgians were furious with the Azeris for being extorted.

Once underway, I got together with five Georgian men also heading to Aktay and then Almaty, where I too was bound. Two were train engineers, two were truck drivers with their rigs on board, and the fifth, Stefan, was an entrepreneur with dual citizenship. He lived in Aktay with his wife and children, where she ran a children's clothing shop at the bazaar. Stefan had gone to Georgia to buy a car for someone and was taking it back to Aktay.

During the ferry ride, we ate, laughed, and drank together, though they did most of the drinking. Alcohol was prohibited aboard, so it came out in plastic water bottles and was clear. The first bottle was the strongest stuff I had ever tasted. I had to water mine down and sip it slowly while they saluted before every drink. We laughed, drank, took pictures, and removed our shirts. It was hot and humid, and we were soaked. The meals onboard were good, costing only two dollars each. I slept in my Jeep while the truckers slept in their rigs and the engineers on couches in the lounge.

Here I was in the middle of the Caspian Sea, the only American, with Azerbaijan to the west, Russia to the north, Kazakhstan to the northeast, Turkestan to the east, and Iran to the south. I told myself that if there was ever a worse place to be during a major conflict, it was right there in the middle of a powder keg.

I bought a watermelon from a roadside vendor for $12. Once he saw what I was driving, he never gave me my change. It should have cost about $1, but it was worth it to get a picture of him, his cart, and his donkey at the stand. I brought the melon to the ferry's kitchen and asked the cook to cut it up for everyone. About twenty people helped themselve. It did not last long on that table.

We arrived at port Sunday night, August 15, and sharply dressed soldiers, immigration, and customs officials came aboard. They were tall, young, well-built, and Asian. I had forgotten Kazakhstan was home to the great Genghis Khan, the legendary Mongol warrior who conquered much of Asia.

20

Jeep Trip Through Kazakhstan

Driving Through Kazakhstan
Day 1 (8/16/2010)
Port of Aktay to Aktobe

Had I known what was ahead, I might have turned around. The roads were some of the most horrific I'd ever encountered, yet many Kazakhstani people managed to keep them busy.

After arriving late on the 15th and clearing immigration, I had to spend the night in a nearby hotel because I couldn't get my Jeep cleared through customs until the next day. I took a $20 cab ride for two miles and got a room for the night, a good decision, knowing what I know now.

The next day I took a ride back to the port and spent four hours chasing officials for stamps. Much of the time was spent waiting for them to show up, and when I reached their offices, some still hadn't arrived. I finally got cleared around noon, but not before a few young soldiers who had helped me took photos with my Jeep. As I drove away, I blasted "I Got the Power" from Coyote Ugly and waved goodbye to my Georgian friends still waiting for clearance.

In Aktay, Stefan spotted my Jeep and pulled up beside me in his Russian Lada. We grabbed a bite to eat and then went to a car wash; the Jeep needed it badly. He helped me find an ATM for Kazakh money and proudly showed me his wife's baby clothing shop at the local bazaar. When I showed him the route I planned to take to Almaty, he pointed to the map and warned me in broken English, "Road no good." I should have listened.

I thought about spending the night in Aktay but decided against it since there was still plenty of daylight and 2,500 miles to go. I found a DHL and sent my passport back to Washington for my final visa. I should have followed my first instinct, for what came next was one of the biggest driving nightmares of my life.

The road began smoothly enough, and I enjoyed the scenery, taking pictures along the way. The camels and herds of horses amazed me everywhere, even on the road. I stopped to photograph them before sunset and asked directions from a man at a construction site who spoke some English. He warned me again about the roads ahead. I figured if the locals could handle them, so could I.

I took more photos of the village, with camel and horse corrals scattered everywhere. Everyone had land outside town where they raised sheep, goats, chickens, camels, and horses. Why so many horses puzzled me, but I soon learned the Mongols are expert riders, and national competitions display their riding skills. As the sun dipped below the horizon, I stopped to capture its peaceful glow in the middle of nowhere.

I remembered reading the U.S. State Department travel advisory, which warned: "Roads in Kazakhstan are in poor repair, especially in rural areas. Poor signage is common. Street lighting may be turned off at night. Drivers often ignore lane markings. Potholes are common and dangerously deep. Pedestrians frequently dart out in front of cars. Visitors should drive defensively. Road rage can be a problem, and accidents involving severe injury and death are common. Traffic police stop cars from extorting bribes on highways. The road between Almaty and Bishkek is especially treacherous at night."

Whoever wrote that report had clearly never been on the road from Aktay to Aktobe.

The roads deteriorated quickly until there was no road at all, only dirt with heavy traffic, including cars, semis, and buses. Luckily, I had filled both my tanks and two Jerry cans. It was now pitch dark, and the only lights were my headlights and the bouncing taillights ahead. To call these holes "potholes" was absurd, they were gullies, some five or six feet deep. At times, the trailer disappeared completely into them. Many drivers created their own "roads" across the desert, headlights scattered like an army charge. Thank God for my pintle hitch. Any other would have snapped.

I saw blown tires and mufflers everywhere and feared a blowout. If anything went wrong, I'd be stranded, with no cell service, no spare parts, no hotels. I was terrified and grateful Colleen wasn't with me. Alone in the dark, I yelled "Hold on!" more than once, though no one else was there.

Suddenly, headlights appeared from the left, racing toward the road. My mind raced. Someone had been tipped off that an American was coming, easy prey. The vehicle joined the road about a mile behind me, lights bouncing closer. I pressed the gas, determined not to let it catch me. For two hours I battled the road, bouncing through holes, weaving onto dirt shoulders, staying just ahead. My top speed was twenty miles per hour; any faster would have torn the Jeep in half. Finally, exhausted, I let the bus pass and pulled over near some semis at a rest area around three in the morning, collapsing into the seat to sleep.

The next morning, I woke in the Jeep and hit the trail again, for it still wasn't a road. In daylight I could better spot the holes, though they were endless. I had no idea how far I'd gone or how much was left, but I pressed on. When my low gas light came on, I had twenty-five miles left. Luckily, I had two full Jerry cans. I stopped near a trucker, cut a water bottle to use as a funnel, and poured in five gallons.

Back on the trail, I noticed the Baja rack on top of the trailer had shifted to one side from all the pounding. I stopped again, and sure enough, it had loosened the top of the trailer, letting dirt fill the interior. I tied the rack down with rope and drove a few more miles before finally reaching pavement again. After twenty-two hours of travel, I'd gone only 120 miles, but sixty miles an hour on smooth asphalt felt glorious.

I reached the next town, found a gas station, and refilled everything. Then I found a car wash, inside a building like a mechanic's shop, and, with help from a local who spoke some English, spent four hours cleaning the Jeep, trailer, and every dusty item inside. We threw away spoiled food and washed everything. With help from two men, I reassembled the Baja rack, vowing that before my next trip, it would be welded solid so this problem would never happen.

Once back on the real road, I continued my drive toward Aktobe, where I expected to pick up what I thought was a highway all the way to Almaty. I came to a major intersection where the good road headed south toward Aktau along with all the traffic, while another road led north toward Aktobe, my intended destination. I went north while everyone else went south, and I should have known then that I was not headed in the right direction. It was clearly the shortest route by distance, but after about forty-five minutes of driving on rough, rocky gravel roads and not seeing a single vehicle, I decided this road was not for me. I turned around and headed back south to Aktau to rethink, regroup, and gather my thoughts about where to go next. I must have had an angel watching over me that night, because what I later learned was that the road I had been on stretched five hundred miles, and all of it was like the section I had just escaped. Many locals refer to that road as the "Road of Death."

Returning to the intersection, I headed south toward Aktau, and after a couple of hours I found the Renaissance Hotel, where this weary and slightly unhinged traveler could finally regain some sanity. I made a promise to myself that night, never again would I drive after dark.

Driving Through Kazakhstan
Days 3 and 4 (August 18–19, 2010)

Aktau and the Renaissance Hotel: It was wonderful to be back in civilization, where there was cell-phone service, internet, and a clean, comfortable place to stay. After my ordeal on the road, I was relieved just to be among people again. I decided to take a couple of days off from traveling to rest, make a solid plan for crossing Kazakhstan, and to completely disregard that damned map that showed every road but none of their actual conditions.

The hotel manager introduced me to a guide and interpreter named Artu, who spoke decent English and was on vacation from his job at the hotel. He offered to spend the day helping me for only $100, and since he was a Renaissance employee, he even managed to reduce my nightly room rate from $350 to $225, clearly well spent money.

Artu took me to the train station so we could explore the possibility of shipping my Jeep to Almaty and avoiding the terrible roads altogether. After discussing the options with some of his friends, they showed me the correct route to take on the map and assured me I would no longer encounter such brutal road conditions. Based on their advice, I decided to continue driving rather than risk the complications of the train, and Artu estimated it would take me about three days to reach Almaty.

While we were still at the train station, a little beggar girl from Turkestan began pestering me for money. Artu tried to shoo her away, but she refused to leave. I had my car door open, and she stood between it and the Jeep, tears streaming down her face, holding out her hand, and refusing to move. I wanted to help but had no change, so I told her to wait.

Artu translated, and I went inside to buy a bottle of water and break a large bill. When I came back about fifteen minutes later, she was still there, waiting patiently. I gave her the equivalent of two dollars, and she finally left. Her older brother immediately grabbed her, snatched the money from her hand, and began striking her repeatedly on the head. He pulled her away roughly, angry that she hadn't brought back more. It was heartbreaking to see such a small child, not much older than Tanner, forced to beg for survival. I feared that this little girl was destined for the kind of hardship and exploitation that haunts so many children in this part of the world.

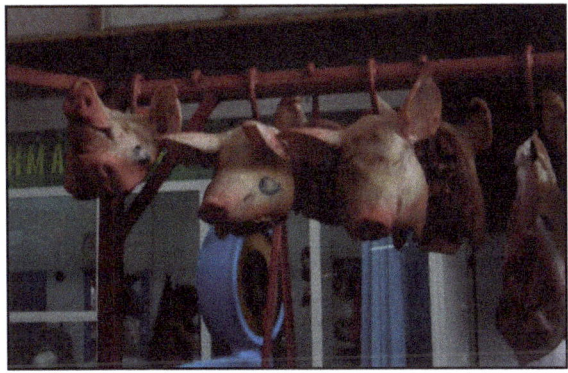

We then went to the bazaar and meat market, where I was shocked to discover that the main meat for sale was horse. The women vendors were slicing and packaging it like it was prime beef, and I couldn't believe people ate horse meat, let alone that it was considered a delicacy. Until then, I had thought the horses I saw along the road were mounts for the Mongols, but

I was clearly in another world. After that, I swore I would never again photograph a horse in Kazakhstan.

As we were leaving the bazaar, I saw a grown man viciously scolding a little boy, no older than Madison. The man grabbed the boy by one arm, lifted him four feet off the ground, and slammed him onto the concrete walkway like a rag doll. He did it five or six more times while the child cried softly between impacts, as if he were used to this kind of abuse. I was sick to my stomach watching it, because in America, Child Protective Services would have been there within minutes, and someone would have gone to jail. Artu just shook his head and said this kind of thing happens all the time, but people prefer not to get involved in family matters.

At the entrance to the bazaar, two women were collecting parking fees. They were dressed entirely in white, long robes, gloves, and sunglasses, so that no one could recognize them. I asked Artu if it was part of a religious custom, but he said it wasn't shameful. They covered themselves because they didn't want anyone to know the kind of work they were doing. I saw similar scenes throughout Kazakhstan, women sweeping streets, doing road repair, and other hard labor that, in most other places, is dominated by men. Aktau, like Baku, is an oil boomtown, driven by British Petroleum, and everywhere you look are big, shiny SUVs with company logos on the doors.

That evening, Artu and one of his friends took me to a restaurant where they ordered horse meat and horse tongue as appetizers, which smelled awful. They tried hard to convince me to try it, but there was no chance of that happening. After dinner, they dropped me off at the hotel, where I got a good night's rest and mentally prepared myself for the long 2,500-mile journey ahead, through some of the most desolate lands I had ever seen.

Driving Through Kazakhstan
(Days 5–10 and Almaty)

Day 5 – Aktau to Kostanay (August 20, 2010)

After leaving the comfort of the Renaissance Hotel in Aktau, I drove 610 miles straight north following the river that flows into the Caspian Sea, the one that technically divides Asia from Europe. There wasn't much to see along the road to Kostanay, where I spent the night at the Medeo Hotel.

The area seemed to have once been a large industrial city back in the days of the USSR. So many buildings stood in disrepair or completely abandoned that it was almost unbelievable. I couldn't help but think how profitable it would be to have a demolition crew here. Just the steel alone would be worth a fortune. It amazed me how much valuable metal sat rusting away with little effort to recycle it.

At one of my stops I met a couple driving to Astana. They asked if we should drive together, and I agreed to follow them for a while. When we reached Kostanay, they turned into what looked like an old abandoned industrial park. Something about it didn't feel right, so I kept going straight ahead until I reached the Medeo Hotel, leaving them behind and wondering where I went. I wasn't about to take unnecessary risks this far from home.

That day I also learned something interesting: every car in Kazakhstan is an unofficial taxi. Along the road I saw covered bus stops every five or ten miles, yet never once did I see a bus. At each stop people waited with their hands stretched out, pointing downward as passing cars approached. Curious, I finally stopped to see what was happening. About eight people rushed toward my Jeep speaking in a language I didn't understand. I held up one finger to signal I could take only one passenger, and a middle-aged woman climbed into the front seat with her arms full of watermelons.

We drove about forty-five miles without exchanging a word until we approached her stop. To my surprise she pulled out about twenty dollars of Kazakh currency and tried to pay me. I politely refused, and she smiled before stepping out of the Jeep. I later learned that this kind of informal ridesharing is a primary mode of transportation across Kazakhstan. Everywhere I went after that I noticed people standing by the roadside with their extended hands, waiting for a driver willing to give them a lift for a few tenge.

Day 6 – Uralsk to Aktobe (August 21, 2010)

Have you ever seen *Lonesome Dove*, where Captain Call drives his herd of cattle through endless dusty plains on the way to Montana? That's exactly how I felt on this stretch of the journey — nothing but wheat fields on both sides stretching as far as the eye could see, no camels, no horses, no people, just endless land.

Occasionally I'd see a large structure rising on the horizon and think it might be a town, only to realize it was one of the enormous grain silos that dotted the landscape. I couldn't help but wonder where they found enough combines to handle such a harvest. It rained lightly off and on throughout the day, which felt refreshing after so many days of heat. For the first time on the trip, I drove with my windows down. The fields reminded me of the Nebraska Panhandle.

After days of temperatures near one hundred degrees, it cooled down dramatically, dropping to forty-seven during the day and even colder at night. Locals were bundled in winter clothes while I was still wearing Bermuda shorts. That day I drove 505 miles and spent the night at the Amsterdam Hotel.

Days 7-8 – Aktobe to Kostanay to Astana
(August 22–23, 2010)

When I don't stop to do something memorable during a day's drive, the places begin to blur together. Much of the route from Aktobe to Astana was more of the same — flat plains, gray skies, and rain that came and went. Each day I covered about 400 to 450 miles, pacing myself since I knew my passport wouldn't arrive in Almaty until the following week.

While in Kostanay I stayed again at the Medeo Hotel for about eighty dollars. I called Colleen from the room phone, which cost seventy-two dollars, money I instantly regretted spending. Unless it's an emergency, I'll never call from a hotel again. My cell phone had stopped working somewhere along northern Kazakhstan, leaving me without any real communication except occasional emails. The isolation made me feel lonelier than ever.

My next destination was Astana, about 420 miles away and the new capital of Kazakhstan since 1997, when it was moved from Almaty. I stayed at the Ramada Inn, where it seemed like nothing in the room worked. Other than sleeping and typing on my laptop I spent most of the time inside.

Astana itself felt strangely modern, tall glass buildings rising in the middle of the steppe. I never fully understood why the capital was moved here, though someone mentioned that Almaty was more prone to earthquakes. I suppose that's something to keep in mind when I finally get there. Along the way I noticed countless cemeteries and roadside shrines, each one built in a slightly distinctive style. Some were elaborate and castle-like, clearly belonging to families of means. I took photos, fascinated by their variety and symbolism.

Days 9-10 – Astana to Balqash (August 24–25, 2010)

I arrived in Balqash toward evening, a small town beside a massive lake. I found the best hotel in town, mainly because it offered internet access. It cost about thirty dollars for the room and an extra three for internet. The building was old, but the night clerk was exceedingly kind and helpful. I gave her one of my cards, and later she surprised me by finding me on Facebook and sending an email. And here is where my problem of getting a potential divorce starts. The lady at the front desk was Alexandra. She had a nice figure, spoke Kazakhstan, Russian, and English.

Unfortunately, that night I was eaten alive by bedbugs. I should've used the bed sheets instead of lying directly on the bedspread, but I was too tired to care. The next morning, to my surprise, Alexandra was still working. I discovered the Jeep wouldn't start. I had left the refrigerator plugged in all night, draining the battery. On top of that I'd somehow lost my jumper cables.

A couple of boys hanging around the parking lot came to help, along with a man who pulled two pieces of house wire from his trunk to use as makeshift jumper cables. Miraculously, the engine turned over. After losing three hours of driving time, I decided to stay another day, get an oil change, and have the Jeep washed. I went back inside to talk to Alexandra about if she knew where I could wash the car and if she knew where one was at. She offered to show me the way if I was willing to wait another hour when she got off work.

The car wash was run by two young boys who charged me only $7.50 for what would've cost at least twenty back home. Covered in dust from days of travel, the Jeep and trailer looked new again. Then I drove around searching for a place to change my oil. With no readable signs, I stopped at a garage that had a car ramp outside. Using hand gestures, I explained what I needed. They sent me to an auto-parts shop for oil and jumper cables. I didn't need a filter since I had spares.

After 6,000 miles since my last oil change in Athens, it was due. The oil cost about ten dollars a quart, but the labor was just a thousand tenge, around $7.50. The two men worked for forty-five minutes, and I gave them double pay out of gratitude. The entire crew came out to shake my hand.

Before leaving, two sisters at another garage offered to detail the inside of the Jeep for the same price. They worked meticulously, cleaning every inch. When I tried to tip them an extra two dollars each, they hesitated but eventually accepted, smiling shyly.

Earlier that morning I asked Alexandria if she likes sushi and she would want to go out and have some that night. She found a Korean restaurant off a side street that served both sushi kebab and sushi. For no better communication skills than what we had, we managed to have an enjoyable time and laugh a lot. Using hand signals, she led me to an enclosed parking lot with a security guard. Once I paid for the car parking, she grabbed my hand and took me to her apartment. Once again, all this was happening with mostly communicating with hand signals. It turned out to be the perfect ending to a long day.

Almaty (August 25–31, 2010)

The drive from Balqash to Almaty felt short compared to the rest of the trip. The road followed the lake's shoreline, lined with roadside stands selling dried fish. I bought a small one to snack on. It tasted like jerky. Later I picked up a larger one to take home to Lincoln. Surely the folks at the office would get a kick out of it.

It took ten days to travel the 2,600 miles from Aktau to Almaty, through brutal roads, endless plains, and some of the most isolated country I've ever crossed. I invented a few new curse words, survived on hard-boiled eggs and dry bread, and constantly prayed to find a hotel before nature called again. I wouldn't have made it without a reliable vehicle; broken-down cars and trucks littered the roadside everywhere.

For all my complaints about the roads, the people of Kazakhstan were some of the kindest I met anywhere. They went out of their way to help me, even when language barriers made communication difficult. Many times, drivers personally led me to gas stations, hotels, or car washes rather than trying to give directions. I understand now why so many Kazakhs prefer to travel east-west by train. It's a long, punishing road.

Not only did the trip wear me out, but it also took a toll on the trailer. A shock absorber broke and needed repair. With help from a taxi driver at the Holiday Inn, I found a shop that fixed it for $250. I also hired one of the hotel supervisors as my guide, a man who proved invaluable in arranging repairs, navigating, and even getting me better hotel rates.

He took me to the American Embassy to handle paperwork, then up the cable car to a mountain overlooking Almaty. My favorite stop, though, was the Green Market, an enormous, covered bazaar full of every imaginable spice, vegetable, and meat, including more horse meat. The Korean section fascinated me most, jars of fermented fish, cabbage aged in buried kegs, and countless pickled creations. The women insisted I taste everything, proudly offering sample after sample. It was like judging a state-fair food contest. I left with dried apricots, spices, and a few rolls of sushi for dinner.

For some reason or another my passport was delayed further, so I called Alex to see if she wanted to come down to Almaty. She arrived the next day after I raised one of the local taxis from the hotel to be at the bus stop and pick her up for, she wasn't getting in until three in the morning. Max, one of the hotel clerks, told us about the world's largest flea market I'd ever seen, five miles long and half a mile wide. Thousands of small stalls filled the area; many built from stacked cargo containers.

The lower container served as a shop, the upper one as storage, with metal roofs bridging the aisles. It was an ingenious way to recycle old shipping containers. The market bustled with traders from all over including Iran, Türkiye, Turkmenistan, Uzbekistan, Kyrgyzstan, and, of course, Kazakhstan. They sold everything imaginable, from baby clothes to industrial equipment, and even single cigarettes. I was there mostly as a tourist not looking to be shopping for anything, but Alexandra wanted to buy a new bedspread.

That night we treated ourselves to a sushi bar, sitting outside near a short wall draped with silk curtains. I made the mistake of moving a candle next to the napkins which quickly caught fire, and then the curtain followed. Smoke filled the air, and the staff rushed over, calmly replacing the napkins as if nothing had happened. We finished our meal surrounded by the faint smell of burnt silk.

The next day, Alex and I drove up to the mountains where the 2011 Asian Games would soon be held. We took a ski lift to the summit, enjoying a stunning view of Almaty. Later we stopped at a Brazilian restaurant for lunch, which turned out to be my worst meal of the trip. I spent the evening nursing a stomachache.

Monday was supposed to be the day I picked up the trailer, but all the shops were closed for a national holiday. I stayed in, caught up on writing, and tried to ignore the frustration of yet another delay in getting my passport. By Tuesday I finally retrieved the trailer and kept myself busy tinkering with small repairs.

Every day I found something to do to keep me from feeling stranded, washing the Jeep, fixing the fuse, or exploring nearby streets. It wasn't always easy, but I reminded myself that every delay was just another part of the journey.

Almaty at Night: It's been too many years for me to claim that I am any sort of expert on nightclubs, the music they play, and what the girls wear these days. When did short miniskirts come back into style anyway? I have been in my Lazy Boy for too many years.

Soho clubs, as they are called, are nightclub-restaurant combinations where you eat dinner while other people may be dancing, while other nightclubs are nightclub-bar combinations. The latter of the two does not seem to be a place where guys take their dates, but where the girls go either alone or in groups of girls and where the guys go alone or in groups as well. Seldom did I see a couple entering together at any of the places I visited, but I did see some leaving together.

The first club I went to on Friday was called Guns and Roses Pub, a very upscale nightclub located within the Hotel Kazakhstan, a rock-and-roll nightclub that was packed. A band tried to imitate American music but was not successful at their fruitless attempt. What was very noticeable there was that most of the women were hookers waiting to be picked by some guy willing to dish out a week's salary. Unlike the Russian bar girls in Bacau, these girls were not trying to hustle drinks but stood there alone waiting, with no drinks before them and a cell phone constantly in their hands, as I am sure they did not want to miss any calls. You could tell the non-hookers, for their cells must have been off and in their bags and they didn't care who was calling. I ate a sandwich for supper and headed back to the hotel after one beer, leaving half of it behind.

At breakfast the next morning, I was visiting with one of the private jet pilots who had been at the Holiday Inn longer than I had. We compared notes as to where we went and where we ate dinner on Friday night. I told the pilot, who was a Canadian, that I did not care for Guns and Roses because it appeared that most of the women there seemed to be workers. He felt the same way, for he had already been there and did not care about it either. He told me of another place, classier than Guns and Roses, with more types of food than the typical pub fare served at Guns and Roses. When Saturday night rolled around, off I went. They had a nice sushi bar on the first floor, karaoke, and a steakhouse on the second floor, and a techno nightclub on the third floor. It was a high-class place with a lot of Land Cruisers and Mercedes parked outside. It amazes me how much money people here in Almaty spend on luxury cars compared to what the average wage earner makes here.

I ate my typical amount of sushi and downed a couple of the best margaritas that I have ever had, because they were extremely smooth. I found my way up to the third floor where they were playing techno music. Is there ever a pause between songs, or does it always play constantly? Girls danced with girls, guys with guys, and some people danced alone. The music was loud but decent, and a fog cloud hovered over everyone. I had never been to any club like this one, so I was surprised, because Colleen had kept me sheltered all these years. I ended up drinking a couple more of those great margaritas and was starting to feel it. I was the oldest guy there and the only one wearing jeans and a beard. Sport jackets, ties, and fancy shirts were the appropriate attire for the men, while the women wore the typical short miniskirts. The age there was younger than that of Guns and Roses, and many of the women and men seemed to be Kazakhs.

It's clearly time for me to leave Almaty, for I have gotten a bad impression about all the women here as being hookers because of the provocative way they dress. I am more accustomed to women being a bit more conservative in their attire than they are here. On a side note, in addition to the flight crew from Canada, there's another crew member from Pakistan. The flight attendant, a young attractive female, dresses in the same manner as the other girls here in Almaty do. Now what does this flight attendant wear when she goes back home to Pakistan, a country that is Muslim?

Leaving Kazakhstan, September 6, 2010: I got my passport today and wasted no time leaving Almaty on my way to China. I have learned a lot about the people after being here for over ten days. I got to know several people at the hotel well, and they, as well as those at the repair shop, were nice to me. Even though I have bad-mouthed the rest of Kazakhstan, especially their roads, I cannot say enough about the people here in Almaty and along the way, for they have only reinforced my feelings that the Kazakh people are the nicest I have met on this entire trip.

Kazakhstan's citizens are basically made up of two groups. First, there are the Kazakhs, who are Asians and descendants of the Mongols and have been natives to this land for several hundred years. Then there are the immigrants, mostly Russians from the time when Russia occupied Kazakhstan for close to one hundred years. Not once did I ever see a Black person in Kazakhstan.

From my impression of the people here, the Kazakhs are a class higher than the Russians themselves. The President of Kazakhstan is Kazakh and elected for life. Of all the soldiers and police officers that I have seen or met, not one Russian was among them. The majority of the Kazakh women, who are thinner and taller than the Russian women here in Almaty, dress as if they are all going to a wedding, and with their big sunglasses and high heels, they walk as if they are Pretty Woman on Rodeo Drive. On the other hand, the Russian women are more casual in their attire as a group.

I gave away the dried fish I purchased on the road to the guys at the shop who fixed my shocks, for I was not sure how long it would have lasted anyway. That giveaway paid off, for on September 1, 2010, when I had to make another trip to the shop to get some fuses for my auxiliary power, they did not want to be paid for their time or the fuses.

Keeping in line with the other days and trying to pass the time, each day I would go out and scout the area and get something done on my trailer or Jeep. On September 2, 2010, I had the Baja Rack reinforced to avoid additional problems down the road. On September 3, 2010, I found bolts for the fenders that needed to be replaced. On September 5, 2010, I washed and reorganized the trailer. That same day, I also made sure to stay up all night so that I could listen to Big Red football on the computer. It is now time to make this last post here in Kazakhstan and hope that my entrance into China will not be as eventful as my entrance into Kazakhstan was.

Back in Almaty, September 7, 2010: Wow, this is one blog I wish I were not writing. All excited about getting my passport back that day, I quickly set my GPS for the border town of Korgas on the China side of the border. The GPS led me north of Almaty on Highway 350 near a large lake. It was a nice, pleasant drive, and I was not in a hurry, thinking that the border crossing was open 24/7.

It was a decent road with not much traffic, and because of the lack of traffic, I asked myself numerous times if I was on the right road to Kata (China). Everyone kept pointing in the direction I was going, so I continued forward. I expected the worst of roads to be in front of me, but I never came across anything too bad. I was able to travel from forty-five to sixty miles an hour for the entire trip. Some of the areas seemed quite isolated in the mountains, and I was always in constant fear of something breaking down or just getting a flat tire out there. I picked up one rider and her groceries along the way at one of those bus stops I mentioned earlier. In all, the total drive there was about seven hours.

When I finally got to the border, it was closed for the night. The soldiers guarding the entrance kept telling me to go to the hotel and pointed toward some shoddy-looking buildings about a hundred yards away. The buildings were what the locals called hotels. The rooms had several old metal beds in them with a two-inch-thick old, crusty-looking mattress that I would not let my dog sleep on. Here they do not rent rooms but beds in a room. I did not feel comfortable staying in one of these rooms, even though the people there were nice. I did, however, decide to eat there and have chicken for dinner, since I know what chickens look like, along with some fried potatoes and dried bread. It served its purpose.

Since this little community of about six shanties had its own security guard walking around and keeping an eye on things while carrying a shotgun, I felt safe parking outside where I ate, and I slept very well in the Jeep, bug-free. The next morning, I had my coffee, two eggs, sausage, and some dry bread, as usual.

I proceeded to the border, where the guards opened the gate and allowed me to pass. I thought I was near the border, but I had to drive another seven miles, through a town and up to another military checkpoint. Once they looked at my passport, I was allowed up to the actual crossing itself. I was there for a total of three hours. The first two were spent showing every customs official, immigration officer, military guard, and anyone else in uniform my Jeep and trailer, for they wanted to know everything about the Jeep Wrangler. They got in behind the steering wheel, started it up, put it in gear, turned on the air, radio, opened the hood, and asked about the price, they wanted to know everything about my Jeep. One guy even brought a 4×4 magazine that had a picture of the same Jeep in the same color. All this was not done as an official inspection, but simply because they had never seen a real Jeep in person before and were in love with it.

Once the gawking was done, along with most of the paperwork, one of the officials looked at my passport and spoke, "BIG PROBLEM." My Kazakhstan visa had expired a week earlier, and they could not allow me to leave Kazakhstan in case the Chinese would not allow me to cross into China that day. I was so heartbroken because I had made a seven-hour drive, spent two days getting there, and now had to go back to Almaty for something I never even bothered to check.

Nevertheless, I had become accustomed to adversity and was not about to let that stop me from accomplishing my goals. I just told myself to relax, get back to Almaty, the Holiday Inn, and get a new visa.

The road back to Almaty was much more pleasant than the road from Almaty to Korgas. I had taken the wrong road before and went the long way around. This road was Highway 351, with plenty of traffic, fruit stands, shish-kebab restaurants, and communities along the way. I took my time and took numerous pictures of the donkeys pulling carts, for they were all over the place, making me laugh and smile every time I saw one. The donkey and buggy were the main sources of transportation for the vegetable and fruit farmers selling their goods along the highway. It was an enjoyable ride back to the Holiday Inn in Almaty.

I got to know everyone at the Holiday Inn well, and they all treated me like long-time friends, especially my good friend Mack, because without him, life for me would be much more difficult here in Almaty. Mack was on duty that night when I arrived back at the Holiday Inn from my attempt to cross into China. We planned to go to the Immigration Police the next morning in hopes of obtaining a new visa for me. I then quickly went to bed because I was physically and mentally exhausted that night.

The next morning, Wednesday, Mack, and I took off for the Immigration Police headquarters, where I quickly saw that this process was going to take longer than I had hoped. One official indicated that it might take two weeks to get this done, while another female immigration officer took both of my passports, gave me a receipt, and told us to call back that afternoon. We went outside, where Mack told me that they were starting to jerk us around and that he needed to get one of his friends, who specialized in these sorts of visa issues, involved. Within a half hour, Mack's friend showed up, and together we went to another part of town, where we waited on the corner near a government building while his friend visited with another individual who had shown up. We headed back to the Immigration Police, where I paid a penalty of $200 for overstaying my visa and got a receipt for my payment, which was handed over to Mack's friend, who then gave it to an official I never once spoke with. About fifteen minutes later, I had to dish out another $10 since the person who typed up the visa claimed to have lots of work to do before he could get to mine. The $10 moved my visa application to the top of the list. Twenty minutes later, Mack's friend showed up with my passport and my new valid visa. Although Mack's friend would not take any money, the government agent requested $400 for his services, which I gladly handed over to Mack's friend to pay off the G-Man. Don't people in America go to jail for these sorts of things?

Might Be Time to Quit, September 10, 2010: Nothing has disappointed me so much as the possibility that I might have to give up, at least for the present time, my current plans, and head home. I was hoping that I could finish my trip either in Singapore or Bangkok, but the Chinese had put a big damper on my plans.

After getting my Kazakhstan visa renewed, I immediately headed out for the border once again. I was hopeful that this time I would not encounter any problems getting around. I spent the night at a hotel that was farther away from the border than the one I looked at a couple of nights earlier, because it was cleaner and newer. I knew that the border would be closed by the time I got there, so I took my time, continuing to take pictures of the donkeys and buggies that were all over the place.

Once again, I stopped at one of the roadside shish-kebab restaurants, where, using my fine-tuned international sign language that I had learned, I let the cook know that I wanted lamb for dinner. I didn't sleep very well that night, for the bed was not as comfortable as my Jeep's lazy boy, and on top of that, I had multiple bad dreams all night long that the Kazakhs would once again prevent me from leaving Kazakhstan.

I was up early the next morning because I could not sleep very well. I headed for the border that morning and was the first one there. Shortly after getting there, I was joined by three buses along with this little old man who just was wandering around, and I had no idea if he was just a local guy or a passenger on one of the buses. After a while, I got the feeling that he must have been a local, for the guards seemed to know his name. This old guy kept hanging around me for some unknown reason. I didn't know if I was just interesting to him or looked like an easy target. I soon found out that it was the latter of the two.

I had my driver's door open for a couple of minutes, listening to the radio, when this old man came up to me and stood between me, sitting in the driver's seat with the door swung open. He only stood there for a second and then walked away, when I noticed my expensive Buck knife, which I used for everything, was gone. I always kept it in the side pocket of the door panel. I quickly looked elsewhere in the Jeep, thinking that I might not have placed it back where I usually kept it. I found the old man and approached him, and before I even mentioned a word, he started defending himself, showing me his hands and letting me know that he did not take anything. To me, there was no other alternative; he had to have taken the knife. I did not want to frisk the old guy for fear of causing a ruckus among the other people in the parking lot, so I started looking around, thinking that he might have tossed it in the nearby grass, but no such luck. I was not happy at the thought of losing this knife, so I decided to try to buy it back from the old guy. I showed him 5,000 Kazakh dollars, or about $40 U.S. The old man took an interest in the money and wanted it first, but I kept insisting that I wanted the knife first. Within a minute, he returned with the knife in his hand, wanting the money. I grabbed the knife while he kept insisting that I pay him the money, and that was not about to happen. He started to pester me when the guards came over and told him to go away, for they knew he was the knife thief. The guard opened the gate and let me pass, leaving the old man behind to go rob someone else.

Back at the Kazakhstan side of the border, I tried to quickly move things along so that I could get myself into China as soon as possible. I made the mistake of leaving my Jeep door open and running, giving the guards the opportunity to start gawking and getting inside the Jeep like the previous time I was there. After an hour, I was cut loose and headed toward the China border about a mile away.

At a distance, the Chinese border crossing seemed newer and cleaner than that of its counterpart in Kazakhstan. There were two fences, one for the Chinese border and the other for the Kazakhstan border about one hundred yards apart, with a road going from Kazakhstan to China. Armed soldiers guarded each gate. As I crossed the line into China (about thirty feet), I was approached by a young Chinese officer who spoke English and was very professional while doing his job. He seemed to me to be a very likeable individual.

He asked if I had a guide waiting for me at the border and told me to call him to escort me across. He also asked for the documentation for the vehicle and the trip. I had neither, for I thought a guide and documentation could be taken care of at the border. No such luck. The young officer called his superior over, and they quickly told him to send me back to Kazakhstan, no discussion, no negotiating, no bribes. The young officer simply told me to go back to Kazakhstan. I was in shock. My trip was ending, and there was nothing I could do about it. I kept telling myself that these Chinese really didn't know what I had gone through to get to the point where I was finally.

I backed out of Chinese territory onto Kazakhstan as requested by the young officer and turned my Jeep around to drive back into Kazakhstan when the Kazakh soldier guarding their gate stopped me and told me to park off to one side while he awaited directions from his superiors to see if I could go back to Kazakhstan.

There I was between two international fence lines, each guarded by soldiers carrying AK-47s, and there was nowhere to go. I felt as if I was Tom Hanks in *Terminal*, stuck in an unoccupied zone. I sat there for about four hours, listening to my music and taking pictures, for neither side told me that it was prohibited since I was between the two borders. I approached the Chinese side of the border and asked a soldier on guard for some water. One of the other soldiers ran to the guard shack and got me a couple of bottles of water and brought them to me. You could tell these guys were nice but just had a job to do. Although they were prohibited from showing much emotion, they smiled and gave me the thumbs-up on my Jeep.

After about four hours in the unoccupied zone, the Kazakh soldier told me to go back to the Kazakhstan border crossing, where I was processed back into the country. I called Mack, and he said, "Get out of that area as quickly as possible and get back to Almaty, where we'll try to figure out what we can do," so back to Almaty I went. I went back the same way I came up to Korgas via the donkey-and-buggy route that I had enjoyed so much before. This time it was not so enjoyable, and I did not take any pictures. In addition to it all, my cell phone quit working, and it was getting dark. What else could go wrong that day?

I went back to the Holiday Inn, where Mack had me a room lined up. I was starting to feel that the Holiday Inn was my home away from home and that I was bound to stay there forever. I did some additional research and blog reading that night that I should have done months earlier; perhaps then I could have avoided some of these problems.

It appears that, for a person to travel freely through China, he must first submit a precise itinerary and hire an official tour guide who would have to always be with him. The Chinese are worried that some foreigner might wander off into a sensitive area and see something they do not want seen. I learned from the American Embassy that the border crossing I wanted to use was in an extremely sensitive area of China, where there is much political unrest in the region.

After settling in once again at the Holiday Inn, I started realizing that my next leg of this trip would have to be back to the U.S. with the Jeep. Personally, I could go to China by train, plane, or bus; I just could not take my Jeep into China. I have never been one to simply quit something that I started, but the time has come to perhaps give up, go back to the States, and reorganize for a future attempt to achieve the goals I want.

On Monday, I would know what my options were as far as either sending my Jeep via train directly to Vietnam, bypassing China altogether while I took the train, or simply sending my Jeep back home. It all depended on how long it would take to get the Jeep to Vietnam from here, for I could not wait forever. I would just have to see what information Monday brought.

Monday, September 13, 2010: Monday came and went with no information from the container company here in Almaty. I was beginning to think that the Kazakh people were not in a hurry to move things along, prolonging decisions that were easy to make. Tuesday started no different than Monday. The cab drivers I asked if they wanted to drive my Jeep to Ukraine, where I would fly and meet them, failed to show up for our meeting at 11:00. I was starting to worry about my Kazakhstan visa once again expiring and that I would have to bribe another official to get another one issued.

It seemed as if nothing was going anywhere for me here in Almaty, and I was afraid nothing would happen, so I decided not to rely on the Kazakhs for any assistance and take matters into my own hands. I went to my room after the cabbies failed to show up, told Tony at the reception desk to prepare my bill, because I would be leaving shortly. I said my goodbyes to my friends at the Holiday Inn and headed back to Astana, where I hoped I could get a transit visa through Russia and back to Europe through either Ukraine, Belarus, or Latvia.

I drove until about two in the morning, until I reached Balqash, where Alexandra lived, a small town that I was familiar with because I had spent two days there washing the Jeep and changing the oil prior to leaving for Almaty. I spent the night in my Jeep near the same area where the hotel I stayed at last time was located. I have come to realize that it is better to sleep in the Jeep than stay in one of the cheaper hotels, because they have one bedbug too many for me. It could be my imagination, though.

I sat in my Jeep outside Alexandra's apartment attempting to call on her phone to no avail. As I was leaving, Alexandra called me, for she had looked out the window and saw me pulling away. We sat in the Jeep talking when she made me promise that one day we would see each other again.

Leaving Almaty, I had the vision of some of the roads having rough construction detours, but I must have been mistaken or on the wrong roads, for the road out of Almaty to Astana was decent. I made it to Astana about five on Wednesday afternoon and checked into a hotel inside a large park near the Russian Embassy. It cost $157 for the hotel, a bit more than it was worth, but I was so exhausted that it did not matter at this point. I quickly went to bed and slept hard, only to be awakened by a few phone calls from the office. I must have slept twelve hours straight that night.

On Thursday morning I immediately went to the Russian Embassy for the transit visa. If I did not get it, I did not know what my next step would be. Time was of the essence, and I only had six days left on my Kazakhstan visa. That morning was the coldest day I had seen this entire trip, requiring me to put on my jeans and break out my heavy red Husker jacket, for everyone in line thought I was nuts for not wearing a jacket. I guess they did not realize how cold it gets in Nebraska and that I was already accustomed to it.

I applied for my visa and paid the express fee, to the surprise of the young Russian taking the application. He did, however, make me fill out a second application since the first one I filled in earlier was sloppy and he couldn't read my writing. The express fee was 40,000 Tenges, or about $275, but it would be worth it knowing that I would quickly have a way out of Kazakhstan. In many cases, that's more money than many Kazakhs make in a month, at least in rural areas.

It was 5:30 p.m., and I was about to pick up my visa in thirty minutes. I was hopeful of being on the road shortly after that, barring any problems.

I might as well mention that after 11,000 miles of driving, I had my first fender bender with a semi. No big deal, it was my fault, and when the police officer came over and asked the trucker, who had no damage, "Problem?" the trucker said, "No problem." Then he asked me, "Problem?" and I said, "No problem," for it was my fault anyway. The police officer quickly said, "You go!" and we left. The fender is now in my back seat.

Heading Home, September 16, 2010: Three days, almost 2,000 miles, wow. With a Russian transit visa in hand, which was only good for four days, I quickly headed north out of Astana, Kazakhstan, toward the Russian border about 250 miles away. When I first indicated on my visa application that I would drive through Russia in four days, I had not looked at a map nor realized that it was one big country. I had to leave it by the 21st of September, something that was going to be impossible for me. Nevertheless, I had to go for it.

To my surprise, most of the roads to the Russian border from Astana were just as good as those in Germany, three lanes of solid concrete with guardrails on both sides separating the lanes. Boy, I was excited. Shame the speed limit was only fifty-five miles per hour, for I really could have made up some time. I was hoping to make it to the border by evening so I could cross into Russia first thing in the morning, but my eyes were starting to get the best of me. I found a safe place to park and sleep for a few hours before crossing the border.

Finishing my drive to the border the next morning, it took less than fifteen minutes to get cleared at the Kazakhstan crossing, for they didn't have civilian customs officials as they did in Kosgove near China. Soldiers ran this crossing very professionally, and there were no gawking looks at my Jeep this time. Getting into Russia was just as easy as getting out of Kazakhstan. I would have to say this crossing was the most efficient and easiest of all those I had crossed during my travels.

The drive to Moscow seemed endless along Highway M-7. At the beginning, it was mostly open countryside with softly rolling hills, quite beautiful with all the colors of autumn on full display. Along the way, there were just as many roadside attractions as in any big city. Vendors seemed endless, selling everything conceivable — four-foot-tall teddy bears displayed in stands on both sides of the road in front of homes, covered with plastic sheeting to protect them from the weather. These bear vendors stood about twenty feet apart and stretched along the road for five miles.

There were also wilderness vendors open 24/7, selling from shacks made of whatever materials they could find. Usually thirty to forty of these stalls clustered together, offering fishing equipment, nets, rubber rafts, camping gear, and all sorts of pellet air guns that looked so real I first thought they were actual firearms. There were arts and crafts from the local region and numerous dried fish vendors selling four-foot-long eels for about forty dollars each. I never tasted any of them, though they looked quite appetizing. Many sold tea along with their fish to make a dollar. Capitalism at work! On occasion, along parts of the road, there were also women selling their own "goods."

Most restaurants catered to truck drivers, so when I walked into one knowing I couldn't read the menu, I simply looked at what others were eating and pointed to the dish I wanted. Most meals cost about three or four dollars, including coffee and water.

If someone ever wanted to make serious money, they should come to Highway M-7 in Russia and build a chain of Motel 6s between the Kazakhstan border and Moscow. The motels that exist are few, far between, poorly maintained, and uncomfortable. In many, the bathroom is down the hall, and the shower might be in another building altogether. During this part of my trip, I didn't see a bed worth sleeping in unless I had no other choice. I'd say most of these hotels have about a 90% vacancy rate, for most travelers east of Moscow prefer to sleep in their vehicles. I only stayed in them for security reasons when I didn't feel comfortable in the area. Drivers often cluster together for safety in parking areas near the roads. There are also private parking compounds enclosed by tall fences with lookout towers, staffed by armed guards all night long. Personally, I always felt safer sleeping in the Jeep than in a bed-bug-infested hotel.

There was one night, though, that frightened me, somewhere between the Kazakhstan border and Moscow on the second night of this leg. Around 2:30 in the morning, after only two hours of sleep parked near a 24/7 vendor area, there came a hard knock on my Jeep window. A man stood there speaking Russian, and the only words I recognized were "Russian Mafia." I had no idea what he meant, but I started the Jeep and left the area immediately. Two miles down the road, I stopped at a well-lit gas station filled with other vehicles and semis, thinking it was safer. Two hours later, the same man was again knocking on my window, repeating the same words. Thinking he was telling me I couldn't park there, I moved forward another two hundred yards, grabbed my pepper spray, and tried to sleep. Ten minutes later, he was back, banging on the window again. I was ready to shower him with pepper spray if he tried anything, but he just kept jabbering in Russian, again mentioning the Mafia. I started the Jeep and drove forty miles before getting any real sleep. To this day, I have no idea who he was or what he wanted, but just hearing those two words, "Russian Mafia," was enough to scare me.

Since the man never tried to harm me, I assume he might have been a private security guard working for the vendors, or perhaps some kind of self-appointed protector looking for payment for "keeping me safe." Whatever it was, once I left the area, I never saw him again.

Moscow, September 19, 2010: After spending only a few dollars per meal on the road, I was shocked to find myself in the most expensive city in Europe. At a BP gas station fully stocked like one back home, a small chicken sandwich and cup of coffee cost twelve dollars. Still, it tasted good enough. Katie had booked me a night at the Budapest Hotel for $125. It was centrally located, and I could park my Jeep and trailer directly in front at no cost, a rare treat. I was exhausted and skipped exploring the city that first night, heading straight to bed.

Moscow – September 20, 2010: Since I couldn't leave Russia within the four-day limit of my original visa, I called the American Embassy. The consular officer, a Russian who spoke English with an Aussie accent, arranged for me to visit the Russian Immigration Office. Within half an hour, I had a second transit visa for five additional days. I'm sure those embassy contacts exchange favors now and then, and I'm still grateful to Krill for helping me. What a difference between Kazakhstan and Russia.

With four extra days, I decided to stay an additional night in Moscow for sightseeing and shopping. Budapest was full, so I moved to its sister hotel around the corner, $500 for the night, the most expensive stay of the entire trip. I left my Jeep and trailer parked safely in front of Budapest.

I exchanged about $450 worth of Kazakh money I still had, though I took a beating on the exchange rate. The money exchange office was in a basement below a high-end clothing shop selling those famous mink hats. I bought one for myself and one for Colleen, $350 for the furry little things.

Throughout this trip, I met some of the kindest, most honest, helpful people. From Amsterdam to Russia, people helped me at every turn, returning lost phones, cameras, and even a credit card I left behind at a sushi restaurant. A waiter chased me down to hand it back.

I noticed two things in Moscow I hadn't seen since leaving Greece, facial hair, and a Black person. By then, I had grown a full white beard, and while having breakfast at the Budapest, I noticed another man with one. Also, I hadn't seen a single Black person throughout Central Asia until that moment at the Russian Immigration Office.

Driving 3,000 miles through Russia, I realized there was no sign of a recession here, the highways were jammed with trucks transporting goods. It was bumper-to-bumper traffic for much of the drive. At times, I zoned out completely and didn't even know where I was. I played the same songs repeatedly; The Bee Gees and Willie Nelson were my companions during that long stretch.

Moscow – September 21, 2010: Leaving Russia was as easy as entering it, aside from a long wait at the border. A strange thing happened there: while waiting in line at the Russian Latvian crossing, a man handed me a cell phone. On the other end, someone speaking broken English told me to skip the line and park in the lot beside the guard shack. I did so. A female border guard waved me over, looked at my passport, and then told me to proceed. I was supposed to pay a "fee" to cut the line, but once they realized I was American, they dropped the idea. No one asked, so I didn't offer.

Crossing into Latvia that afternoon, I was back in the European Community for the final time, no longer needing to show my passport at borders. I drove to the city of Rezekne and spent the night at a local hotel Katie had arranged.

Latvia and Lithuania – September 22, 2010: After one of the best breakfasts of the trip, I headed toward the Baltic Sea ports hoping to find passage for my Jeep back home without having to drive all the way to Amsterdam. I crossed into Lithuania at Zarasai and drove to Kaunas, where I found a sushi bar along the main road before continuing into Poland. I was now on a mission, to get home as soon as possible.

Crossing into Poland late that afternoon, I spotted the Golden Arches. At the start of my journey, I had sworn I'd starve before eating at McDonald's, but this time I couldn't resist. I ordered two fish sandwiches, a Big

Mac, two cheeseburgers, fries, and a Coke. I couldn't finish half of it but seeing that McDonald's bag on the seat next to me somehow made me feel closer to home.

I tried a shortcut to Gdansk that looked shorter on the map but wound through small villages where the houses practically touched the road. At times, I felt like I was driving through people's front yards. Eventually, I reached the Hyatt, where Katie had booked me a $125 room — the best value of the whole trip, with a panoramic view of the river just fifty feet away.

The next morning I searched online and by sheer luck found Andrzej Burdynske's company while reading an article about a new roll-on roll-off car carrier ship. I contacted Andrzej, and after overcoming some language issues, we arranged to drop my Jeep at the Gdynia Port later that day. My friend Yunnan joined me; we found a car wash to rinse off the Kazakh mud before delivering the Jeep and trailer to the cargo storage area. Andrzej met us there and handled the paperwork. Though I was uneasy leaving my Jeep and everything I owned for the last three months with a stranger in a foreign country, Andrzej assured me payment would be arranged once shipping was confirmed. I trusted him.

With everything settled, I took a taxi back to Gdansk and spent my final night at the Radisson, since the Hyatt was full.

September 24, 2010: I woke up early, ate my last breakfast of the trip, and caught a taxi to the airport. A short flight to Warsaw, then to Chicago, and finally to Lincoln, where I saw my favorite sight of the entire journey: my family waiting for me.

Trip Conclusion

My wife constantly asks what I learned about myself on this three-month journey, and some days I've learned a lot; other days, nothing at all. Looking back from Amsterdam to China, and failing to cross into it, I realized one major truth: reaching a destination isn't as rewarding as the journey itself. The road, with all its challenges and surprises, became the real adventure.

Those who followed my blog asked why I would "torture" myself for three months only to fall short of my goal. But to me, the journey was more important than the destination. After all, what would I have left to strive for if I had reached my goal too easily?

Returning home from the east rather than the west was hard, but what some might call failure gave me new motivation, to build my "Mud Wagon," a 1974 Dodge Power Wagon that I disassembled piece by piece, sandblasted, painted, and rebuilt in my shop. This new travel wagon would be a state-of-the-art four-by-four home on wheels, dependable and ready for my next adventure.

Once I left Almaty, I was constantly looking for opportunities to plan future trips. No longer thinking about reaching Thailand or Singapore, I began to see those destinations as milestones rather than final goals, part of a larger journey still waiting to unfold.

Looking back, I realize that a touch of my Asperger's may have helped me endure the solitude of driving so far, for so long, and through so much uncertainty. The ability to focus intensely, to be content alone, and to face danger without fear was, in its own way, a blessing that carried me safely across continents.

As for Alexandra, I will miss her. Someday, I hope to keep my promise to her, and we'll meet again. We spent thirty days together, and though those memories will always stay with me, I was ready to go back home. As for the Jeep, I still own it; it made its last trip to Playa de Carmen, Mexico where I spend some of my time.

21

One Lousy Salmon

Colleen and I set out with our dog, Leo, on a long road trip through the American Northwest, crossing South Dakota, Wyoming, Montana, and Idaho before finally reaching Washington State. It was a region neither of us had seen, a part of our own country we had too long overlooked. This year, instead of boarding a plane for Europe as we had so many summers before, we decided to travel the open road, to rediscover America at our own pace.

Our first stop was the Tatanka Trading Post, a quiet spot just south of the Badlands and the little town of Wall, South Dakota. The wind carried the smell of sage and dust, the same scent that must have hung over the plains a hundred years ago. The place stirred old memories for me, of another time when I'd been "locked up for a while" near to there, a reminder that every road trip also passes through personal history.

From Tatanka we drove west to Deadwood, an historic mining town where legends and gamblers once walked the streets. We spent the night at a local casino hotel, leaving Leo to rest in our room while we tried our luck downstairs. Neither of us struck it rich, but the mix of neon and nostalgia gave the evening its own charm.

The next morning, we crossed into Wyoming and stopped at Devil's Tower, one of nature's most extraordinary monuments. Its columned rock face rose straight from the earth, a solitary sentinel surrounded by miles of open grassland. The tower seemed alive, changing color as the sun moved across the sky, its surface shifting from gray to gold to amber. Local tribes once called it Bear Lodge, and standing there, it wasn't hard to understand why. You could almost imagine the ancient stories, of giant bears clawing at their sides, of spirits dwelling within their shadows. We walked part of the trail that circles the base, listening to the wind whisper through the pines, before continuing north into Montana. That stop lingered with us, a place both sacred and mysterious, as though the land itself was trying to speak.

By the time we reached the Little Bighorn National Monument, the late-afternoon light had turned golden, stretching long shadows across the grasslands. The air felt heavy with silence, the kind of silence that holds memory. Once called Custer Battlefield National Monument, the site was renamed in 1991 to honor both sides of the conflict, giving the long-overdue recognition to the Native American warriors who fought and died there. That simple change in name carried a quiet power, a gesture that acknowledged history not as a single story, but as a shared one written in blood and loss.

The visitor center had closed, so Colleen and I drove the narrow ridge road that winds through the battlefield. Marble markers and bronze plaques stood scattered across the rolling hills, each one a voice from the past. I drove slowly while Colleen read aloud from the inscriptions, her voice carrying softly in the quiet. At every marker, the imagination filled with the thunder of hooves, the smoke, the chaos, and the cries of men who knew their end was near. We drove all the way to the cul-de-sac at the far end, turned around, and retraced our path, reading the plaques again in reverse, like rewinding time itself.

It was sobering to stand where the battle had taken place, knowing that 210 men under Colonel George Armstrong Custer and another fifty-three under Major Reno of the Seventh Cavalry were killed there, along with fewer than a hundred Sioux, Cheyenne, and Arapaho warriors. What happened at Little Bighorn wasn't simply a military defeat, it was the collision of two worlds, one fading and the other rising, each convinced of its own destiny. The wind seemed to carry that weight still, whispering across the ridges as if reluctant to let the memory rest.

The visit touched me deeply, more than I expected. The Sioux, especially, were never far from my own past. Their descendants live at the Pine Ridge Indian Reservation, barely thirty miles from where I grew up in Chadron. When I was young, I saw firsthand the effects of what history had brought down on them: poverty, alcoholism, drug abuse, and finally hopelessness. The proud faces of warriors replaced by the weariness of survival. It is impossible to stand on that battlefield, to see where Custer fell and where the Sioux stood victoriously, without feeling both sorrow and admiration, for what was lost and for what endured.

We drove west to Bozeman, where Midwest Demolition had a project underway at the state college. We stayed at a small bed-and-breakfast just outside of town, framed by open meadows and mountain peaks. That evening, as we took Leo for a walk, we finally understood why Montana is called Big Sky Country.

The air was clear and cold enough to sting the lungs, yet it felt clean, honest. The stars hung so low it seemed we could reach out and touch them. Their light was so bright we hardly needed lamps. It was a kind of peace neither of us had felt in years, a silence that healed something deep inside.

From Bozeman, we continued south into Yellowstone National Park. Passing beneath the great stone arch at the northern entrance wanted to cross into another world, one that belonged more to nature than to man. The air smelled faintly of pine and sulfur. Steam drifted from the ground in ghostly veils, and the earth seemed to breathe beneath our feet. We stopped first at Mammoth Hot Springs, where terraces of limestone shimmered like melted ivory, and then at Norris Geyser Basin, where boiling pools bubbled and spat in shades of turquoise and gold.

Further south, Old Faithful lived up to its name, erupting right on cue, sending a plume of white water into the sky as dozens of travelers watched in reverent silence. Colleen stood there with Leo at her side, the mist catching her hair, and I remember thinking how small and magnificent the world can feel all at once.

We spent the afternoon driving the park's winding roads, past herds of bison and elk grazing near the Madison River, past the deep blue of Yellowstone Lake, and finally along the Grand Canyon of the Yellowstone, where the waterfall roared with a force that shook the air. The colors of the canyon walls, red, yellow, and rust, seemed painted by fire. By the time we exited through the west gate, the sun was sinking, turning the sky the color of copper. We stopped and stayed in West Yellowstone where we enjoyed a well deserved meal after driving all day.

After leaving West Yellowstone, we headed north to pick up Interstate 90. We drove most of the day before coming across a place called Coeur d'Alene. I'm not sure where the name came from, but it had to be one of the most beautiful places we'd seen so far on the trip. The lake glowed under the fading sun, surrounded by thick pine hills that dipped right into the water. We found a quiet hotel that would take Leo, with the understanding that we wouldn't leave him alone in the room. After so many miles on the road, it felt good to rest in a place that seemed carved out of peace itself.

The first couple hundred miles after entering Washington could have passed for the Mojave Desert — dry, sunburned, and lifeless. Then, little by little, green fields began to return, followed by thick forests and the first signs of the Pacific air. As the skyline of Seattle came into view, the famous Space Needle rose above the city like a silver beacon reaching into the mist.

In Seattle, we leaned into the tourist thing like the Space Needle, Pike Place Market, and the waterfront. The Space Needle was more than just a tower; it was a symbol of how the city always seems to look toward the future. From the observation deck, we could see the whole sweep of Puget Sound, the Olympic Mountains in the distance, and the ferries cutting through the gray-blue water like threads on a quilt.

Pike Place Market was pure energy. We stood among the crowds as vendors tossed fish across the counters, the air thick with the smell of salt and fresh catch. It was noisy, chaotic, and people yelling and laughing, while the cameras flashing, the famous flying fish sailing overhead like a choreographed dance.

Every stand told its own story — flowers, fruit, baked bread, and coffee that defined Seattle itself. It was one of those rare places that make you feel both small and part of something big at the same time.

That evening we walked to the waterfront, it was near our hotel, stopping at Joe's Crab Shack for dinner. It was our first time there, and we both agreed it wouldn't be our last. The food was fresh, the sea breeze cool, and the glow of the ferries sliding across the harbor made it a perfect evening. Later, we found a small sushi bar tucked away on a quiet street, where the chef worked behind the counter with the calm precision of a man who loved what he did. It was, in every sense, peaceful.

I was concerned that because of my felony, I wouldn't be allowed to leave the country and go into Canada. So, after discussion with Colleen, we thought we'd try it and see what happens. To my surprise, the border guards barely gave us a second look, and soon we were crossing into Canada without a problem. It felt like a small victory, another reminder that sometimes in life, you just must take the chance and see where the road leads.

Arriving in Vancouver was like driving into a field of light, as if the whole city had been draped in Christmas decorations. The tall glass condominiums shimmered against the black sky, their reflections dancing on the surface of the harbor. It was breathtaking; the kind of sight that makes you forget the miles behind you. As we crossed one of the bridges downtown, the glow from the city seemed to wrap around us, soft and golden.

We found our hotel without trouble, parked the Jeep, and checked in. The air outside carried the faint scent of rain mixed with sea salt. Exhausted but content, we went straight to bed, eager to wake up and see what the city looked like in daylight.

The next morning, we decided to do a little sightseeing around the city. We hadn't been gone long before I got a call from the front desk at our Hilton Hotel, letting us know that Leo had been barking and disturbing the guests. So, we drove back, took Leo out of the room, and decided to bring him along with us for the rest of the day. For a while, we kept him in the car with the windows cracked and the weather cool, then continued exploring. It wasn't ideal, but that's life on the road, you adjust, and the journey keeps moving forward.

We spent the rest of the day enjoying Vancouver, walking the seawall along Stanley Park, eating the best sushi we'd ever had, and wandering through the Granville Island Public Market, with its artists, food stalls, and street performers. Later, we browsed through a weekend flea market before deciding we wanted to try deep-sea salmon fishing.

To do that, we'd need to head for Vancouver Island and hire a charter boat. The morning air carried that crisp ocean scent, and as we watched the boats sway in the marina, it felt like another small adventure waiting to unfold.

To reach the place where we planned to go salmon fishing, we first had to take a BC Ferries boat across the Strait of Georgia to Vancouver Island. What we didn't know was that the ferry terminal wasn't in downtown Vancouver, it was the Tsawwassen Ferry Terminal, about twenty-five miles south of the city. Once we arrived, we joined a long line of cars waiting to board the MV Spirit of Vancouver Island, bound for Swartz Bay near Victoria.

The wait was long, but the moment we drove onto the ferry and felt the engines hum beneath us, it was worth every minute. The deck offered sweeping views of the Gulf Islands, the blue-gray waters stretching out beneath a pale morning sky, and the faint outline of mountains beyond. After crossing the Strait, we landed on Vancouver Island and began the long drive toward the opposite coast. The farther we went, the wilder it became, dense forests of cedar and spruce, rivers flashing silver through the trees, and small villages tucked into deep green valleys. At one point, we slowed to watch what we thought was a large black dog by the roadside, only to realize it was a black bear patiently waiting for traffic to pass. For a moment, everything stopped — the cars, the noise, even time itself. Then the bear crossed the road and disappeared into the woods, leaving us quietly amazed and grateful for the encounter. It felt like the island's way of welcoming us, wild, beautiful, and unforgettable.

We found a small hotel near the coast and decided to eat dinner there that evening. Most of the people staying at the hotel were either heading out fishing the next morning or just returning from a trip. After asking around, we managed to find someone who agreed to take us out the next day. Morning came quickly. We arranged for someone at the hotel to watch Leo, then headed down to the dock. The air was cool and heavy with the smell of salt and seaweed as we climbed aboard the charter boat. Once we were out on open water, Colleen quickly realized she didn't have sea legs and started feeling sick, while I still had mine from my Navy days. We fished for about two hours and managed to catch one salmon, not much for the cost of the trip, but the experience was worth it. Still, I couldn't help but think about the money and miles it took just to get there.

After returning to port, we drove south to Victoria, the capital of Vancouver Island, where we planned to catch the ferry back to Seattle. By that time, Colleen was frustrated and upset with me for reasons I couldn't quite figure it out. Once we were back in the United States, we didn't waste any time, we headed straight for Nebraska and somehow made it back in record time.

Looking back, that trip was more than just a drive through the Pacific Northwest; it was a journey through patience, partnership, and discovery. From the hum of Seattle's streets to the quiet waters of Vancouver Island, every mile carried its own lesson. Sometimes the best parts weren't the landmarks or the meals, but the pauses in between, the laughter, the small arguments, and the moments of silence that said more than words ever could. We had quite a venture from Nebraska, South Dakota, Wyoming, Montana, Idaho, Washington state, Vancouver, Vancouver Island, back to the United States — all for the great reward of one lousy salmon.

22

Hong Kong

Hong Kong: Once I left Almaty, I was constantly looking for opportunities to get onto my laptop so I could research means of transportation for my future adventure plans. No longer was I thinking about reaching Thailand or Singapore as I once did. I now thought of those destinations only as milestones on an overland adventure that would lead me to places I had not yet even imagined. After my trip, and coming back on such short notice, I was having withdrawal syndrome, an emptiness that only the road could fill. Never again will I set a goal of journeying from one place to another. It is the journey itself that keeps me alive.

It was not a good day. The Asperger's really came out in me this afternoon. The problems with Zane at the office, him not passing his drug test, filtered into the family, and I lost it with Katie and my mom. I need to learn how to control myself when others cannot or do not have all the facts. I am having a tough time coping with myself here. I get nothing done at the office other than thinking about my next trip and when I can get out of here. It feels as if there is a large hollow hole in me that can only be filled with adventure.

We started working on the Dodge today. The M866 ambulance arrived on Friday, and it will work perfectly on the Dodge. Today I fired Klein Williams after Dick Garden screwed up the trustee sale. Christmas is approaching, and I am already thinking about building a new expedition truck.

The Mud Wagon is coming along well. The new Dodge 360 engine we installed has required quite a bit of modification to several of the brackets, but it is finally starting to look like something rather than a thousand pieces. I worry, though, that it might not get done on time. Walt is hitting the bottle again, and although he is a great mechanic and fabricator, he might end up getting fired for other reasons. I am hoping he cleans up his act, so I will not have to fire him.

I got Charley in September 2011, against the wishes of Colleen, who thought I was crazy for taking on the responsibility of caring for a dog. Charley was a full-registered German Shepherd, born July 8, 2011. I got him to accompany me on my next overseas adventure and to provide some sort of deterrence or protection if I ever needed it. Colleen hated him and showed no emotion toward him whatsoever. But Charley travels where I go.

On December 1, 2011, I purchased the Overdraft Bar and Saloon at a foreclosure sale for $50,000. I had no idea what I was going to do with it, but I knew I could add its value and income to my retirement portfolio.

Arrival in Hong Kong: December 26, 2011, I arrived at Hong Kong International Airport after a grueling fifteen-hour flight, with Colleen arriving only an hour behind. Back then we never flew together, nor have we flown together ever since we had our first child. It seems like I did not want to jeopardize having to leave our children without a parent. From the moment I stepped into the terminal, I was struck by how clean, efficient, and modern everything felt. Immigration and customs went without a hitch, and the signs and facilities seemed built for calm, clarity, and order. We took the Airport Express Train, the dedicated link between the airport and downtown Hong Kong, from the airport to the city center in about twenty-four minutes. The ride was smooth, silent, and comfortable, with ample room for our bags and minimal fuss. I remember thinking that if travel could always be like this, I might never resent being off the road again.

After customs, we went through a fever checkpoint. They used a scanner that could detect if you had a fever without even stopping you. No hats were allowed inside the airport — security reasons, I am sure. Someone came up and asked me to remove mine, and Colleen, who was behind me, had to remove her Seattle ball cap as well.

The hotel Katie had booked for us turned out to be far less than I expected. For what they called a four-star hotel at $370 a night, I would not have given it more than two stars, and even that would have been generous. It should have cost no more than $150. My Asperger's started to kick in while I was checking in. The lobby was no bigger than my living room, and I immediately felt disappointed and restless. I started to lose my patience until Colleen calmed me down, reminding me we could find another place tomorrow. It seems that both Colleen and I have grown accustomed to a little more comfort and service when we travel, and we have always been willing to pay for it, but this hotel was absolute crap from top to bottom.

For a "deluxe room with a city view," it was anything but. The carpet was worn, the walls were scuffed, and the window looked out on a tangle of rooftops rather than any skyline. There was only one working plug, no light switch in the bathroom, and barely enough space to open both of our suitcases at once. It felt claustrophobic. I sat there wondering how a place like this could call itself four-star. It was hard enough to charge our electronics, let alone our patience. I told myself that tomorrow we would find something better, and we did.

As I wrote a bit, Colleen slept. She had managed some rest on her flight. Mine was smooth, but I could not sleep at all. Still, we both made it safely and on time. I was looking forward to exploring this city with its history, culture, and seven million people living within four hundred square miles.

Exploring Hong Kong: December 27, 2011, we spent most of our first day walking, exploring, and taking taxis. The air was warm but crisp, and the city pulled with energy that seemed to come from every direction at once. We took the tram up to The Peak, where the view opened like a painting, skyscrapers rising from the harbor, mountains curling behind them, and the water dotted with ships from all over the world. Standing there beside Colleen, I felt both small and incredibly alive, realizing just how far I had come from Nebraska to this far corner of the globe.

Although cab fares were reasonable, we still managed to spend a small fortune that first day. Every driver had his own shortcut through the city's maze of hills and narrow streets, weaving us through traffic with a mix of confidence and madness. I was glad we had not rented a car; people drove on what I still call the wrong side of the road, and I am sure I would have ended up in the wrong lane before the first turn. Someday they will figure it out, but in Hong Kong, I doubt it.

We spent the afternoon wandering through shops without any goal, simply enjoying being together in a place so different from home. From narrow side streets packed with market stalls to glittering malls filled with designer brands, Hong Kong offered everything and nothing we really needed. Colleen and I talked about how fortunate we were to have reached a point in life where we did not crave more things. What we value most now were experiences like this, new sights, shared laughter, and the quiet moments between adventures. Traveling with Colleen always brings us closer, though it is never easy convincing her to go in the first place.

That evening we ended the day with sushi for supper, but honestly, I have had better sushi in Nebraska than in Hong Kong. Still, the city was alive, the streets glowed with neon lights, the air was thick with the smell of street food, and the noise of traffic blended with laughter that rose from every corner. Despite my exhaustion, I could not stop thinking about the constant movement around us. By the time we returned to the hotel, neither of us could sleep. Around four in the morning, Colleen and I played a few games on her Nook, trying to relax, but rest never came easy. When she finally drifted back to sleep, I slipped quietly out of the room in search of a traditional Chinese breakfast, curious to see what the locals ate before another day in this restless city began.

Boy, was I in for a surprise!

I walked up a narrow flight of stairs into a large room filled with three hundred men sitting shoulder to shoulder at round tables while women pushed carts stacked with bamboo baskets. A waiter motioned for me to take any open seat. In front of me were a teacup, bowl, spoon, and chopsticks.

Watching the locals, I realized there was a whole rhythm to breakfast here. A man came by to pour boiling water into each bowl, which everyone used to rinse their cups and utensils before drinking their tea. I tried to follow along but mostly ended up splashing water across the table. When the women rolled by with steaming baskets, I just pointed to a few and soon had four small dishes in front of me, none of which I could identify. After a few bites, I decided I needed Andrew Zimmern to tell me what I was eating. I left smiling at my own curiosity and headed straight for the nearest bakery, where I found a ham sandwich that felt like a small victory. Later that morning, when Colleen woke up, she wanted one too.

Anniversary Reflections: That day we switched to the Marriott, a much better experience with comfortable rooms, modern amenities, and good restaurants nearby. The moment we walked in, I knew we had made the right choice. The lobby was beautiful, with a grand staircase that seemed to rise forever, and a breakfast buffet of which you could only dream. It was exactly what we were used to, and I did not have a problem paying for it. It felt like a reward after the previous hotel disaster, and both of us finally started to relax and enjoy Hong Kong for what it was meant to be — a blend of energy, order, and elegance unlike anywhere else I had been. It was our anniversary, and as I sat by the window that evening, watching the city lights flicker across the harbor, I could not help but think about how far Colleen and I had come. Thirty-three years of marriage, it still amazes me. She has endured so much over the years, stood by me through every up and down, and somehow still manages to travel halfway around the world with me when most would rather stay home. The Marriott was first-class, great service, though expensive, but it was worth every penny.

Back home, Katie was dealing with collections issues at the office, her first major test while I was gone. I hope she will handle it well. Our children are grown up now, with families of their own, and for us, travel has become the thread that keeps us connected to each other and to the world around us.

We visited Lamma Island, a place I had once seen on No Reservations with Anthony Bourdain. We even ate at the same restaurant he featured in, though I was not impressed. The shrimp were hard to peel and not that good.

Later, we took the Star Ferry to Kowloon. The ferry system was the backbone of Hong Kong's public transportation.

Kowloon felt bigger, older, and more congested than Hong Kong Island. We wandered through the Ladies' Market, which reminded me of the garment district in Los Angeles, same products, same feel. We bought a few T-shirts for the grandkids and got a good walk in before heading back to the hotel.

That night, in honor of our thirty-third wedding anniversary, Colleen and I went out for dinner at a quiet little restaurant near the harbor. The meal was not fancy, but it was peaceful, just the two of us sitting side by side, watching the lights of Hong Kong shimmer across the water. After more than three decades together, we have learned that the best moments are not the ones filled with excitement or crowds, but the ones when time slows down and we can simply enjoy being together.

Macau and Farewell: December 30, 2011, we extended our stay another night to visit Macau and do a little gambling enclave before heading to Bangkok for warmer weather and better seafood. The breakfast buffet at the Marriott was one of the best I have ever had.

After an hour-long ferry ride, we arrived in Macau and went through immigration again. A shuttle took us to The Venetian Macau Hotel and Casino, where I discovered that blackjack was non-existent. The Chinese love baccarat, tables everywhere. Minimum bets were about 500 HK dollars, or sixty US dollars, and it did not take long to lose. The dealers were young, polite, and efficient. Unlike Las Vegas, it was conservative, no flashy uniforms or shows. I even wondered if China had strip joints at all. Doubt it.

After another ferry ride back, a chaotic immigration line, and a taxi driver who thought he was in a Grand Prix, we finally returned to the hotel. Colleen went straight to bed while I stayed up to jot down a few notes before exhaustion took over.

Macau was not my favorite. From what I could see, the strip was mostly under construction or being redeveloped. The big players had taken over, and the smaller casinos were fading away, leaving blighted stretches in between.

King and Country headquarters was in Hong Kong even though their manufacturing plant was in China. They had a museum at their office. So being the big collector that I was, we decided to visit a museum.

The Chinese people, as I saw them, seemed always in a rush, cutting in lines without a thought. Colleen kept reminding me to stay calm, but to me, they were plain rude, though I am not sure they even realized it.

23

Bangkok/Phuket

(December 31, 2011 – January 12, 2012)

December 31, 2011. The last day of the year had finally arrived, and we were on our way to Bangkok for a few days before continuing to our final destination, Phuket. Colleen and I were on the same flight, something I always dreaded whenever we had to fly together, which, in truth, had only happened a handful of times over our thirty-three years of marriage. But still, I hoped all would go well.

January 1, 2012, we arrived safely in Bangkok and quickly hired a private limo service for 1,600 BHT, about fifty-three dollars, for a forty-five-minute ride to the Marriott. After checking in, Colleen and I took a long nap, hoping to have enough energy to stay up until midnight to celebrate the New Year, something we hadn't done in a very long time.

That evening we ventured out to the famous Night Market in the Patpong red-light district, and what a sight that was. We took a three-wheel taxi-scooter for 300 BHT and stayed away from the two main streets lined with go-go bars, notorious for scams and rip-offs. The infamous "ping-pong" shows were still a draw there, though I had no interest in seeing one. I always try to read about the areas we visit, just to avoid putting us in awkward or unsafe situations.

For the most part, the evening went smoothly. The vendors were polite and never pushed their wares unless you showed interest. We, as usual, limited ourselves to buying only a few souvenirs, T-shirts and magnets for the girls back home. What struck me most were the countless massage parlors everywhere. Colleen insisted some might be legitimate, catering to reflexology or spa services, but I had my doubts. Some of them were surprisingly elegant, almost luxurious, but I still wasn't convinced.

January 2, 2012, We set out for the Floating Market, about a two-hour drive by taxi, we hired a driver for the day at 2,000 BHT, and the journey was filled with views of beautiful shrines and colorful roadside life. When we arrived, I was initially frustrated. I didn't understand how the market operated, and that lack of control always triggered my Asperger's tendencies. Thankfully, Colleen stayed calm, as always, and helped steady me.

Right away as the boat was floating by one of the locals' homes, a gal was sitting outside taking a bath as if nothing was going on nor the fact that the tourists were drifting by where she was bathing.

Once we negotiated a fair price, we boarded a long, narrow riverboat that took us through winding canals lined with vendors. Many of the boats were rowed by older women, some of whom also cooked small meals aboard their boats. We couldn't resist ordering soup, a mixture of squid, shrimp, chicken, and a few mystery ingredients better left unknown. After finishing it, I began to sweat so profusely my shirt was soaked through. I won't even mention what the rest of my body was doing.

On our way back, we stopped in Chinatown and wandered through its narrow, crowded alleys. It was chaotic, noisy, and fascinating all at once. We ate dinner there and returned to the hotel exhausted, collapsing into bed and sleeping fourteen straight hours.

January 3, 2012. From the floating market's timeless charm to the ultramodern, today we spent the day inside one of the most impressive malls I've ever seen or visited. Christmas seemed to be in full swing, despite being long over, for a Buddhist country. There were plenty of Christmas songs, lights, and one of the tallest trees I've ever seen.

We shopped a little and even ordered custom-fitted suits that would be ready in a couple of days. The highlight of the day was the food court, or rather, the realization that Thai food just wasn't for us. We tried four different dishes before giving up. Back at the Marriott we ordered a pizza, devoured it, and promptly ordered a second.

January 4, 2012. Today was our temple tour. We hired a driver and a guide named Nancy, who took us to several magnificent temples — the Golden Buddha, the Emerald Buddha, and the Grand Palace. Each was breathtaking in its own way, but the Grand Palace stood above them all with its endless courtyards and dazzling architecture.

Nancy's explanations were thorough, and Colleen hung on every word. For me, after a while the temples began to blur together, my feet hurt, the humidity was unbearable, and I finally told Nancy, "No more temples." We returned to the hotel, grabbed lunch, and promptly fell asleep again for twelve hours.

January 5, 2012, the day began lazily. After breakfast, we strolled around the neighborhood before heading for our final suit fitting. Our salesman, persuasive as ever, talked us into buying a few more pieces. We then explored the Indian fabric district, where Colleen hunted for material she liked.

We grabbed lunch from a busy street vendor — fried chicken and rice, simple but delicious. Getting back to the hotel, however, was a fiasco. Our taxi driver had no idea where the Marriott was and drove in circles. After paying 150 BHT instead of the usual 80, we gave up and caught another cab for another 100. When it started to rain, the first rain of our trip, the driver refused to use the meter, asking for 150 BHT instead. I hate getting cheated, but Colleen reminded me it was only about four dollars.

That evening, we dined in the Arabic district near our hotel, where no alcohol was served. The restaurants gleamed with stainless steel, spotless and welcoming. The atmosphere was lively but modest. By now, our internal clocks had finally adjusted to Thai time, waking in the morning and sleeping at reasonable hours. Of course, we'd have to readjust all over again once home.

January 6, 2012, we slept in late, checked out around mid-afternoon, and realized we'd lost our small camera. We retraced our steps back to the Indian fabric area but never found it. We did, however, enjoy another round of fried chicken. After checking out, we took a short walk, got foot massages, and made one last visit to Bangkok's red-light district, just to see what all the fuss was about. Massage, Massage, Massage, Massage.

Phuket: By evening, we hailed a cab to the airport for our 11 p.m. flight. 20 minutes to Phuket. Once we landed in Phuket and after the usual haggling over fares, we finally made it. We checked into the Radisson around 3:00 a.m., exhausted but relieved.

January 7, 2012, our first day in Phuket began with renting a car and driving across the island to Patong. Driving on the left side of the road was an adventure, to say the least. Colleen was terrified, white-knuckled the whole way, while I did my best to stay focused.

Patong was pure chaos, wall-to-wall shops, beach umbrellas, massage parlors. We had breakfast at a small Thai restaurant across from the hotel that charged nearly the same as the Radisson. We spent the day by the pool before heading to the Siam Show in the evening, a spectacle similar to one we'd seen in Cancun. The buffet was disappointing, but the performance itself was grand and full of color.

January 9, 2012, the Phi Phi Islands. What can one say, absolutely stunning. We took a speedboat from the marina, about an hour's ride, and visited Maya Bay where *The Beach* was filmed. Monkey Beach was unforgettable. I could have stayed there for days. We stopped at Krabi Island for lunch, swam, snorkeled, and soaked up the sun. On our return, one of the boats got stranded on a sandbar, and passengers had to push it back into deeper water. It made for a memorable laugh before a long nap back at the Radisson.

January 10, 2012, we ventured out again in our rental car, but it turned into a comedy of errors — three minor fender benders, getting lost multiple times, and one very frustrated wife. For the first time in years, I'd actually bought insurance on a rental car, and thank God I did. I returned it the next day, a little wiser and much calmer.

January 11, 2012. These were slower days. We lounged around the hotel, played a game we called "Bubbles," and enjoyed each other's company. On the twelfth, we packed up, said goodbye to Phuket, and caught an earlier flight back to Bangkok. Our friendly cab driver from the week before gave us two keychains as a farewell gift. We stayed at an airport hotel that night, $150 with shuttle service, and slept soundly before an early morning departure.

January 13, 2012. It was hard watching Colleen leave for home. I wished she could have stayed longer, but we travel differently. She enjoys comfort, and I thrive on adventure. After seeing her off, I wandered through the airport unsure of what to do next. A sign for the train caught my eye, and soon I found myself riding thru downtown Bangkok, aiming for the main station. I knew from reading earlier that a train to Cambodia left around five in the morning, and sure enough, I'd just made it in time.

January 14, 2012. Cambodia was eye-opening. I hired a driver named Vivian for $50 for the day, a fortune for him, as he normally made less than $10. We toured the Angkor Wat temples, awe-inspiring yet haunting in their age and decay. A seven-year-old girl, fluent in English and a bit of Spanish, tried to sell me trinkets. I gave her a dollar just so she'd stop asking. It broke my heart to see children working like that.

Later we visited the city center, where I ate lunch at the Red Piano Bar in the middle of Siem Reap's bar district. I realized most of the young tourists weren't there for temples at all, they were there to party. After lunch, Vivian drove me to the floating village. Along the road, rows of wooden shanties stood on stilts, with open sewage flowing beneath. Life was unimaginably hard there.

At the pier, I refused to pay the inflated ticket prices for tourists, $40 per person compared to $11 for locals, and simply walked away. My Asperger's tendencies kicked in hard at that moment. I couldn't tolerate being ripped off. Back at the hotel, I tipped Vivian generously, grateful for his patience and honesty.

January 15, 2012, the long journey home began, from Cambodia to Seoul, then Tokyo, then across the Pacific. I barely slept, and the flights blurred together. Somewhere between Tokyo and Toronto, I calculated how much this entire adventure had cost me. Nearly $4,300 in airfare alone. Poor planning, yes, but unforgettable memories. From Hong Kong to Bangkok, Phuket, Cambodia, Seoul, Tokyo, Toronto, Chicago, and finally Lincoln, the journey had come full circle. I crawled into bed at last, unsure whether it was good night or good day.

24

CAMBODIA

ONCE I FOUND THE TRAIN STATION IN BANGKOK, I was told that the train for Cambodia had already left, although I could not verify it, since I did not speak Thai and had to rely on the people who were hustling us. It was one big setup between all the drivers, for suddenly, there was a shuttle bus going to a bus station about ten miles away, and from there we could catch another bus to the Cambodian border.

At the bus station about ten miles out of Bangkok we were more isolated than at the train station. We waited an hour with other expats when we concluded that there was no bus coming to take us to the Cambodia border. It felt like another part of the big hustle, but we didn't have many options. About six of us agreed to pay around twenty dollars each and squeezed into a small car for the long, uncertain ride.

When we finally reached the border, the chaos was immediate. The line of foreigners wanting to enter Cambodia stretched half a mile, snaking past dusty storefronts and small roadside stalls. I didn't want to wait all day, and when a Cambodian immigration officer approached me, I handed him fifty dollars. He took my passport, disappeared briefly, then returned and escorted me straight to the front of the line. Moments later, my passport was stamped, and just like that, I had crossed into Cambodia.

Once we crossed the Cambodian border, there were again several drivers acting as taxis, waiting to take travelers deeper into the country. Many expats quickly jumped into these so-called taxis, paying a fee to be driven to Siem Reap, a major hub for backpackers heading to explore the country's temples and ancient ruins along with bars and discotheques full of young women wanting to hustle you for money.

As we drove toward Siem Reap, all packed in like sardines inside that small car, I didn't know exactly where we were going, and I didn't feel comfortable. They said there was a house we could stay in, but I didn't want that. As we passed by a nice-looking hotel, I asked the driver to stop, and he let me out. I checked in right away, it was a clean, nice, and quiet place, much needed after a long and uncertain day.

That evening, the clerk asked if I wanted a massage since they offered in-house massage therapist service. I agreed, paid twenty dollars, and before long a massage therapist came up to my room to give me my massage.

The next day, on January 14, 2012, I asked the front desk clerk if he knew of a guide, and he told me about an off-duty clerk named Vivian who had a car and could take me around. Within half an hour, Vivian showed up, friendly, polite, and eager to please, and we began touring the Siem Reap area. Vivian and I are still Facebook friends, and in fact, when I returned to Cambodia two years later, he was the one who picked me up at the Cambodian border.

Cambodia was eye-opening. I hired Vivian for fifty dollars for the day, a fortune for him, as he normally made less than ten. We toured the Angkor Wat temples, awe-inspiring yet haunting in their age and decay. Built in the early twelfth century by King Suryavarman II, Angkor Wat was originally dedicated to the Hindu god Vishnu before later becoming a Buddhist temple. It remains the largest religious monument in the world, surrounded by massive moats and intricate carvings that depict ancient battles, heavenly dancers, and the daily life of the Khmer Empire at its height. The air was thick with history — centuries of power, loss, and rediscovery.

A seven-year-old girl, fluent in English, approached me trying to sell trinkets. I gave her a dollar just so she would stop asking, but it broke my heart to see children working like that in the heat, their innocence traded for survival. Beyond the grandeur of the temples, the poverty surrounding them was impossible to ignore.

Later we visited the city center, where I ate lunch at the Red Piano Bar, a popular spot in the middle of Siem Reap's bustling bar district. It was famous for its connection to Angelina Jolie, who had dined there while filming *Lara Croft: Tomb Raider* in 2001, a movie that had unexpectedly revived global interest in Cambodia and Angkor Wat.

As I sat there, I realized the young tourists weren't there for history or temples at all, they were there to party. After lunch, Vivian drove me to the floating village on Tonle Sap Lake. Along the road, rows of wooden shanties stood on stilts, with open sewage flowing beneath them. Life was unimaginably hard there, yet somehow the people smiled, waving as we passed.

At the pier, I refused to pay the inflated ticket prices for tourists, forty dollars per person compared to eleven for locals, I simply walked away. My Asperger's tendencies kicked in hard at that moment; I couldn't tolerate being ripped off. Back at the hotel, I tipped Vivian generously, grateful for his patience and honesty. Siem Reap, for all its beauty and history, had also become a party town for young people looking to drink and for men seeking women and prostitutes. I wanted nothing to do with that lifestyle, so I decided to cut my trip short. After two nights in Siem Reap, I packed my bags and prepared to head home.

January 15, 2012, the long journey home began, but unforgettable memories. This trip took me from the United States of America to Hong Kong, to Bangkok, Thailand to Phuket, Thailand to Cambodia, to Seoul, South Korea, to Tokyo, Japan, to Toronto, Canada, to Chicago, USA, and finally home to Lincoln, Nebraska, the journey had come full circle. I crawled into bed one last time, thankful to be home, carrying with me the images of an ancient kingdom that had once ruled Southeast Asia, and the faces of those still living among its ruins.

25

SINGAPORE

In 2013, Colleen and I had the opportunity to travel to Southeast Asia once more. Midwest Demolition had secured a government contract to remove three radar towers in the Marshall Islands, specifically at Kwajalein Atoll, one of the largest coral atolls in the world. The site carried deep historical significance, having served as a major U.S. military base during World War II and later as a missile testing ground throughout the Cold War. Even decades later, remnants of those turbulent times lingered in the air and in the stories of the locals.

My journey began in Lincoln, Nebraska. From there, I flew to San Francisco and onward to Honolulu, Hawaii, where I spent the night before boarding a special flight to the Marshall Islands. It was a long but peaceful journey across the vast Pacific. From my window seat, I gazed down upon the endless blue expanse and reflected on how far life had carried me, from the plains of Nebraska to remote islands halfway around the world.

Colleen followed on a separate route, flying directly to Singapore while I completed my work on Kwajalein. Our task was to dismantle the three radar towers safely and ensure full compliance with environmental protocols. I could not help but think about the history beneath my feet, the very ground once held by American soldiers during the Battle of Kwajalein in 1944, a fierce conflict that marked the first major defeat of Japan's Pacific defenses.

Upon completing the work, I boarded a small aircraft bound for Guam. The flight was memorable for its multiple stops at remote islands along the route, where groups of scuba divers disembarked to explore the untouched coral reefs surrounding each atoll. The runways on these islands were so short that the plane's wheels brushed the ocean's surface before touching down. Each stop offered a fleeting glimpse of paradise; tiny green specks set against an infinite sea of blue.

Once in Guam, I caught a connecting flight to Manila, Philippines, where I spent two days exploring the city. Manila, with its striking blend of Spanish colonial heritage and bustling modern vitality, captured the layered essence of Southeast Asia, ancient yet evolving, chaotic yet kind. From there, I continued to Singapore to reunite with Colleen.

After checking into our hotel and catching up on much-needed rest, we decided to visit the Singapore Zoo, often regarded as one of the finest in the world. It was there we saw our first panda. Though I found the animal's calm demeanor unremarkable, Colleen was utterly delighted, her face lit with joy throughout the visit. Her enthusiasm alone made the experience worthwhile.

Later that afternoon, we visited Marina Bay Sands, an architectural marvel that has come to symbolize Singapore's skyline. The three towering structures are connected at the top by an enormous sky park and infinity pool that appear to float in the clouds. From that vantage point, we could see ships anchored off the coast, the meticulously landscaped gardens below, and the organized hum of one of the cleanest and most efficient cities in the world. Singapore felt futuristic and disciplined, yet deeply respectful of its cultural heritage.

We also attempted to visit the local casino, but the regulations were strict. Foreign visitors were required to apply for special permission, while Singaporean citizens had to pay a substantial entry fee to discourage excessive gambling. It struck me as another example of the nation's distinctive balance, allowing indulgence, but always under careful governance.

After three days in Singapore, Colleen and I flew back to Bangkok, Thailand, returning to the same Hyatt Hotel where we had stayed two years earlier. The city was as vibrant as ever, alive with traffic, color, and the fragrance of street food drifting through the humid evening air. I told Colleen that I wished to continue to Vietnam, a country I had never visited. She was less enthusiastic about extending the trip, so the next day we hired a taxi to the Bangkok airport, and she boarded a flight home.

I, on the other hand, arranged for the same taxi driver to take me to the Cambodian border. Along the way, we passed rice fields and small villages where children waved as we drove by. Once at the border, I spent a brief time at a nearby casino while waiting for my Cambodian friend and guide, Vin, whom I had met on a previous trip, to collect me. Remembering the complications of past border crossings, I kept the process simple this time.

After Vin arrived, we drove toward Siem Reap. Having already visited the major historical sites during my earlier journey, I stayed only one night at the boutique hotel Vin now managed, a clean and comfortable establishment in the heart of the city. This time, I was determined to take the boat tour of the fishing village on Tonlé Sap Lake. On my prior visit, I had refused to go after feeling overcharged by local guides, but this time I resolved to experience it, regardless of the cost.

As we drove toward the lake, scenes of poverty unfolded before us, families living in stilted houses above muddy riverbeds littered with debris, where children played freely in the water below. When we arrived, I was surprised to find the docks modernized and professionally organized. Vin declined to join the tour, so I went alone. As the small boat glided across the water, I saw entire communities living upon the lake — houses, schools, churches, and clinics all raised on wooden stilts. The people survived by fishing, selling their catch at the local markets, and keeping only enough for themselves.

After this memorable excursion, I decided to continue my journey. The next morning I boarded a flight to Ho Chi Minh City, Vietnam, formerly known as Saigon, a place that had fascinated me for decades due to the war that defined much of my generation's youth.

In Vietnam, I visited the War Remnants Museum, where the narrative was presented entirely from the Vietnamese perspective. The exhibits portrayed American soldiers as aggressors, a depiction that was difficult to absorb, yet understandable given the nation's suffering. Outside the museum stood relics of the conflict: rusting tanks, old Huey helicopters, and captured jets, silent reminders of a violent era.

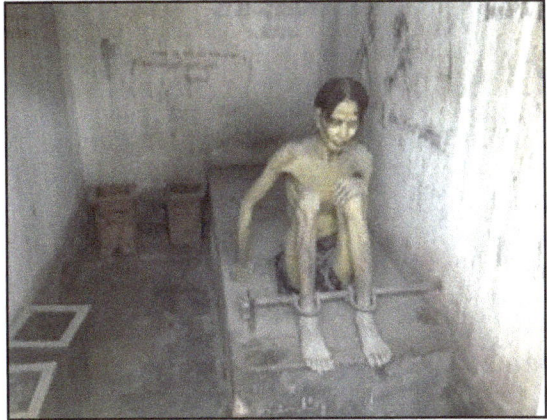

I stayed at the Majestic Hotel, an elegant French colonial building overlooking the Saigon River. From my window, I watched cargo boats drift slowly beneath the tropical sun as vendors called out in the early morning. I visited the former South Vietnamese Presidential Palace, now known as the Reunification Palace, where the war had effectively ended when North Vietnamese tanks crashed through its gates in 1975.

During my stay, I explored the city's open-air markets by cyclo, a two-wheeled rickshaw pedaled by a wiry man who navigated gracefully through the chaos of motorbikes and pedestrians. The markets overflowed with life and color, offering everything from exotic fruits to wartime memorabilia.

After three days in Vietnam, I boarded a flight to Seoul, South Korea, and from there connected home. As the plane crossed the Pacific, I reflected on how fortunate I had been to see so much of the world, and how each journey had deepened my understanding of history, humanity, and my own place within both.

All the Asian people are true and loyal to their cause. Once they make a commitment, they stay with that commitment. I found out through Vin because he became a good friend.

26

2012

Olympics

I'm hoping Joe steps up to the plate and takes over the new Wild's Bar and Grill.

January 22, 2012: It has been a few sad days for me, for I have lost my good friend and companion, Charlie, a six-month-old tan and black German Shepherd who was with me all the time. Never once did he miss a day of going to work with me. I remember the day I came home from my trip. Never has one seen a pet so happy to see me. It was an awesome homecoming, to be greeted with so much love. Charlie was born in early July and was very large for his age, he slept in my den and was always at my side. We made several trips to the ranch together, and when we were there, he would run and leap around as if he had been born for that place. I will miss Charlie.

February 11, 2012: Missing Charlie has not been easy for me, although he was "just a dog," he meant more to me than any other I've owned. I now have Bo, Mr. Bojangles, from the same breeder. He's Charlie's stepbrother, a German Shepherd too, with shorter legs and a different personality. We'll see how things go with Bo. Last night at the St. Peter's annual chili cook-off, I purchased a seven-night stay at the Grand Cayman. Looks like my next trip is coming soon.

February 20, 2012: President's Day, back to work after spending a week at the ranch and at the bar in Chadron.

March 1, 2012: Another year down, four more until social security. Time moves fast.

March 21, 2012: Leaving San Juan, Puerto Rico. After going to trial with José Pérez, I left behind the wristband I purchased at the UNL football game almost two years ago. Closing that chapter in my life. It may seem trivial to others, but such things have deep meaning to me. I'd worn it for over two years, longer than my wedding ring, and now I must move on to another cause to support. I fired Zane a couple of weeks ago, on the Monday after Easter, which caused problems between Sammy and me. I've always thought of Zane as a drifter, a loser making little effort to better his family's life. If it weren't for Sammy, he'd still be living on the street, and his two boys would be wards of the state. Money at work has been tight. We've maxed out our line of credit with Union Bank.

May 22, 2012: We bid again on Building 1526, but it looks like Cheever is in line for the contract. I guess I got what I deserved. Brett Kindig was in a serious car accident in Hastings and had to be flown in. He nearly lost his life. Colleen, Michael, and I spent time at the hospital while Tom and Erin drove up. It brought back memories of the day I drove from Overton to Hastings nearly twenty-nine years ago. Life is so fragile. I can't complain about medical costs anymore. One never knows when those same technologies will be what save our lives.

June 30, 2012: Going to the cabin today to celebrate the Fourth of July since the holiday falls on Wednesday. Our neighbors have grown accustomed to our annual fireworks display and often set up their lawn chairs, not knowing for sure if we'll do it again. We also built a new dock this year and it looks great. The bar in Chadron is now open and doing well for Joe and Tori. I also purchased The Red Zone, the former Elk Club, for my next project. I remember taking Audrey Linglebach there to our fraternity dance when I attended Chadron State College.

It looks like Maggie will be going with Colleen and me to London for the Olympics in August. This adventure will be different with her along. I hope we can get tickets for some of the events. We wanted to take Maggie along because we thought that perhaps someday she herself would be competing at an Olympics. The Opening Ceremonies weren't like Beijing's but still impressive. Only a couple more days and Colleen, Maggie, and I will be off to London, then I'll continue alone to Paris for some time by myself.

We just finished the Data Center for Lincoln public schools, the first government job I've done since California. It's not something I want to undertake often. It brings back memories I'd rather not relive.

August 1, 2012: We're off to the Olympics. I flew Aer Lingus from Chicago to Dublin, then to London, while Colleen and Maggie flew Lithuanian Airlines from Chicago to London. We should arrive within fifteen minutes of each other, then head to the Holiday Inn Express for some much-needed rest. Once settled at the Holiday Inn Express in Swiss Cottage, I met with Paul, who found us tickets to several events, $3,300 in total. It was a relief to finally have everything arranged.

August 6, 2012: After five nights in London, we're starting to wear out, I need to remember that I'm getting older and these long trips take their toll. The hotel room is small, and with no Wi-Fi in the room, I must go to the lobby for internet access, something I'll never tolerate again on future trips. Colleen and Maggie have teamed up, and I seem to be the third man out. Maybe it's a girl thing. They enjoy shopping and laughing together, and I often find myself looking in on the outside. So far, we've visited Westminster Abbey, Tower Bridge, Piccadilly Circus, Buckingham Palace, Harrods, and last night attended our first Olympic event, the U.S. vs. Turkey basketball game, which the U.S. won. My Asperger's seems to worsen with age; it frustrates me when Colleen doesn't follow through on what we've agreed upon.

Yesterday, we planned to meet at 5:30 at a specific spot. I arrived early, walking nearly five miles to ensure I was on time, but she texted me later saying to meet elsewhere. To her, it was nothing, to me, it was everything. When I finally met her at the pub, she'd had trouble with her bank card and somehow upset the bartender. Some beer spilled, and she tried to clean it with my jacket. I stopped her, and she got upset, then turned it around as if I were the one at fault. I wasn't angry, just confused about why things always seemed to twist this way between us. Despite the frustrations, we kept exploring Chinatown, Trafalgar Square, and the London Eye.

We returned to the hotel around 11:00 p.m., exhausted but fulfilled. At bedtime, Colleen and Maggie sang Mary Poppins songs, teasing me in British accents. It made me laugh. Those are the moments I'll remember most.

August 9, 2012: Every day in London has been full. We usually start around noon after breakfast and time on the iPad, then hop on the Tube toward a new destination. We watched another U.S. volleyball match and even ran into John Burroughs, whose future daughter-in-law, Jordan Larson, plays for the U.S. team. I've gotten to know Maggie better on this trip. She's a good kid, focused, strong, and bright, she's a lion in her own way. It will be hard for her to find a man who can out-run, out-throw, or out-think her. All the walking and stairs are taking a toll on my body. I wonder if my health will allow me to keep traveling the way I used to. My mind also feels less sharp. Colleen often takes my hand when we cross streets, traffic moves in the opposite direction here, and though it makes me feel like a child, it's also comforting. I'm thankful to Jan Ashby for connecting us with Paul; without him, our trip would have been uneventful. He found tickets for almost every event we attended. I dearly love my wife, but I also look forward to my time alone in Paris and maybe Barcelona. She enjoys her solitude too, though probably for different reasons. Sometimes I think my Asperger's grows more pronounced as I age. I don't always follow simple conversations easily. I function best within the comfort zone I've built over the years. Without that structure, I'd feel lost.

August 11, 2012: Only two days left in London before Colleen and Maggie return home. I'll take the Eurostar train to Paris, through the tunnel under the English Channel, something I've always wanted to do. I remember the first time I crossed the Channel in the 1970s, I hitched a ride on a lorry for free because I had no money. That driver's kindness got me to London, where I earned enough to buy my ticket home. Now, decades later, I'm crossing with plenty of cash and a lifetime of memories. Yesterday, while the girls visited St. Paul's Cathedral, I went to buy my Paris ticket.

Deep down inside of me, I knew the real reason why I wanted to go to Paris and it wasn't because of the English Channel. It was because I was going to meet Alexandra in Paris, like I promised two years earlier.

I first went to Trafalgar Square Station, only to realize that back in 1975, the Channel Tunnel didn't exist. It was one of those Asperger moments, funny in hindsight. The last few days have been packed: two volleyball games, the women's gold-medal soccer match, and the men's basketball semifinal, USA vs. Argentina. Paul joined us for that basketball game.

Wembley Stadium was incredible, holding nearly 90,000 fans. The U.S. beat Japan 2–1 in soccer and hearing the national anthem at the medal ceremony brought tears to my eyes. We didn't get tickets to the volleyball or basketball finals, but we watched from the Australian pub near our hotel. The U.S. women lost in four matches. Today we visited the Tower of London, then relaxed at the Walkabout Pub to watch more Olympic coverage.

August 13, 2012: The Closing Ceremony was one of the best I've seen, music everywhere, the Spice Girls, The Who, and so many British legends. I was hoping Adele would perform, but no such luck. Colleen and Maggie flew home the next day while I took the Eurostar to Paris. Two hours and twenty minutes from London to Paris, incredible. Traveling has changed so much since my first trips. What once took a full day now takes just a morning. In Paris, I checked into the Hotel Ponce Royal, took a nap, and went out for a sandwich while waiting for Alexandra.

August 17, 2012: Over the next few days we revisited the familiar sights — the Mona Lisa, the Louvre, Notre Dame. The crowds are larger than ever, filled with travelers from every corner of the world, even Russia and China. The world feels smaller now, and freer.

I don't like Paris much. Maybe it's the language barrier or the lack of control over my surroundings. After three days, I decided to move on to Barcelona, a place that feels like home.

August 19, 2012: Barcelona remains one of my favorite cities, La Rambla is still alive, though different from years past. This must be my ninth visit. I met two guys from Holland, a math teacher and a policeman, both good company though a bit drunk. Colleen would have liked them. The backpacker spirit is fading; hostels are giving way to hotels that charge over a hundred euros a night. Meals that once cost ten now cost seventy-five. Still, the tapas are unbeatable. I took a cab to Castelldefels for a day at the beach, a little sunburn, good food, and memories. Mostly, my days have been quiet, naps, walks, and reflection. Today I took a sightseeing boat ride up the coast while waiting for my flight. Tonight, I begin my journey home, but first I'll take Alexandra to Venice where her sister will be waiting for her. We did alternative areas and after a couple of days I headed home. I have never seen Alexandra again.

Venice first, then Amsterdam, Minneapolis, and finally Lincoln. I miss Colleen and the comfort of home more with each passing year. Barcelona grows more expensive every time I return. My first trip was as a child with my parents, then with the Navy, then hitchhiking with Mark from Paris, then with Colleen and Michael, then on the Harley, then driving en route to the 2004 Olympics in Greece, and now this one. I wonder if there will be another.

August 20, 2012: Venice is as beautiful as ever, but this is my third visit and perhaps my last. There are fewer pigeons in St. Mark's Square, probably due to the new feed that made them sterile. It seems to be working; the plazas are cleaner. I bought Colleen a gold chain with a cross from a jeweler near St. Mark's. The shop we'd visited on our first trip together is gone, but I found something I liked. As I wait to board my flight to Amsterdam, I can't help but think this might be my last time in Venice, not as a destination, but as a stop on the road to somewhere else.

August 22, 2012: The flight home from Venice to Lincoln was smooth and uneventful, about fourteen hours total, including layovers. I made it home in time to stop by the office. I received sad news upon returning. My aunt in Spain, my Uncle Pepe's wife and my cousin Millie's mother, passed away from cancer. It's even sadder knowing that Millie herself only recently underwent cancer surgery. Now she is alone.

27

Costa Rica/Belize/Cuba

Whenever I went on a trip, either alone or with Colleen, I always took the opportunity to look for a second home, a place where we could vacation regularly. I was constantly checking local real estate prices. In the fall of 2013, I decided to make a trip to Costa Rica to see what it had available for homes as a possible second home for us. After driving around to various locations, both to the north, then the south of the country, near the beaches. I don't know what it was about Costa Rica, but I simply didn't like the country. It was too much jungle, and the beautiful areas were too far away from the capital, San José, where medical care would be available if I ever had an emergency. Stupid me I forgot to bring my insulin. I quickly called home and talk to Maggie Malone and asked Maggie if she would FedEx it to me at my hotel in San Jose. Once again, instead of getting my insulin delivered to the hotel I received notification that I had to go to customs to pick it up because of the medicine. This ordeal was so horrible that I wasted an entire day, for had I known better, I could've walked across the street from the hotel to the pharmacy and bought insulin, for in Costa Rica insulin is considered an over-the-counter item.

So, I decided to fly to Belize. While at the airport waiting to board my flight, the plane was canceled. There were two girls, one from Colorado and one from Australia, Shawnee and Stephanie, who didn't understand what was going on. In addition to the three of us, another gal who was from Costa Rica and who happened to be American joined the group for the next day's flight to Belize via El Salvador. The airline rebooked us for the next day and gave us all separate hotel vouchers, so the four grabbed a taxi and headed to the hotel together.

Once we got to Belize I rented a car. I was there to look at real estate. Shawnee and Stephanie were there to sightsee, and the American gal was there to run a marathon. So we drove for about three hours until we reached the far end of Belize where we found accommodations for all of us. I didn't like the looks of Belize either. But the American gal along with Shawnee decided both would run the marathon and to everyone's surprise, Shawnee won it.

We talked about whether any of us had been to Cuba or wanted to go. We agreed that I would go as their interpreter, since I could speak Spanish, which would help make them feel safer, and in truth it would make me feel safer too, because I had no idea what to expect from Cuba.

From Belize city we had to take a five-hour bus ride to Playa del Carmen. We found a motel near the beach and booked two rooms just steps away from the shoreline. The American gal went back to San Jose, Costa Rica. After arriving, we were so exhausted that we all went straight to our rooms and to bed. The next day, I went around to the local ATM machines to withdraw enough cash for the upcoming trip to Cuba, since it was my understanding that credit cards would not work there. Later, after I got home, I found out that you do not want to use the ATM machines that are not affiliated with the banks, for those on the streets are run by the cartel.

In the little time I spent in Playa del Carmen, I genuinely enjoyed it and thought it might be a good place to buy or build a home. The following morning, we shared a taxi to Cancún, where we caught a short flight to Cuba. The tickets cost us just $50 apiece, an easy price to pay for the adventure that lay ahead.

After arriving in Cuba, I quickly learned my iPhone would not work in Cuba. I went to the telephone company on occasions to place my phone calls to the U.S. and to Colleen. Once inside, you could not simply dial on your own, you had to have an assistant help you make the call. This is where I met Lissandra Cavajar-Garcia, who was employed as a phone operator. I made so many trips to the phone company trying to have Colleen wire me money that I got to know Lissandra well over the next couple of days. She was 23 years old, had a boyfriend, a two-year-old son and lived with her mom and dad, along with her boyfriend. During that time, I also went back and forth between the phone company and the Cuban Western Union, trying unsuccessfully to arrange the wire transfer. In the process, I lost my passport. I was so scared when I realized it was gone that I couldn't get out of Cuba fast enough once I finally found it. Shawnee and Stephanie headed out for other parts in Cuba, and I was tired, scared, and ready to go home.

The U.S. had no relationship with Cuba at the time, and legally I wasn't supposed to have been there in the first place. Once I recovered my passport, I headed back to Cancún to catch a flight home, because by then I was finished with traveling. Prior to leaving Cuba, however, Lissandra and I exchanged email addresses, and from there comes the rest of the story.

I had received emails from Lissandra, but I never read them because I could not read Spanish. One day she called me directly and asked if I had read her emails. I told her no, and she asked me to please read the last one. So, after I read her email, I decided to go back to Cuba in early 2014, hoping that Lissandra would be able to show me more of the true and real Cubans that I had hoped to see my first time around.

On the way back from Cuba, I stayed in Playa del Carmen for a couple of days because I liked it so much and wanted to look at the local real estate development. I found a site in an area called El Cielo, the very same development that Colleen and I had driven through on our trip to Cancún years earlier. Lissandra, her boyfriend, and I were only friends. I would never try to have a relationship with her, because I could no longer perform my manly duties, and I did not want to embarrass myself.

Sometime in the spring of 2014, I told Colleen that I was going to Playa del Carmen because I wanted to make an offer on a lot there. And I did make an offer and then took a quick side trip to Cuba, but then I lied to Colleen about that trip. Colleen eventually figured it out. She suspected that I had gone to Cuba again, and she thought I had a girlfriend down there. The truth was that I had gone to Cuba, but I did not have a girlfriend, nor was I looking for one.

Construction on the new second home began in late 2014, and I made several trips down to Playa del Carmen during that time. I would also take a side trip to Cuba. I always asked Colleen if she wanted to go with me, but I knew in my heart that she wouldn't. In a way, which gave me a sense of relief, more of a relief, because it meant I could make the trip without the tension that always seemed to come with her presence.

Summer turned into fall of 2014, and things between Colleen and me continued to deteriorate. After I started building the new house, she told me flat out that she would never move down to Mexico. That November, we attended one of my daughter Megan's friend's weddings in Lincoln, and it was there that the last picture of Colleen and me together was ever taken. In that photograph, Megan stood with us, like a referee, as if she were holding the fragile peace between her parents.

It was the stupidest decision I ever made in my life. I chose to go to Cuba right after Colleen told me our sexual relationship had ended. It was just after Christmas and right before our anniversary. On top of it all, I intentionally refused to call Colleen on our anniversary, the first time that had ever happened. Looking back, I know I should have stayed home and tried to work things out with her instead of running away. Instead, I ran from the pain, not realizing that in doing so, I was running straight into the greatest loss of my life.

Things between Colleen and me were already strained, and deep down I could feel the distance growing like a shadow over our marriage. When she told me there would be no more sex between us, I should have known then that something more was behind it, that she might have already been talking to an attorney. Based on the timing of when she filed for divorce, I have always believed those conversations were already happening before I ever left for Cuba. That knowledge makes my choice to go feel even more reckless, as if I had walked blindly into the storm and sealed my own fate before I even knew it. For years I always thought that Colleen married me not out of love, but more so out of pity.

The decision I made to leave cost me the love of my life. I was not a good husband, and she was a great wife. It was a moment of weakness, an escape that turned into a permanent wound, one I will carry for as long as I live.

On the way back from Cuba, I had a connecting flight through Toronto, Canada. The moment I switched my phone back on, my screen lit up with message after message that hadn't been able to reach me while I was gone. And then came the one that shattered me: a text from Colleen telling me not to come home because she had already filed for divorce. Standing there in that airport, surrounded by strangers hurrying to their gates, I felt as if the entire world had gone silent. My heart raced, and tears burned in my eyes, but there was no one to turn to, no one to understand the weight of the words that had just destroyed me.

I still had to fly from Toronto back to Lincoln, Nebraska, with all of that on my mind. It was the longest flight of my life. Trapped in my seat, I stared out the window into the dark sky, replaying everything in my head. I knew that what I was returning to was no longer the life I had left behind.

Back at the office, the reality closed in even harder. I was at my desk, trying to push through the fog in my mind, when the sheriff walked in and handed me the divorce papers. In that instant, my world collapsed. The cold official envelope felt heavier than stone, heavier than anything I had ever carried. I took it upstairs to the apartment, shut the door, and finally let it out. I cried until I could not breathe, until my chest ached and my body trembled. I cried until there was nothing left inside me but emptiness.

That was the moment I knew I had lost Colleen forever, gone because of the foolish choice that I made. And no matter how much I wished I could take it back, there was no going back. Yet I blame myself more for not making a bigger effort to fix the problem.

While writing this chapter about Colleen, I also reminisce about the past thirty-eight years: from the first day I met her at the union, to skiing trips together, to the joy of buying our farmhouse, to holding our first baby in our arms, to the Amtrak ride we took to San Francisco, and the drives we made out to the coast. And the trips overseas, still the memories bring tears to my eyes even now. It has been ten years since we separated, yet the ache of her absence still feels fresh, as if no time at all has passed.

28

The Age of 77

All my adult life I have carried a quiet question inside me: Do people somehow know the year they are meant to leave this earth? I can't explain why, but something in me has always whispered that my own journey might end when I reach the age of seventy-seven. That thought has hovered in the back of my mind for decades, a shadow that follows me even in bright sunlight. Now, standing at the threshold of that year, I find myself looking both backward and forward, trying to make sense of the path I've traveled and wondering whether fate has been whispering my number all along.

Part of this feeling comes from my Tito Juan. For as long as I can remember, I believed he died at the age of seventy-seven. Perhaps it was just a misunderstanding, a detail carried down through memory and family conversation, yet because I sometimes wondered if he might have been my true father, that number began to feel personal, like an echo that belonged to me as much as to him.

Was it only coincidence, or am I, without realizing it, racing against a clock of my own imagination, driven by the thought that I must finish my memoir before I reach that age. I feel the urgency like a low drumbeat beneath everything I do, a steady reminder that my days are not endless. Every word I write feels like a stone laid carefully into the foundation of a legacy I don't want to leave unfinished.

Still, I hope I am wrong in my feelings. I would like to believe that I can carry on well into my nineties, just as my mother has done, for Laura's sake too. She is still learning many of our ways here in the United States, and I want to be with her through those steps. My mother's quiet resilience through hardship has always reminded me that strength can carry us further than we expect. Even so, after my stroke, I've become more aware of time's fragility, and I know I can't take a single day for granted.

All my life, I have felt an uncanny sense of things before they happened, I would catch a glimpse of a moment before it unfolded or feel a certainty about an event before it came to pass. Some people call that ESP, extrasensory perception, the mysterious ability to sense things beyond the ordinary five senses. Others call it premonition. Whatever the name, it has always felt like a quiet companion, whispering truths I wasn't always ready to hear.

I remember moments when that strange knowing touched my life, times when I would think of someone I hadn't spoken to in years, only to receive their call or news of them within hours. Or times when I woke from a dream with a clear picture of something that later happened exactly as I had seen it, never dramatic enough to make headlines, but always powerful enough to make me pause and listen. I learned not to question it too much. Instead I came to see it as a kind of guidance, a nudge from something beyond my understanding, perhaps from God, or from the quiet corners of the human spirit that we rarely acknowledge. And yet, even now, when a sudden feeling passes through me, I can't help but stop and wonder what it's trying to tell me. Maybe it's protection, maybe it's memory, or maybe it's the simple awareness that we are more connected to the unseen world than we care to admit.

When I thought of Tito Juan, who I believed had passed away at the age of seventy-seven, I couldn't help but wonder if that number was waiting for me as well, and if this sense I carried all these years was less a warning and more preparation, a quiet acceptance of life's rhythm before the final note plays.

Nevertheless, I tell myself I will simply have to wait and see what the age of seventy-seven brings. I imagine it will be a long year, waking each morning with the question: Is this the day? if it is, then this memoir will become my farewell, my voice preserved on the page, a final letter to the world, a gift for those I love most.

29

Solitude

I do not know why, but I have always enjoyed solitude when I was driving. There is something peaceful about being alone on the open road, no schedule, no voices, just the steady hum of the tires and the rhythm of my own thoughts. The miles have a way of quieting the noise inside your head.

One day, out of nowhere, I decided to drive to Veracruz, Mexico. Santos, a former employee from Midwest Demolition, had moved back home there after being employed by me for years. Before leaving Nebraska, he had said, "Come down sometime, boss. I will show you where I grew up." I had not thought much of it then, but later, when life felt heavy and quiet, his words came back to me. I was looking for something, or running from something, but either way, I packed up my white Expedition and headed south.

My first stop was Galveston, Texas, just south of Houston. I remember it clearly. I parked right on the sandy beach that night. The surf was close enough that the sound of the waves lulled me to sleep in the back of the truck. By morning, the sky was painted in soft pink and gold. I lowered the tailgate, pulled out my small camping stove, and made a cup of coffee. Sitting there on the edge of the Gulf, watching gulls drift over the water, I realized how good it felt to be alone. Not lonely, just free.

From Galveston, I drove toward Corpus Christi, hugging the coastal road whenever I could. Somewhere along that stretch, I drove into a storm of butterflies, thousands of them, fluttering into my headlights like falling leaves of gold. For a moment it was mesmerizing, a living cloud of color shimmering in the air. But soon they began striking the windshield, one after another, until it was completely covered.

I had to stop three times to wash the glass at roadside gas stations because I could hardly see ahead. I could not help but laugh at the old saying that everything is bigger in Texas, even the butterflies. I remembered Corpus Christi from my old Navy days, when one of my girlfriends, who got me thrown into the brig, was from there. For one reason or another, I had to drive through it.

By the time I reached Brownsville, the last Texas town before Mexico, the air was thicker, the sun hotter, and Spanish filled the streets. Crossing the border wanted to step into another world. The road narrowed, the signs were hand-painted, and life seemed to move at its own rhythm.

I did not rush. I stopped for tacos at roadside stands, cold Cokes in glass bottles, and fuel from dusty stations where children waved as I drove away. The landscape changed with every mile, from dry brush to lush green hills that rolled toward the sea.

Although the GPS showed it was not the best route to reach Barracudas, I wanted to stay close to the coast. There was something about being near the water, seeing the Gulf appear and disappearing through palm trees and fishing villages, which made me feel connected to the journey itself. At one point, I came across an area that had been devastated by a hurricane. For miles, there were rows of identical block houses built at higher elevations than the shoreline. Families were living there temporarily, rebuilding their lives. Children played in the sand, and laundry fluttered from makeshift lines strung between the walls. It was humbling. Those smaller, rougher roads told more of the real story of Mexico than the highways ever could.

When I finally reached Veracruz, I found Santos living in a modest home on the edge of town. I stayed at the Holiday Inn near the seaport and spent the next day visiting the downtown square with his entire family. It was the first time I had ever heard real Mexican mariachis, their music filling the plaza with energy and emotion. The trumpets cut through the night air, sharp and bright, while the guitars and violins carried warmth and heart. Couples danced, children clapped in rhythm, and even the old men smiled beneath their wide-brimmed hats. Santos greeted me like family, surprised that I had made the trip. That evening, we sat outside under a bare light bulb, drinking a beer while music drifted from a nearby cantina. Santos talked about his family and how life there was simpler, slower, and somehow richer. I listened, watching the last light fade over the Gulf of Mexico and thinking about how far I had come, not just the miles, but the years.

After three days in Veracruz, I decided to drive over to Mexico City and do a little sightseeing. The route took me inland through rolling green mountains, past sugarcane fields, and small villages where people sold fruit and pottery by the roadside. After reaching the outskirts of Mexico City, I encountered my first case of crooked police officers. Before entering the city, I got stopped by the state patrol and told that I was driving on a day I should not be. Apparently license plates were restricted to certain days of the week, depending on their numbers, and I had the wrong one. Regardless, it cost me two hundred dollars to get out of that mess.

After driving around Mexico City, I found my way to the Hilton Hotel near the American Embassy. I used the hotel as a base while visiting the area. It was a modern, comfortable place with an air of familiarity that made me feel closer to home. From there, I explored the city's grand boulevards, parks, and plazas, taking in the energy and chaos that only Mexico City can offer. While staying at the Hilton, I found a tour guide who took me the next day to the Pyramids of the Sun. The scale of the ancient site was breathtaking, endless stone rising from the earth, silent witnesses to civilizations long gone. Climbing to the top, I looked out across the Valley of Teotihuacán, feeling both small and deeply connected to something far older than myself. I did not know it then, but someday I would marry a beautiful Mexican woman from Mexico City. At that time, she was only fifteen years old, living her own young life somewhere in that vast, vibrant city.

After about three days at the Hilton, I decided it was time to leave and head back home. So, without hesitation, I turned north toward the U.S., crossing the border at Laredo, Texas. From there, I made my way back to Nebraska. The long drive gave me time to think, to process everything I had seen and felt. I was re-energized, grateful, and ready to get back to work.

That trip was not about visiting Santos. It was about rediscovering something I had lost, the peace that comes with motion, and the kind of quiet you only find when you are alone on the road. In that solitude, with butterflies fluttering into my headlights and the sea whispering beyond the horizon, I felt more like myself than I had in a long time.

30

Last Vacation

In the fall of 2014, Colleen and I decided that we would take a vacation and head out to the East Coast, a place we had never been to together, in our RV. She had a conference to attend in Des Moines, Iowa, and we agreed that I would pick her up there. From Des Moines, we would head east. At the time, I did not know it would be our last trip together, but something deep inside me must have sensed it. There was a heaviness between us that neither of us wanted to acknowledge, an unspoken distance that had slowly crept into our marriage over the years.

With the wind at our back, we rolled eastward toward Pennsylvania, watching the landscape change from flat fields to the soft green hills of the Appalachians. We stopped to explore old cemeteries and dig through local archives, searching for traces of Colleen's family history. She was fascinated by every discovery, tracing names, and dates with her fingertips as if they were clues to her own identity. I watched her, quietly proud of her determination, though there was a lingering sadness in me, perhaps because I knew I was losing her in ways neither of us could fix.

From Pennsylvania, we drove down to Washington, D.C., where we parked the RV at a nearby campground and took the Metro downtown. Together, we wandered through the monuments and museums, surrounded by the echo of history and the hum of tourists. We met up with my nephew Matt, who lived nearby, and shared a few good laughs over dinner. On the surface, it was a wonderful trip, but inside, I could feel our silence growing longer, our conversations shorter.

Next, we made our way to New York City. We left the RV in New Jersey and took a cab into Manhattan, checking into the Hyatt near Times Square, a trip we had once planned for our 10th anniversary but canceled when life and four kids got in the way. From the Hyatt, we could walk anywhere. The bright lights, the bustle, the noise all reminded me of how alive the world could be when love was still new. The last time we had been there, I was too sick to leave the room while Colleen spent her days shopping alone. This time, I was determined to make it different. We took the ferry to see the Statue of Liberty and Ellis Island. Watching Colleen gaze up at Lady Liberty, her eyes full of wonder, I wished I could capture that moment and keep it forever.

We continued north toward Massachusetts, getting close to Boston before turning west. Along the way, we stopped in Buffalo, visited Niagara Falls, and even spent an evening at a small local casino. The sound of the rushing water at Niagara was powerful, both beautiful and deafening. It mirrored the noise in my own head, the confusion of love fading and the ache of not wanting to admit it.

When we finally began the long drive back to Nebraska, we stopped briefly in Des Moines so Colleen could pick up her car. She kissed me on the cheek before leaving, and I remember watching her drive away, feeling as though something inside me had quietly closed. No matter what I did, it seemed I could no longer reignite the old flame between us. When we fought, it was not with shouting or anger, it was silence. That cold, unbearable silence. Colleen slept in the bedroom, and I slept in my La-Z-Boy chair in the den, even when I did not want to. The distance between us had grown so wide that even sharing the same house felt lonely.

For two years before that trip, I had thought about filing for divorce, but I never did. I felt a sense of duty, to help Colleen finish her master's degree in psychology, to see her succeed in starting her own business, to do right by her after all the years we had shared. But love, once lost, does not come back easily. That East Coast trip, as ordinary as it seemed at the time, marked the quiet end of our marriage.

A few months later, in January, Colleen filed for divorce. I did not fight it. Deep down, I knew the decision had already been made long before the papers were signed. That last vacation was not just the end of a journey across the country; it was the closing chapter of us.

31

THE LOVE OF MY LIFE

How can one condense 38 years of love and marriage into a short story? Colleen's and my story begin in January 1977, when I transferred from Chadron State College to Kearney State College. Before settling in, I took a short ski trip to Loveland Basin, Colorado, with a friend I had met at Chadron. When I returned from that trip, I packed up my 1966 blue Chevy Impala and drove down to Kearney, where I moved into Randall Hall on campus.

Once I had settled into my dorm at Kearney State, I wandered over to the campus Union, and that is where she first caught my attention. She stood out immediately: athletic, full of energy, with long straight blonde hair and a light complexion. Her bright blue eyes carried both strength and grace, and she moved with a natural confidence that drew people in. She had chosen Kearney State to compete in track, for she was a truly gifted all-around athlete. Whether she was sharing a laugh, leaning over a foosball table, or simply carrying on a conversation, there was always a spark about her. I found myself drawn to those moments, making a point of speaking with her whenever I had the chance. I did not realize it then but meeting her that day would shape the next 38 years of my life. Years later, Colleen told me that when she first saw me, she somehow knew I would be the man she married, even if, at the time, she did not care much for me.

With her long straight blonde hair, she looked strong and graceful with her bright blue eyes. She was by far the most beautiful women I have ever laid eyes on. She was truly an excellent all-around athlete. She was always pleased to talk to me. I made a point of speaking to her whenever I had the chance.

Her name was Colleen Marie Kindig, from Hastings, Nebraska. At the time, she was a junior at Kearney State, studying to become a teacher in physical education and health. She had originally gone there with the intention of running track, for she was an excellent all-around athlete. After her first year, however, she decided to set aside track to focus on their education, though the discipline and drive she carried from her athletic background never left her. Colleen came from a very athletic family in Hastings, where she attended St. Cecilia, a Catholic elementary and high school. Her sister Nancy was a particularly good athlete, and her younger sister Barb was just as talented, though she did not want to run as much as Nancy or Colleen.

That spring, while I continued my studies at Kearney, I would see her from time to time, most often in the Student Union, or through the window as she walked from the Union to the gymnasium, wearing a green sweatsuit and passing by the Industrial Arts Building where most of my classes were held. I also noticed her in the Union having coffee with an older gentleman, a small man with gray hair who was also a student at the college. At times, I felt a twinge of jealousy, until I learned the truth: he was her best friend, an Irish priest who had been her track coach for years and who also taught in the Catholic school system.

As spring rolled around and the sun came out, I could tell that Colleen still did not have much interest in me beyond being friendly in social settings. At one of the school events, I was walking around with a six-pack of something hanging out of the back pocket of my shorts, shirtless and trying to look cool. She reminded me of that moment years later and laughed, telling me she thought I looked foolish.

I met Julie Hellman that summer, a wealthy young woman I ran into at a local discotheque called Dickey Dugan's. Julie and I spent that summer together. One day Julie left me a dear John letter before she went back to school in Arizona. I was heartbroken so I climbed into my blue Impala and drove all the way to Regina, Canada, to see Deanna and Connie, friends who I had previously met in Barcelona, Spain. I stayed in Regina for about a week, but before coming back to Kearney, I sent Colleen a postcard and, in my nervousness, I managed to mess up her address badly. After arriving back in Kearney from Regina, I stopped by to see her at her apartment on the second floor of a two-story building, and she reminded me of that screwed-up address on the card. I told her I was heading out to Denver, Colorado, where I left my car with Jerry and Shirley before catching a flight bound for San Diego, California.

I spent a couple of days in the San Diego–Tijuana area, just messing around, even making a trip to Black's Beach. From there, on a whim, I hitchhiked to Tempe, Arizona to see Julie, without giving her any warning. When I arrived, I called her from the Holiday Inn, and she came over to meet me. Instead of the welcome I had hoped for, she gave me the cold shoulder and sent me back to Kearney, leaving me to hitchhike the long road home.

Once I was back at Kearney State in the fall of 1977, I continued my quiet pursuit of Colleen, though she had no idea of the depth of my feelings. She kept me at a distance, politely turning me down in her own subtle way, not even realizing that I was falling deeply in love with her. Yet, in spite of those rejections, our friendship slowly grew stronger.

That fall, around Thanksgiving break, opportunity quite literally knocked on my door at 3 AM in the morning. Colleen had gone home to spend the holiday with her family, and one of her friends stopped by to visit. They had decided to head to Kearney for a night of barhopping, but Colleen had left her car at home along with her keys thinking that her friend would return her to Hastings. Something happened between Colleen and her friend causing Colleen to leave wherever they were at. Without her apartment keys, and with all her other friends out of town for the holiday break, she had no choice but to come to my trailer house, where I was living with Madeline. It was bitterly cold that night, so much that if she had stayed outside any longer, she might have frozen to death. That night, Colleen slept shivering on the sofa while Madeline brought her a blanket, and the two of us went back to our bedroom. The next morning, Madeline fixed Colleen breakfast, and soon after, Colleen asked if I would drive her to Hastings so she could pick up her car and retrieve her keys. It turned into a pleasant trip, with an easy, enjoyable conversation during the drive down. Not long after, Colleen made an off-the-cuff remark that struck me deeply: if we were ever going to go out on a date, she would never do so as long as I was living with another girl. When those words finally sank in, in December I asked Madeline to move out of my place, and I even helped her find another apartment of her own.

I took Colleen out for lunch one day at Cattleman's, a fancy steakhouse in Kearney, and I remember her telling me that she really was not interested in going out with a guy without ambition. She was more interested in a relationship with a guy who wanted a good future, someone like a businessperson. I was only a recreation major at the college. Soon after I went to the registrar's office and changed my major from recreation to industrial tech. It would be tougher classes and more work in a longer stay at the college, but she was worth everything to me.

December 11th was Colleen's birthday. I went to the flower shop and bought her a dozen red roses. It was a freezing night, the kind where the cold cuts right through you. The flower lady asked if I wanted her to wrap the bouquet, but I foolishly said, "No, thank you." For I was in a hurry to take the flowers to Colleen. I walked out with the roses in my hand and carried them the short thirty feet to my car, thinking only of giving them to her.

When I brought the roses to her apartment, Colleen was exceedingly kind and gracious, thanking me warmly and telling me I did not have to do that. She asked if I wanted something to eat, and I said, "Sure, why not?" Curious, I asked what she had made, and she told me it was beef. To my surprise and amusement, it turned out to be beef heart from a cow, something I had never eaten in my entire life.

On my way out that evening, Colleen was standing in her doorway while I stood one step down. Just then, Roger came up the steps, hoping to see his girlfriend, Julie Molely. He greeted us politely, realized she was not there, and then went on his way. That night, though, is still etched in my memory because it was then that I received my very first kiss from Colleen, just a small, peck kiss on the lips. I walked away knowing it was the best day of my life so far.

Although the 11th had been a momentous day for me, with Colleen's kiss still fresh in my mind, the 12th was not as bright. That day I found out from Colleen that the red roses I had bought her had frozen on their way to her apartment, and by the next morning they had all withered and drooped.

After the thrilling night of December 11th, a night I will never forget, filled with chills, excitement, and hope for the future came the dreadful next day. As the semester ended, that contrast between joy and disappointment stayed with me. During those final weeks, Colleen and I began spending more time together, and with Madeline moving into her own apartment, I suddenly had the chance to deepen my relationship with Colleen, an opportunity that felt both natural and long-awaited.

Feeling more comfortable with myself, and with Colleen planning to move into a trailer with a friend, I took the opportunity to ask them both if they wanted to go skiing over Christmas break. After some thought, Colleen agreed to go along with her new roommate, Sandy. Deep down, I was hoping that Sandy believed in the old saying "two's company and three's a crowd" and would withdraw from the trip, leaving Colleen and me to share the experience on our own.

When Colleen asked if I would help her move into the trailer where Sandy would also be living after leaving their apartment, I agreed without hesitation. On the very first night Colleen was officially settled there, I stayed with her. We lay together in bed, both of us fully clothed, she was in a football jersey, me beside her with my arm draped gently over her. I simply held her, never attempting to go further. Later, she told me how much she valued that night just lying there without any pressure or intent to make it something physical. For her, it was comfort; for me, it was quiet reassurance that our connection rested on something deeper than desire.

Once the semester ended and the holidays arrived, Colleen spent time with her family while plans for the ski trip took shape. As it turned out, Sandy decided not to go. She thought it would be best to let the two of us go alone. With a mix of excitement and anticipation, we set out in my Monte Carlo and drove west toward Colorado, spending our first night with Jerry and Shirley at their home near Hudson. Their warmth and hospitality gave us a soft landing before we continued deeper into the mountains.

The following day we continued our journey, driving into the mountains until we reached Silverthorne, Colorado. We checked into a hotel there for the night, our minds already set on the slopes. The next morning, we would go skiing, just the two of us, free from the distractions and complications that had lingered back home.

The next morning, when I woke up eager to hit the slopes, my Monte Carlo refused to start in the bitter cold. I found myself outside in the freezing mountain air, crouched over the engine with a hair dryer, trying to warm the battery and the carburetor. After some persistence and a few anxious minutes, the car finally turned over, and with relief we headed off to the ski slopes, ready to make the best of the day. We spent the next few days skiing, enjoying the crisp mountain air and the freedom of being away together. Those days on the slopes brought us even closer, turning shared laughter and simple moments into something deeper.

One day while skiing in Vail, Colorado, we ran into a friend of Colleen's. We were standing on an old wooden bridge, just having a conversation when another skier was passing by and I asked if they would take a picture of the three of us. With me on one side, Colleen in the middle and the other guy on the other side of Colleen. In the picture I had a big Afro with a beard and the other guy was a blonde hair clean-cut-looking young man. I developed that picture in my photography class and made an 8 x 11 which I still have today. Colleen took that picture home to show her parents. When her parents looked at the picture, they automatically assumed that the blonde well-trimmed guy was John. Colleen quickly pointed out that the guy with the Afro and beard was John and not the other guy.

When the trip finally ended, we decided to head back to Kearney. By then, after those few days in Colorado, Colleen and I had grown close. On the way home back to Nebraska, it grew late, and we decided to stop for the night in Georgetown, Colorado, a small town nestled on the eastern slope, just below Loveland Pass. The quiet streets and mountain backdrops gave the stopover a peaceful feeling, a pause between the excitement of our ski trip and the return to everyday life.

Although what came next might sound a bit grotesque, it became an important turning point in the future between Colleen and me. In Georgetown, we checked into a small motel to spend the night, planning to continue our drive the next day. It was on January 2nd or 3rd, 1978. The room had two beds, and we chose one to share. That night, we decided to make love. What I had not realized was that Colleen had just started her monthly cycle, and the moment carried with it a surprise I had not expected. Afterwards, we moved over to the other bed and spent the rest of the night calmly in each other's arms. There was no rush, no tension, just a quiet closeness that felt natural and reassuring. The next morning, we got up, packed our things, and continued our drive back to Kearney.

From January onward, Colleen and I were inseparable. She came to see me every day, and our time together grew more intimate. We often made love, most tenderly in the quiet moments before she left for work. But by the end of January, Colleen realized she had missed her monthly period, and fear began to weigh heavily on her. The possibility of pregnancy brought a new and sobering dimension to our relationship.

On February 14th, Valentine's Day, I took Colleen to the local medical clinic in Kearney, where she went in for a checkup. When she walked out, she looked at me with a mix of nervousness and excitement before offering her congratulations, because I was about to become a father. The news hit me with a rush of emotions — excitement, fear, and a sense of responsibility all at once. Valentine's Day, a day meant for love and celebration, had suddenly taken on a much deeper meaning. I was going to be a father, and as Colleen and I drove away from the clinic, the weight of that reality began to sink in. Our lives were about to change in ways we could only begin to imagine. I planned to remain in Kearney and continue my education, while Colleen looked ahead to Omaha with hopes of starting a new career. The distance between us was already beginning to take shape, and though I did not fully grasp it at the time, our paths were moving in different directions.

About a week before she was to leave, Colleen called and said she wanted to come over and talk. She did not want to come inside, so we sat together in her car. That was when she told me she had decided to go to Omaha early, have an abortion before starting her student teaching, and that this would also mark the end of our relationship. I told her I did not want her to do it, in fact, I begged her not to. We both cried there in the car, and after she drove away and left me at my trailer, I broke down again. I was madly in love with Colleen, and I knew that if she went through with the abortion, it would weigh heavily on her emotionally for the rest of her life, for she was a particularly good Catholic. But despite that conflict, she had already decided it was the best path forward for her future. It was one of the sorriest days of my life. It was a sad day when Colleen left for Omaha, both to begin her student teaching and to end her pregnancy.

During that time, I stayed connected with her, calling the house where she stayed with an acquaintance daily. I made trips to Omaha, determined to keep our relationship alive despite the distance and the weight of what had happened. On one of those trips, I even changed the spark plugs in Colleen's car, which had not been running well. It was a small gesture, but it gave me another reason to be close, to feel useful, and to remain connected to her world in whatever way I could. On another trip we went camping in Louisville State Park.

Over the years, whenever I was in Omaha, I would often drive by the small abortion clinic just off Dodge Street, just to see where it was, or just to see if it was still there. Each pass stirred up memories I could never leave behind. At times that building would just disappear, so perhaps then my memories of that horrible event would disappear.

Colleen also came to Kearney to visit me on occasion, and during one of those visits her neck began bothering her so badly she could no longer drive. I took her back to Omaha in her own car and then hitchhiked my way back to Kearney. A difficult trip, but one more reminder of how far I was willing to go to be there for her.

When her student teaching was over, Colleen returned to Kearney, where I had found a small cottage for her to rent. It was owned by an elderly lady who lived in the big main house, and Colleen had made a connection with her. The woman was a hoarder. When we went into her house, she must have had every newspaper ever printed, stacked up in all corners, and a path had to be made to maneuver through the house. Still, she was kind enough to offer Colleen the small one-bedroom cottage for only fifty dollars a month. Colleen stayed there until she decided about where she was going to work. She was offered a teaching job both in Fairbury, Nebraska, and in Lexington. She chose the Lexington job so she could be close to me while I finished my schooling.

Easter of 1978 was the first time I officially went to Colleen's parents' house as her boyfriend. I arrived the Saturday before Easter, sporting a new haircut, and spent the night in her mom and dad's basement. The following Sunday, she wore a beautiful blue dress that I can still picture even now, its color bright and cheerful, perfectly suited for the spring day. I also met her entire family for the first time, Steve, the oldest, along with Nancy, Barb, and Tom. We all went to church together at St. Michael, and it marked the moment when I was introduced not just as Colleen's friend, but as her boyfriend.

It was August of 1978, and Colleen was just preparing to begin her new job teaching at Lexington Senior High School. We had planned a trip to the Southwestern United States to spend time together before her school year officially began. The thought of getting away, just the two of us on the open road, gave the trip a sense of freedom and excitement for both of us.

That summer, I bought an old Ford Econoline van somewhere in Kearney, and we were planning to take it on the trip to the Southwest. The van was running well after I put new spark plugs in it, made sure all the belts and hoses were in decent condition, and, in general, gave it an overall checkup, for I did not want to have any problems while on the road. The inside had been converted into a small camper, which made it feel perfect for the kind of adventure we had in mind. It was white, and it had good tires. I threw some camping equipment in the van along with a cooler, some sleeping bags, pillows, and a few pots and pans so we could at least cook some meals while we were on the road. This was going to be Colleen and my first road trip together aside from going skiing the previous December to Colorado.

Somewhere in New Mexico, on our first night, we pulled into a campground along a wide, beautiful river and set up camp. It was there Colleen was falling in love with me more deeply than ever before. She was tired and sleepy, yet she felt at peace in that quiet setting. I pulled out the cooking utensils, peeled some potatoes, mixed them with eggs, and proceeded to make her a Spanish tortilla. She was so tired after that first day of traveling, and hungry as well. But she indicated it was the best thing she had eaten in a long time. She also told me she was so happy and felt comfortable, knowing that I was going to be taking care of her. That moment, simple as it was, seemed to draw us closer together than ever before.

Our first destination was to go to Albuquerque, New Mexico, where one of her dad Jim's sisters used to live with her family prior to her death. She had a cousin by the name of Bobby Gore, and his dad was Robert Gore. They were all part of the connection to Colleen's family back in Hastings and visiting them gave us a sense of belonging as we paused on our journey. Our destination was going to be Los Angeles to visit Colleen's Aunt Velma and her great-uncles and great-aunt, and as we continued onward from Albuquerque, we headed toward Arizona with the plan of reaching Los Angeles before heading back to Nebraska via Las Vegas.

Once we got going through Arizona, we decided to make a side trip and visit Old Tucson up in the high desert to see the old western town that was used in western movies. Walking through the dusty streets, we could almost imagine the cowboys and outlaws who had played their parts there, with the saloon doors, wooden storefronts, and stagecoach props adding to the feel of stepping back in time. It gave both of us a sense of being part of those classic westerns we had watched growing up. After leaving Yuma, Arizona, where we had stopped to go through the old federal penitentiary, we drove a little further into California and then decided to head south into Mexico. At that time, passports were not needed, nor did we have any current ones with us. Once in Mexico, we drove toward Tijuana, traveling parallel to the American border as close as we could while staying on the main road. During this long haul of a journey, we noticed concrete troughs along the side of the road, particularly at the tops of the hills. At first, we thought they were meant for watering horses or donkeys pulling carts, or any sort of animal. What we later found out was that they were tanks of water for travelers to use in filling radiators if their vehicles overheated. Thank God we never had to do it. Of course, while in Mexico, Colleen had to try out the local Mexican beer.

We finally reached Tijuana that afternoon and did the usual tourist trip around the city, sampling Mexican food and wandering through the market. We could not help but notice the flies swarming over the food everywhere we went. We also saw old school buses converted into public transportation, still carrying chicken baskets tied to the roof. That night, as we were preparing to leave Tijuana, I accidentally ran a red light. A young police officer pulled us over and asked for my driver's license. He then told us to sit on the curb while he spoke with us, but during that time he received another call on his radio and instructed us not to move. So, we sat there for two hours, waiting for him to come back and wondering what was going to happen to us. When he finally returned, he simply sent us on our way without any fines or bribes, and back into California we went.

We were exhausted and had no intention of sleeping overnight in a hotel or motel in Mexico, so we found the first place available after we crossed the border into the US and sacked it in for the night. Since I had been to San Diego the summer before, I knew Black Beach was located on the northern part of La Jolla, and I decided to take Colleen to Black's Beach, a nudist beach. Once we were at the beach, Colleen had absolutely no reservations about taking her clothes off and heading straight for the water without a thing on. I, on the other hand, still felt uneasy and kept my shorts on, more content to watch than to join in.

That same day we headed into Los Angeles and tried to find Aunt Velma's home, which was in the city. Once in L.A., we were lost. There were no GPS devices or cell phones at that time to help us, only the old-fashioned way, a map, and a phone book. Finally, we found the street where Velma lived, and to our surprise, she was standing outside of her apartment waiting for us to come by. She then directed us to a nearby motel where we gladly spent that night.

The next day, we visited other relatives of Colleen who had moved out to L.A. many years earlier to work in the film industry in one capacity or another. After spending some time with them, we were anxious to start heading back east to Nebraska through Las Vegas, so we left the following day. The drive from L.A. to Las Vegas was long, but by the end of the day we finally arrived. Earlier that summer, I attended a seminar, and to attend I was given a discount coupon to a hotel called The Mariner, located in the southern part of Las Vegas. Once we reached the city, we found The Mariner, checked in, and then set out to find the first casino we could. The Mariner stood on the site where the current MGM is now located. When the new wedding MGM was built, it went up right over the Mariner and replaced the Marina Casino, which happened to be the first casino we visited. After our short stay in Vegas, we headed back home by way of Utah and Colorado, returning so Colleen could start her teaching job, and I could continue with my roofing business.

That fall, after Colleen began teaching in Lexington and I was running my roofing business, I moved into her little fifty-dollar-a-month cottage in Kearney. Each day we made the thirty-five-mile drive back and forth, until eventually I settled in with her full time. Still, I kept my own cottage in Kearney because Colleen wanted our living arrangement to remain a secret. Holding on to that place gave me somewhere to stay whenever her parents came to visit Lexington, allowing us to keep up appearances.

That fall brought many difficulties for us, and amid it all we began talking seriously about marriage, imagining what our future together might look like. Later that season, we went to Hastings to attend her mom and dad's twenty-fifth wedding anniversary at Southern Hills Country Club. It was there that Colleen thought I would officially propose to her. The proposal never came, though, because I had not had the money to buy an engagement ring. I was waiting for my VA check to arrive so I could buy her the ring.

Once I had the money from the VA, along with some savings I had put aside, I went into a jewelry store in Kearney, Nebraska, and bought her a gold with a diamond ring with black markings. It was not just a simple ring, it had delicate engravings etched into it, the dark patterns standing out sharply against the gold. Both her engagement ring and wedding ring, along with my own wedding band, matched the same type of pattern: gold etched with black.

Once Colleen let her family know that we were going to get married, for some reason they began checking around about me. The family did not like what they saw. I had made plans to go to Chadron to see my parents when Colleen told me that her dad was planning to come up and see her while

I was gone. I had no clue why he was coming to talk to her without her mom. It was the longest six-hour drive from Lexington to Chadron that I've ever had, giving me plenty of time to wonder and worry about why her dad was making that trip to speak with her alone. Once I arrived in Chadron, I called Colleen from my mom and dad's house to let her know I had made it all right and to ask about what her dad had said. He was there for the sole purpose of trying to convince her not to marry me, bringing up things from my past as reasons why. But it was nothing new, for Colleen already knew everything about me, since we had been together for a year and a half, first as friends and then as boyfriend and girlfriend. She understood that it had not been an easy start for me in business, and none of it came as a surprise to her. After that hurdle with her family, we decided to go ahead with our plans and get married in December during the Christmas break. So, with the final hurdle behind us, the wedding plans were underway.

I could not have been a happier man than I was with Colleen. Over the two years we had known each other, we had weathered both difficulties, yet I never gave up on us. She was, without question, the love of my life, and I wanted her with every part of me. It was my persistence, something I have often connected to my Asperger's that gave me the strength to hold on until this moment.

It was January 1, 1979, just three days after our wedding, and we were on our honeymoon in Aspen, Colorado. We had skied all day and were too tired to go out that night, so we chose to stay in our room, lie in bed together, and watch the Nebraska–Oklahoma Orange Bowl game. Nebraska lost 31–24, even though they had beaten Oklahoma earlier in the season.

Once the wedding plans were underway, December 29th arrived in what felt like the blink of an eye. I spent Christmas with Colleen and her family, learning some of their traditions.

As soon as the holiday was over, the week grew hectic with people bringing over various pieces of china that Colleen and I had carefully chosen from a local gift store, along with other presents for us. When my family arrived in Hastings, Bonita, Colleen's mom, sent me to stay with my parents, feeling that I was only in the way.

On the morning of the wedding, my mom decided that I had to cut my beard off, so I walked into the church with only a mustache, though I normally wore a full beard.

The church was still decorated for the Christmas holidays, so it looked especially beautiful combined with our wedding decorations. Colleen had her sister Nancy as maid of honor, with Barb, my sister Millie, and two other friends as bridesmaids. I had my brother Bobby as the best man, along with groomsmen Danny Wild, Randy Vrbka, and Tom Kindig. When the music started, the bridesmaids began walking slowly up the long aisle toward the front of the church, where the groomsmen met them. My cousin Darren Sydow served as the ring bearer, and next to him was the flower girl, Christie Kealy, Colleen's cousin. The altar servers were Johnny and Rick Kealy, also cousins of Colleen. As I watched them all take their places, I grew more nervous with every passing second. Then came Colleen, arm in arm with her father, walking slowly down the aisle in her beautiful white wedding dress with a long flowing veil. I will never forget how radiant she looked; the kind of beauty that makes the entire world stop. Her father looked so proud that he handed her to me, and in that moment my nerves eased, replaced with a deep sense of joy and gratitude. We were married at St. Michael's Catholic Church, which was, the Kindig family's own church. Officiating the ceremony was the local parish priest and Colleen's good friend, Father Patrick O'Byrnea, the little Irishman who always shared coffee with her at the Union in Kearney.

It was a snowy, wintry night, so one had to drive carefully. Our reception was held at the Southern Hills Country Club, where we had a live band providing the music. My brother got the crowd going by singing Proud Mary by CCR about five separate times, which was the only song he knew. The band kept the dance floor alive, and I can still picture Colleen laughing as she twirled in her gown, with guests pinning money to her as part of the celebration. The wedding cake was cut and shared, and the toast, though simple, filled the room with love and encouragement. It was a very enjoyable evening filled with dancing, laughter, and plenty of cake. It was the kind of night you could never forget. When we left the reception before everybody else, we went to Colleen's mom's house, where she changed clothes. We picked up our luggage and then drove north to spend the night at the Holiday Inn near Interstate 80. Our first night as a married couple was one of the most wonderful and exhausting nights of my life, because we were so tired that we were ready to go to bed. The next day, we got up and started heading out for Aspen, Colorado, with a short stop at our apartment in Lexington, Nebraska. The snow still lay on the ground as we drove west, and I remember thinking that the cold outside only made the warmth I felt inside even stronger. I was beginning my new life with Colleen, and nothing could have been better.

In early 1979, we were just back from our honeymoon. Colleen went back to teaching school, and I continued to look for work. We were living at 1204 North Madison Street, a two-bedroom apartment. One room we used for ourselves, and the second we used as an office for me. Money was tight in those early months. We ate Campbell's soup, and I even poached a deer, which we hung up on our back porch before grinding it up and making steaks.

That spring I started to build a new home on the corner of 15th and Constitution in Lexington. I had obtained a loan and began construction, but about four months in, Colleen found an acreage just east of Lexington on 13th Street, which she immediately fell in love with. It was centered around an old farmhouse, surrounded by five-foot-tall weeds and a scattering of sheds.

By now, we were connected to the community of Lexington, and we had earned enough money to continue the construction of the house and buy the acreage on 13th Street. Prior to moving into the acreage, Colleen surprised me by saying she was ready to have a baby, even though she had previously told me she wanted to wait a couple of years to see how our relationship was doing. Shortly after that conversation, we moved into the farmhouse on 13th Street.

Once we moved into the house, Colleen and her sister Barb set to work cleaning the immediate area around the farmhouse and mowing down the tall weeds with a push mower. I still remember seeing them slowly working, a little at a time, farther away from the house, uncovering piles of old scrap metal scattered across the acreage. There were rusted tools, broken parts, and bits of machinery, remnants of years gone by. Every piece we hauled away felt like progress, one step closer to turning the neglected property into a real home.

Once Colleen surprised me by telling me she was ready to have a baby, we started the process immediately, but with no luck at first. At one point, she became concerned that because of her abortion, she might not be able to conceive. She went in to see a doctor for a checkup, and everything with her turned out fine. The doctor then asked me to come in and give a donation. I did, and after running tests, the doctor informed her that I had a low sperm count, though he assured us that we could still conceive. It was a mixture of relief and worry. We knew it might not be easy, but we still held on to hope.

The months rolled on, I was busy with my work, and then one day after a doctor's visit in 1980, Colleen came home and told me the wonderful news that she was pregnant. We were both so happy, filled with excitement, and ready to begin our family.

I clearly remember it was the morning of November 23, 1980, a Sunday.

Colleen and I were sitting on our bed just talking when, suddenly, I heard a sound like a water balloon popping. Her water had broken. We called the doctor immediately, and he told us to head to the hospital. We grabbed the emergency bag Colleen had previously packed, called her mom and dad from our house to let them know, and then drove straight to Lexington Hospital.

Once we arrived at the hospital emergency room, the nurses quickly took Colleen into the delivery room and began monitoring her. It felt like a countdown, first eight centimeters, then eight½, then nine. By then the contractions were so severe; her face turned red with tiny red dots bursting all over it. I sat next to her, near her head, holding her hand, and with each contraction she squeezed so hard I thought she might break it. Finally, the doctor arrived at the hospital, and Colleen was getting ready to deliver. The nurse told me to put on a gown, and off to the operating room we went to have our first child.

In the operating room, Colleen continued to scream and push while squeezing my hand with all her strength. I could not stand to watch the birth itself, but I could hear everything — her cries, her pushing, the intensity of the moment. Then finally, the baby was born. Right away, I could tell it was a boy, because as soon as he came out, a stream of pee shot up into the air, and in that instance, I knew we had a son. And his name was Michael John Lecher; I could not be a prouder father and husband.

By this time, after two years, Colleen had quit teaching school since I was making enough money to support us. I remember her cashing in her retirement, and we used that money to buy a refrigerator after ours went out. Around then, I was also attending night school in Kearney two or three times a week. During this period, I had hired a young woman by the name of Christy Swanson to be my secretary, and Colleen suspected that I was having an affair with her. While sitting in my drafting class in the Industrial Arts building, I saw Colleen driving by. This time she was in her Jeep Wagoneer instead of a green sweatsuit she wore while in college. I would often go out with the boys after class to the Fort Kearney Inn, where there was a lounge with live music. One time, I was in the lobby when I saw Colleen pulling up in the parking lot, suspecting I was with Christy Swanson. She was so wrong about that. I never had a relationship with her,

Colleen breastfed Michael for nine months, and almost immediately after she quit breastfeeding, she became pregnant with our second child. In May of 1982 Katie was born. When Colleen got pregnant with Katie, it was an easy detection. Almost right after she conceived, her breasts became very sore and painful, and that was how we knew she was pregnant.

Katie was the easiest child for Colleen to give birth to. Even though she was late and went past her due date, Colleen would ride around the yard on a riding lawn mower, hoping it would help her water break. Eventually, it did, and once again we rushed to Lexington Hospital. They immediately took Colleen into the operating room, and before the doctor could even arrive, Katie was born. Our beautiful little girl arrived on May 19, 1982, exactly eighteen months after Michael was born. She was tiny, covered with a head full of hair, and had jaundice. Although Katie's birth was the easiest, she turned out to be the meanest of the four children. Everything was always for her, and she made sure she got her way. Each streak of meanness carried through Katie's whole life, remaining part of her personality well into adulthood, when it often felt as though anything I had was something she believed should belong to her as well.

One of the scariest days of my life came in August of 1983. Colleen had driven to Hastings to visit her mom and dad, taking along little Michael and Katie while she was seven months pregnant. I stayed back in Overton, never imagining how quickly the day would turn into one of the darkest moments of my life.

Colleen took the kids to a nearby park, where other family members were playing softball. The sun was shining, the game was lively, and everything felt normal. As she crossed the street with Katie on her hip and Michael's small hand clasped in hers, there was no reason to think danger was only steps away.

Just as they reached the other side, Michael looked up and saw his grandpa Jim walking toward them from across the road. His little heart leapt with excitement, and before Colleen could react, he slipped free of her hand and darted back toward his grandpa. At that very moment, a car came roaring down the street, driven recklessly by a drunk driver. In an instant, Michael was struck. The sound, the impact was every parent's worst nightmare. He was thrown to the pavement, his small body breaking under the force. The accident shattered his shoulder and fractured his skull.

At the time of the accident, I was at our house in Overton when the phone rang. On the line was Colleen's mother, her voice trembling. Her first words pierced me like a knife: "John, he is all right, but Michael got hit by a car. He is in the hospital." In that moment, my knees nearly buckled. My mind could barely hold on to the word "all right." Everything else felt like a blur of panic and fear.

I immediately jumped into my 1976 Corvette, my fastest vehicle, and tore out of the driveway. Normally the drive to Hastings took two hours, but I made it in less than an hour, the engine screaming as I pushed it to its limits. I did not care if the highway patrol saw me, I was not slowing down. Every second felt like an eternity. My only thought was getting to my son, to see him, to hold him, and to know he was still alive.

When Colleen became pregnant with our third child, Samantha, it felt like both an exciting and uncertain time. Our longtime doctor in Lexington, who had guided us through the births of Michael and Katie, had retired and moved to Arizona. That left Colleen with the challenge of finding a new doctor in Kearney, Nebraska. For the next eight months, with steady determination, she made the drive back and forth for her checkups, never complaining, though I knew the trips were tiring.

On the day her water broke, the weather turned rough, and I felt a nervous weight in my chest. All we had was our small Ford Fairlane, and I remember gripping the wheel, knowing I had to get Colleen to the hospital safely. We debated which route to take, and rather than risk Highway 30, we chose the interstate. It added about ten more miles to our trip, but at that moment, safety was far more important than speed.

As we pulled up to the emergency entrance at Good Samaritan Hospital in Kearney, the tension of the drive gave way to nervous laughter as we talked about names one last time. If the baby was a boy, I suggested calling him Mike, after Mike Rozier, the Nebraska football hero who had just won the Heisman Trophy. Colleen gave me that look only she could give, gently reminding me that we already had a Michael. Thankfully, it was a girl. The moment we knew it felt like everything had come together, we already had her name ready: Samantha Josephine Lecher.

Back home, life continued. One of the neighbor girls kindly stepped in to watch Michael and Katie until her mom and dad came from Hastings. I will never forget the relief of knowing they were cared for while Colleen was in labor. The next day, after Colleen gave birth, Bonita and Jim brought

Michael and Katie to the hospital. Seeing them walking wide-eyed and curious to see their mother and meet their new baby sister for the first time is a memory I will carry forever. In that moment, our family was complete, and my heart overflowed.

That same year, just before Christmas, and only a month after the birth of Samantha, Colleen received the heartbreaking news that her father had passed away. We were both asleep in our upstairs bedroom when, at about 3 a.m. in the morning, the phone rang. It was Steve Kindig, Colleen's older brother. He said to me, "John, can I talk to Colleen?" Immediately I knew something was wrong. When Colleen hung up the phone after talking to her brother, she turned to me with tears in her eyes and told me that her dad had passed away. Her voice trembled with grief as I pulled her into my arms, holding her tightly while she cried. The very next day, our family headed for Hastings. The drive to Hastings felt long and heavy with silence, each of us lost in thought, with only the children's voices occasionally piercing the stillness along the way.

For reasons I will discuss in other chapters, in 1984, with three children, Michael, Katie, and little Sammy still perched on Colleen's hip, we packed our furnishings into a 28-foot trailer van that belonged to Lecher Construction and headed west to California. It was a big move, a big decision, but also a wrong decision, one that would shape the next stage of our lives and mine forever.

We spent our first Christmas in California on Paulson Street. Colleen was nine months pregnant when the landlord unexpectedly sold the Paulson Street house from under us. Fortunately, he offered us another home just a block away. We shifted over quickly, trying to make it livable before the baby arrived. The landlord felt so guilty about evicting us so suddenly before the birth that he sent Colleen a bouquet of flowers.

On December 19, 1986, we went quickly to Fresno Community Hospital while our landlord's mother came over to watch the other three kids. This delivery seemed to take longer than the others. Instead of moving from the delivery room to the operating room, we stayed in the same room. Between contractions, Colleen kept asking me where the doctor was. At one point, I stuck my head out, looked to the right and then to the left, and did not see anyone, only what I thought must have been a janitor walking toward me wearing scrubs. A so-called janitor walked into our room, introduced himself with, "Hello, I am Dr. Brown," and then proceeded with his duty. Colleen looked at me, and in her eyes, I could see the question, was he really the doctor? She asked me if he was Black, and if he was, his accent gave it away. It was there that Megan took her very first breath, and we named our beautiful little girl Megan Elizabeth Lecher.

I do not know exactly where the name Megan came from, but Elizabeth came from an old friend of mine. Our children grew up in California. They attended Catholic school, spent countless afternoons playing soccer, made friends, went on many vacations, and were often looked upon as spoiled kids. All the while, they were finding their way far from Nebraska.

From our second home, we eventually moved farther east of Clovis, about six miles out, into a larger house. It was there that our family settled more firmly into California life, with the steady rhythms of school, soccer practices, and the daily demands of raising four children. Once again, Colleen found a much larger home on an acreage just east of Clovis. It was on an acreage, and it was beautiful. This house had five bedrooms, a large living room, a spacious family room, a big kitchen, and a large primary bedroom. Out back was a big yard, which we fenced in and later added a swimming pool. The kids loved that pool, and it quickly became the center of our family's summers. And since we had a substantial amount of cash to put down, we were able to buy it quickly.

While living in California, Colleen and I often enjoyed taking trips on Amtrak from Fresno to the San Francisco Bay Area. We would stay in downtown San Francisco, where the energy of the city always made us feel alive. I remember taking Colleen shopping at Nordstrom, where I picked out beautiful clothes for her. On one occasion, we made a stop at a local salon, and I insisted she treat herself to the works. She spent the afternoon there while I waited nearby, and when she finally stepped out, it took my breath away. Her hair was styled to perfection, her face glowed with fresh makeup, and she carried herself with the quiet confidence of a woman who knew she looked radiant. To me, she had never been more stunning. That night, as we walked together through the city streets and later dined in a fine restaurant, I could not take my eyes off her.

We also ventured farther along the West Coast, visiting Monterey and the surrounding areas. Strolling together along the Wharf, we breathed in the salty air mixed with the aroma of clam chowder drifting from the restaurants. We spent hours at the famous Monterey Bay Aquarium, marveling at the sea life, watching the playful sea otters, and being mesmerized by the giant kelp forest swaying gently in the water. The rhythm of the ocean, the cries of the seagulls, and the sight of boats rocking in the harbor created a backdrop of peace and wonder.

It was in those moments that I realized just how deeply I loved her. I knew, without a doubt, that if she had ever left me, I could not live without her. She was not just the woman by my side; she was the very center of my world.

Colleen's sister Barb lived east of Los Angeles. On many occasions, Colleen made the trip there with Michael as her guide. Before setting out, we would spread the map across the table, carefully tracing the highways and side roads that would take us through the sprawl of Los Angeles. With Michael as her guide, the drive felt less intimidating, and he often pointed out landmarks and shortcuts that helped make the long journey easier.

While in California, we started four-wheeling, both at Pismo Beach and at San Felipe, Mexico, which is part of Baja California. Each kid had their own four-wheeler, and I had a dune buggy. We really enjoyed going out to Pismo Beach in our RV pulling a trailer full of four wheelers.

About a year after Megan was born, Colleen became pregnant again. It was Colleen's sixth time in her life. About three months into the pregnancy, she began to bleed. In a rush of fear, we drove straight to Fresno Community Hospital and checked her into the emergency room, praying everything would be all right. Waiting for us was Dr. Brown, the same calm, steady doctor who had delivered Megan, and was ready to assist Colleen with whatever needed to be done. His reassuring presence steadied us during overwhelming uncertainty. Nazi, a good friend of mine, and his wife, Howla, who happened to be a pediatrician, met us at the hospital and stayed with us the entire evening. Their support meant the world to us, helping ease the long hours of waiting and worry with just a little less fear.

Shortly after Colleen's miscarriage, the doctor advised her that it would not be safe for her to carry another child. The walls of her uterus had become dangerously thin. It was heartbreaking news, but also a turning point. After a long talk, Colleen and I made the difficult decision that she would have her tubes tied. It was not the future we had once dreamed of, but it was the choice that gave her the best chance to protect her health. It was sad knowing that we could no longer have any more children.

Life moved forward. The kids grew up attending Cathedral of the Rising Christ, while Colleen poured herself into coaching track and tennis at one of the Clovis schools. At home, we installed a large swimming pool and landscaped the backyard. The kids learned to swim quickly, spending endless summer days splashing and laughing in the water. Those were golden times, our little oasis of joy and peace.

Then, in what felt like an instant, everything came crashing down. The company's financials were crumbling, and I made choices I should never have made. One day, while Colleen and the kids were in Nebraska visiting my mom and dad, I was in Las Vegas working from a small office when the federal government in California indicted me on mail fraud. I had long feared that day might come, but when it did, the weight was unbearable. Colleen desperately called me after a friend read an article from the Fresno Bee over the phone. She was scared.

From there, life began to unravel like a row of dominoes. Colleen and I filed for personal bankruptcy, and not long after, she gave me an ultimatum: either we moved back to Nebraska, or she would take the kids and go home alone. She was exhausted with my mistakes, my self-imposed problems, but she also told me she would stand by me through it. Afterward, she said we would decide whether our marriage could survive or if it was truly over.

We moved back to Lexington, Nebraska, where our life together first began when we were young, and where we had started from nothing. But things were not the same. We had sold our farmhouse only about four years earlier, and now we had no money, no jobs, no home and were living on public assistance. With no other option, we moved into a two-bedroom apartment in a low-income development. It was hugely different from the home and life we had once built, and the change weighed heavily on both of us.

All of this unfolded during the start of the O.J. Simpson trial. Day after day, I lay on the sofa watching every moment of it. At the time, I did not realize I was so deeply depressed, but later I came to see just how much it had consumed me. Still, we did what we could to survive. Colleen found a job at the Lexington newspaper, while I tried to pick up small construction projects while facing the looming court hearing back in Fresno.

One Saturday, Katie, and I went to a soccer tournament in Omaha. On the way back, I picked up a Lincoln Journal Star and flipped to the hiring section. There it was: Cathedral of the Rising Christ in Lincoln Catholic school was looking for a health and physical education teacher. I knew instantly that if Colleen applied, she would get the job. She was perfect for it, a good Catholic girl from Hastings, Nebraska, with a respected Irish priest as a friend. She applied, and sure enough, she was hired.

We could not leave Lexington fast enough. Colleen had gone to Lincoln a week earlier to start her new job, staying with friends. I packed up the kids and followed her. After spending a couple of days with Nancy in Geneva, we finally found temporary housing and began to settle into a new rhythm.

Back in Fresno, I pled guilty to one count of mail fraud and was sentenced to fifteen months at the federal prison camp in Yankton, South Dakota, where I could at least be closer to my family. During that time, Colleen carried the weight of supporting the family entirely on her salary. To make ends meet, we downsized into a smaller, more affordable house doing whatever we could to keep the family afloat. Luckily for us Colleen landed a public-school teaching job in Lincoln that paid somewhat more than she was making at the Catholic school.

When I was released on December 24, 1996, Colleen picked me up so I could make it home in time for Christmas Eve. Soon after, I found a job in Omaha working as an estimator. When I brought home my first paycheck, the kids were overjoyed. They said it felt like we were rich again. For the first time in years, we had extra cash. But deep down, I was not happy. I hated working for someone else. I knew I needed to be my own boss again.

That is when I decided to take a risk. I borrowed money from my son Michael's trust, money he had received from his car accident, and bought about thirty used pop machines from the University of Nebraska for $30 apiece. Over the next couple of months, I sold every one of them for about $400 each. That gave me the money that I started Midwest Demolition with. Colleen wanted nothing to do with it. She refused to sign any papers and made it clear she was not interested. It was my burden to carry, and my chance to rebuild.

As Midwest Demolition grew, we bought a new home on Old Dominion

Road in a pristine part of Lincoln. This time, it was not Colleen who found the house, it was Megan and me. We drove through neighborhoods until we spotted the right one, a quiet street lined with tall trees and well-kept lawns. It felt like a fresh start, a place where we could begin to breathe again after so many years of uncertainty. Colleen did not even see it until after we had already bought it, which said about how much trust she had left in me at that point.

As the years rolled on, Midwest Demolition gave us a steady living. We began traveling again and slowly marrying off our daughters. For a while, life felt stable, almost bright again. Colleen and I traveled every year. We traveled to Spain on several occasions. We also traveled to Europe, Cancún, Mexico, Vancouver, Thailand, Singapore, Hong Kong, Canada, and Cabo San Lucas. We went to Alaska to do deep-sea fishing with friends. We went wherever we wanted, chasing our adventure. Colleen did not realize it then, but we drove though those vacant lots where I currently own a home in Playa De Carman.

My most memorable trip with Colleen was over a three-year period when, we shipped our Harley-Davidson to Paris, France in 2002, where we planned on traveling from France down to Spain, and we would meet our kids in Madrid. The kids spent the next 30 days having the most wonderful time one could have with my family and their cousins.

In 2003, we decided to ride our Harley-Davidson motorcycle to Tangier, Morocco, to see how far we could travel down the coast of Africa. In 2004 we shipped our Harley-Davidson back to Lincoln. Nebraska.

Our final trip together to Europe together was in 2010 when we decided to ship our 2009 Jeep Sahara along with a matching trailer to Amsterdam, with the goal of driving as far as we could. My dream was to make it all the way to Thailand. Colleen only made it partway, as far as Hungary, before deciding to return home. I pressed on, determined to keep going, eventually reaching Kazakhstan.

But the downfall of our marriage had already begun. Whenever Colleen and I fought, it was not a knock-down, drag-out fight, it was more of a cold-shoulder, do-not-talk-to-each other kind of fight, which absolutely drove me nuts. Throughout our marriage, Colleen usually slept in the bedroom, while I often slept on the sofa or in my La-Z-Boy chair in my den. It left me feeling alone, even inside my own home. We were not happy with each other, nor getting along the way we once did. For the previous two years, I had even contemplated filing for divorce, by now we were not making love very often. I chose not to file because I felt responsibility for Colleen, supported her, and made sure she completed her master's degree in psychology, since she wanted to start her own business.

Sometime in the spring of 2014, I told Colleen that I was going to Playa del Carmen because I wanted to make an offer on a lot there. Once I made the offer on the lot, I took a quick side trip to Cuba, but then I lied to Colleen about that trip. Colleen eventually figured it out. She suspected that I had gone to Cuba again, and she thought I had a girlfriend down there. The truth was that I had gone to Cuba, but I did not have a girlfriend, nor was I looking for one.

Construction on the new second home began in July of 2014, and I made several trips down to Playa del Carmen during that time. Often, I would also take a side trip to Cuba. I always asked Colleen if she wanted to go with me, but I knew in my heart that she would not. In a way, which gave me a sense of relief, more of a relief, because it meant I could make the trip without the tension that always seemed to come with her presence.

Summer turned into fall of 2014, and things between Colleen and me continued to deteriorate. After I started building the new house, she told me flat out that she would never move down to Mexico. That November, we attended one of my daughter Megan's friend's weddings in Lincoln, and it was there that the last picture of Colleen and me together was ever taken. In that photograph, Megan stood with us, like a referee, as if she were holding the fragile peace between her parents.

It was the stupidest decision I ever made in my life. I chose to go to Cuba right after Colleen told me our sexual relationship had ended. It was just after Christmas and right before our anniversary. On top of it all, I intentionally refused to call Colleen on our anniversary, the first time that had ever happened. Looking back, I know I should have stayed home and tried to work things out with her instead of running away. Instead, I ran from the pain, not realizing that in doing so, I was running straight into the greatest loss of my life.

Things between Colleen and me were already strained, and deep down I could feel the distance growing like a shadow over our marriage. When she told me there would be no more sex between us, I should have known then that something more was behind it, that she might have already been talking to an attorney. Based on the timing of when she filed for divorce, I have always believed those conversations were already happening before I ever left for Cuba. That knowledge makes my choice to go feel even more reckless, as if I had walked blindly into the storm and sealed my own fate before I even knew it. For years I always thought that Colleen married me not out of love, but more so out of pity.

The decision I made to leave cost me the love of my life. I was not a good husband, and she was a great wife. It was a moment of weakness, an escape that turned into a permanent wound, one I will carry for as long as I live.

On the way back from Cuba, I had a connecting flight through Toronto, Canada. The moment I switched my phone back on, my screen lit up with message after message that had not been able to reach me while I was gone. And then came the one that shattered me: a text from Colleen telling me not to come home because she had already filed for divorce. Standing there in that airport, surrounded by strangers hurrying to their gates, I felt as if the entire world had gone silent. My heart raced, and tears burned in my eyes, but there was no one to turn to, no one to understand the weight of the words that had just destroyed me.

I still had to fly from Toronto back to Lincoln, Nebraska, with all of that on my mind. It was the longest flight of my life. Trapped in my seat, I stared out the window into the dark sky, replaying everything in my head. I knew that what I was returning to was no longer the life I had left behind.

Back at the office, the reality closed in even harder. I was at my desk, trying to push through the fog in my mind, when the sheriff walked in and handed me the divorce papers. In that instant, my world collapsed. The cold official envelope felt heavier than stone, heavier than anything I had ever carried. I took it upstairs to the apartment, shut the door, and finally let it out. I cried until I could not breathe, until my chest ached and my body trembled. I cried until there was nothing left inside me but emptiness.

That was the moment I knew I had lost Colleen forever, gone because of the foolish choice that I made. And no matter how much I wished I could take it back, there was no going back. Yet I blame myself more for not making a bigger effort to fix the problem.

Colleen had no justification for filing the divorce when she did. I was not having an affair with any gals in Cuba. However, she did have justification for filing for divorce for the affairs she did not know about.

While writing this chapter about Colleen, I also reminisce about the past thirty-eight years: from the first day I met her at the union, to skiing trips together, to the joy of buying our farmhouse, to holding our first baby in our arms, to the Amtrak ride we took to San Francisco, and the drives we made out to the coast. And the trips overseas. Still the memories bring tears to my eyes even now. It has been ten years since we separated, yet the ache of her absence still feels fresh, as if no time at all has passed. Colleen, if you ever read this, you will always be the love of my life.

32

My CHILDREN

Colleen and I were blessed with four wonderful children: Michael John, Katie Marie, Samantha Josephine, and Megan Elizabeth. Michael, Katie, and Samantha were born in Nebraska, while Megan was born in California. Each one brought their own personality, laughter, and challenges, shaping our journey as parents in ways we could never have imagined.

Each of their middle names carried special meaning. Michael's middle name, John, was my own, a reflection of the bond between father and son. Katie's middle name, Marie, came from her mother, Colleen. Samantha Josephine was named after Colleen's grandmother, Josephine Beriger, and Megan Elizabeth's middle name came from an old friend of mine. A story that I will explain later. Those choices were deliberate, connecting our children to the people and memories that shaped our lives.

From the beginning, Colleen and I made it a priority that each of our children earn a good education. As young parents while we still lived in Overton, Nebraska, we set up a checking account deduction for each of the kids of $50 a month for their college education. We acquired $64,000 in savings, but when times got tough, we had to cash them in to survive in California. I told Colleen that I would find a way to pay for their education when the time came.

Michael John and Katie Marie pursued degrees in business from the University of Nebraska. Samantha Josephine studied social work and received a two-year degree from Southeast Community College, then followed up by earning a four-year degree from Wayne State College, all while raising three kids. Megan Elizabeth followed her passion for interior design. Education gave them the tools to build their own paths, and we remain proud of the dedication each one showed in reaching their goals. All four of the kids eventually walked down the aisle with diplomas in hand, and each one of them asked me the same question: "Hey Dad, what are you giving me for graduation?" I told each the same thing: "I just gave you your college degree with a debt-free future." We managed to pay their way through college without going into debt.

Katie Marie went on to build a career in business for herself. Samantha Josephine became a manager at the Nebraska Regional Center, where her compassion and leadership skills made a lasting difference. Megan Elizabeth works as a plan reviewer for the City of Lincoln, recognized for her mindfulness and her fairness in treating everyone equally. Michael John, on the other hand, chose a more complicated path that included business and theater a mixture that brought both pride and frustration over the years. Of all the kids, Katie was by far the boldest and most defiant of them all.

Colleen and my four children, however, claimed to have another son and brother, which I have never accepted as my own. His name was Antonio Taylor, a young Black man whom Colleen met on the track and brought home like a stray dog. She chose to bring him into her life around the age of fifteen, when she was coaching at Lincoln High. Antonio was originally from St. Louis, where he grew up surrounded by the mentality of the hoods and gangsters of that city from an early age. With my marriage to Laura, I gained two stepchildren: Jonathan Sanchez-Villagoma and Stephanie Sanchez-Villagoma. Both are from Mexico, and their presence has brought new dimensions and bonds into my family life. Jonathan is the older of the two. Jonathan is married to Jenny, and they have one son, Geovani. We call him Geo. Stephanie, who we call Fanny, is married to Beto, and they have one son called Nicholas, who we call Nico. They are all wonderful and treat me as if I was the real father and grandfather.

Michael John: Of all my children, Michael John was by far the smartest of the four. He was also very conniving and always wanted to make a fast buck. From about the age of twelve, when he went to Clovis Lake, only a couple of blocks from our house in California, it became clear that he had a sharp mind and a natural ability to think ahead, setting him apart from his siblings.

At Clovis Lake, Michael John found a way to make money by collecting abandoned inflatable inner tubes and reselling them to the people waiting in line. Each time, he doubled his money, showing both creativity and business instincts even at an early age. That early glimpse into his entrepreneurial side hinted at the direction his life might take later, though not always in the ways I would have hoped.

As he grew older, Michael's independence sometimes worked against him. Independence ran through all my children, but in Michael's case, it came with a defiant edge that both impressed and frustrated Colleen and me.

Katie Marie: Katie was our second child and, in her own ways, the most driven. She was born in Nebraska during a time when Colleen and I were still building our lives and businesses. From an early age, Katie Marie had a keen sense of independence and ambition.

During her school years, Katie Marie was known for her determination and charm. She had a knack for making friends easily and could talk her way through almost any situation. In high school, she worked hard at whatever job she held while maintaining good grades, always keeping her eye on the future. After earning her degree in business, she carved out her own career working for Kiewit Corporation before coming back to Nebraska with her fiancé and then started working for me at Midwest Demolition.

Katie Marie worked at Midwest Demolition for sixteen years as president and controller, where she was deeply involved in the company's operations and once appeared to be the successor to inherit it. However, things changed after internal conflicts, and she eventually was let go. Still, Katie's resilience carried her forward. She went on to build a life centered around her four children, Madison, Hardin, Avery, and Ruby, all wonderful kids who brought her joy and grounded her in ways that business never could. I gave Katie not only a four-year degree but 16 years of experience and growth that a twenty-two-year-old would never get anywhere else.

Samantha Josephine: Samantha Josephine, our third child, was anything but a peacemaker. She was the hothead of the four, quick to speak her mind. She never shied away from confrontation and made sure her voice was heard. But behind that fiery attitude was strength, conviction, and a determination to stand her ground no matter who she was up against.

Her passion for helping others led her to pursue a degree in social work. She began her career working with the elderly and eventually rose to the position of manager at the Nebraska Regional Center. Her ability to manage conflict and speak directly, even when others avoid it, made her well-suited for the job. People respected her because she did not sugarcoat the truth, and in her own way, that honesty became her strength.

Samantha carries a no-nonsense attitude, but beneath that rough edge lies loyalty and heart. She is a resolute employee for the State of Nebraska and a devoted mother of three children, Christian, Tanner, and Bryson. Her husband, Jake, has stepped up to be both a solid father and a partner, making tough decisions and providing balance to Samantha's fiery spirit. Together, they have built a life that works, one shaped by honesty, grit, and a touch of chaos.

Megan Elizabeth: Born in California, Megan Elizabeth's arrival marked a new chapter in our family's story. She was the youngest of the four and grew up surrounded by the energy of her older siblings. From the start, she had an artistic eye and a natural sense of style that set her apart.

Megan worked at Midwest Demolition during her college years, and I gave her a flexible schedule so she could study and complete her coursework while still earning a paycheck. It was during those years that she met Adam Talbott, who has now been with me for twenty years and has become both a trusted employee and her husband. Megan has built a strong future with the City of Lincoln, where her creativity and professionalism continue to open new doors for her.

Together, Megan and Adam have three wonderful children, Reed, Nora, and Judah, who light up their world. Megan balances family and career with the same steadiness she showed as a young girl, and I take extraordinary pride in the woman and mother she has become.

Reflection: All my children are fiercely independent, each carving their own path in life. Sometimes that independence brought tension, but it also gave them strength. Watching them grow, through mistakes, successes, marriages, and parenthood, has been both humbling and rewarding.

Our children have been both our teachers and our greatest blessings. Each one has carried us through distinct stages of life, adding depth and meaning to our family story. As parents, we may not have done everything perfectly, but we gave them roots and wings. And in the end, that is all any parent can truly hope for.

33

MILAGROS

At ninety-two years old, my mother carried herself with the unpredictability of youth. At times, she could act like a spirited sixteen-year-old, full of spark and mischief, quick to laugh, and just as quick to stir things up. Yet beneath that playfulness ran a streak of iron will, stubborn enough for not just one mule, but two combined. I do not ever remember my mother apologizing to anybody for anything. That mix of youthful energy and immovable determination made her unforgettable, sometimes exasperating, and always uniquely herself.

I always told my mom she was going to live to be over one hundred years old. With her fire, her humor, and that unshakable stubbornness, it seemed less like a hope and more like a certainty. Even now, living alone on a five-acre parcel, she carries herself with independence and grit. She still hauls the laundry up from the basement washroom, mows her own grass, does all the weed-eating, shovels her own stone, and even shovels her own snow. Every day, she makes the twelve-mile drive into town, whether it is rain, shine, or snow, showing the same resolve that has defined her whole life.

My mother was the most wonderful, loving, and warmest mother one could ever ask for. She cared for her family with tenderness, wrapping every moment in care, and making even the hardest times bearable with the strength of her love. She always told me that she would do anything in her power to take care of her kids and make sure her children were cared for. And over the seventy-one years that I have known my mother, I have always believed that to be true.

Known to everyone in Chadron as Millie, she was also one of the best cooks anyone could ask for. Her kitchen was the honest heart of our home, always filled with the aromas of her meals, the warmth of her presence, and the comfort of knowing every dish was prepared with love. Many times, as

I grew up and came home from school, she would have fresh baked bread and cinnamon rolls waiting for us. She did that for years, and it became one of the sweetest comforts of my childhood. Even later, whenever she visited me no matter which part of the country I lived in, my wife would simply step aside and let her have the kitchen, for now, she was the boss. Millie's meals were not just food; they were love served on a plate.

Holidays and family gatherings were where Millie shined most. The table always seemed to overflow with her cooking, roasts, casseroles, and desserts that made every occasion feel special. Yet her greatest specialty never required a trip to the store. She could create a wholesome meal out of whatever was in the refrigerator, the freezer, or on the shelves. With a bit of ingenuity and her natural gift in the kitchen, she could whip up anything and feed a family of six without buying a single thing. She always made what her children and grandchildren liked best, and whenever she visited them, she brought enough to feed everyone. Her most famous gift was her banana bread, a simple loaf, but one that carried her love in every bite. Through it all, she remained determined to hold her family together and provide a better future for her children.

A beautiful Spanish lady with pitch black hair and a beautiful figure, she carried with her the toughness born out of survival. As a child, she lived through the Spanish Civil War, trotting across the countryside near her hometown of Puerto de Santa María, Spain, with her brother Juan, searching for anything they could find to eat. Those early struggles shaped her into a woman of remarkable strength, resilience, and resourcefulness — qualities that never left her, even decades later. My mother and her brother Juan were inseparable. For Tito Juan, as we called him, it was more than just a sibling, he was her lifelong companion and support. He helped my mother in those early years of childbearing, standing by her side when times were hardest and offering the kind of strength only a brother could give. Wherever Tito Juan went, my mother followed. It was as if they were spouses rather than siblings, bound together by loyalty, trust, and an unspoken devotion that lasted throughout their lives.

My mother had other siblings as well. Besides Tito Juan, she had a sister by the name of Teresa, whom we called Aunt Teresa, and another brother named Pepe. Together they formed a family bound not only by blood, but by the hardships and resilience of growing up in Spain during some of its most difficult years. They lived in a rundown Hacienda-style structure, with numerous families crowded throughout the building, each surviving the best they could with what little they had.

My mother received little formal education. In fact, my mom was thrown out of a Catholic school in the second grade by a nun, not for her honey-ness, but for her unruliness. After moving to the United States, she never did learn to read and write very well, although her English improved over time and she eventually spoke it well. What she may have lacked in schooling, she more than made up for in determination, resourcefulness, and common sense. She knew how to manage a household, raise her children, and face life's challenges with courage. Her wisdom came not from books but from experience, and it proved far more valuable in guiding her family and shaping the lives of those around her.

My mother married my stepfather, Robert Wayne Lecher, in Barcelona, Spain, where he was serving his last couple of years of his Navy enlistment around 1961–1962. At the beginning, my stepfather was a drunk, a womanizer, and physically abusive toward both my mother and me during those early years. It was a difficult and painful time, but my mother's strength and resilience never faltered. She married my stepfather not so much for love, for he was a true asshole, but for the hope of moving to the United States and creating a better life for her children, like so many other women with children from developing countries. Together, they had one child, my brother Bobby. My mother brought myself and my sisters, Maria and Millie, into the marriage. One child tragically died at birth.

My mother became a widow after nearly 60 years of marriage when dad no longer wanted to live. In 2017 my dad simply gave up and wanted to die. He chose to let go, leaving mom to face life without him. His passing marked the end of a difficult chapter, but it also revealed once again the depth of my mother's resilience as she continued with quiet strength, determined to keep going despite the loss.

My stepdad left my mother with a very small pension. When he retired from the federal government, he had her sign documentation that allowed him to receive a larger pension while he was alive, but it meant my mother would receive almost nothing after his death. As a result, she lived on a small pension, along with her Social Security.

My mother's entire life was devoted to her children. From her younger years in Spain to her later years in Nebraska. As a child, she endured war and hunger, learning resilience the hard way. In America, she raised a family and held it together through many hardship. She never had much in the way of money or possessions, but she carried within her a fierce determination to provide for her children and a heart that gave without limit. Her life was never easy, yet she bore every burden with grace, always putting the needs of her family before her own.

All four of her children built lives of independence, a reflection of the determination they inherited from her. Maria pursued a successful career in sales. Millie and her husband worked on the land, on their ranch outside of Chadron, living by the values of hard work and family. Bobby ran a store in downtown Denver, carving out his place in the heart of the city until he passed away. And I continued in my construction business, following the entrepreneurial drive that had always defined me. Each of us stood firmly on the foundation our mother had given us, strength, resilience, and the will to make our own way in the world.

Though she never said it aloud, my mother achieved her greatest goal: seeing her children live better lives than she had known. Each of us found our own path, built good homes, and earned a living through our own work. That quiet triumph was the legacy of her sacrifice and devotion and a life of hardship transformed into opportunity for the next generation.

In her later years, my mother's devotion extended well beyond her children. She became the heart of a much larger family, with more than forty-one grandchildren, great-grandchildren, and great-great-grandchildren to care for and worry about. Each of them carried a piece of her love and strength, and though she could no longer hold them all as close as she once had, her concern and pride reached the generations. Her influence lived on not only in her children's success, but in the countless lives that followed.

34

If You Only Knew

For a guy who never dated much, nor ever had a girlfriend in high school or in the Navy, I somehow turned into a bit of a Casanova afterward. In this chapter, I will talk about things I should never have done with the ladies. I will describe them only briefly, just enough to paint the picture, but never in a way that would hurt anyone's feelings.

When I first came home from the Navy, I bought a small old trailer on North Morehead, just two blocks north of Mom and Dad's house. It cost only five thousand dollars, but that little place was my kingdom, and I became the king of it right away. Not long after settling in, I started dating a girl named Deb, a local girl from the Hay Springs area who attended Chadron State College. We were on again and off again for about a year, more off than on.

Shortly after being released from the Navy and taking a job with the City of Chadron at the cemetery, I stopped by to see Eva, the owner of the local bar called the 77 Cave, a smoky little joint everyone simply referred to as *the Cave*. It was known for its go-go dancers, its music, and the late nights that never seemed to end. I told Eva I wanted to work nights and asked if she would let me a bartender. She smiled and said, "All right, you've got it."

The Cave really was a haven, a place where people drifted in after long days or bad nights, looking for company, laughter, or simply an escape. For me, it became a refuge of another kind. The music was loud, the lights dim, and the conversations easy. Anything could happen there and often did.

I met all kinds of gals: single students from Chadron State, waitresses trying to forget their shifts, and married women whose marriages had long gone stale. I wasn't looking for anything serious, and neither were they. Most of those short-lived flings faded as quickly as they started, rarely lasting more than a week.

Deb later introduced me to her friend Brenda, who was five years older than I was. Brenda stopped by my place occasionally for about a year. Her husband managed the movie theater in downtown Chadron and worked evenings most of the time, which made it easy for her to visit when I wasn't tending bar.

Then life took its usual turn, and we drifted apart. Thirty years passed before Brenda's name surfaced again. My daughter Katie was speaking with an administrator at a company we had done business with for over fifteen years. When the woman asked Katie her name, and Katie answered "Katie Lecher," the woman paused and said, "Do you have family from Chadron?" When Katie added, "Yes, my dad's name is John Lecher Zapata," the woman nearly fell off her chair.

It was Brenda. All those years, she had handled our paperwork as the contract administrator, and neither of us knew. Time had changed us both, but there was no mistaking who she was when we eventually crossed paths again. Life has a strange way of circling back on itself.

Eventually, I decided it was time to move on. I transferred to Kearney State College because I knew that if I stayed in Chadron, I would never get anywhere. At the end of the fall semester, I quit my cemetery job, told Eva she would need a new bartender, and loaded my life into my '66 Chevy Impala. Shortly after New Year's Day, I headed east toward Kearney.

Once settled into my dorm at Kearney State, I laid eyes on **Colleen Kendig**, an employee at the college who was also a student working her way through school. I didn't know it then, but meeting Colleen would change the direction of my entire life.

Two years later, we were married on December 29, 1978. I loved her deeply, but I didn't always know how to express my feelings, and that often bothered her. I was still young and proud and learning what it meant to truly share a life with someone.

In the summer of 1977, I met Julie, a local girl home from Arizona State University. She was polished, well-spoken, Catholic, and clearly raised with money. We met at a discotheque called the Back Lot in Kearney. She was there with her boyfriend, also from Kearney and attending ASU. I asked her to dance, and she agreed. Her boyfriend was deep in conversation at the bar.

I don't remember exactly how Julie and I ended up seeing each other regularly, whether it started that night or later when I picked her up after her parents had gone to bed. She always treated me like I was from "the other side of the tracks," especially with my gangster look and Afro. Colleen used to think that way sometimes too.

Julie and her friend Becky often went to the Fort Kearney Inn on Wednesdays to listen to a band, and I would meet them there. Becky was fond of one of the band members, who happened to be married. Julie and I took trips to Johnson Lake near Lexington and even planned a road trip to the Black Hills.

One day, I waited all afternoon for Julie's call to finalize the trip. The phone never rang. Frustrated, I almost gave up, until I realized the phone wasn't hung up properly. The moment I placed it correctly on the receiver, Julie called, furious that I hadn't answered. Within hours, I was in North Platte picking her up, and we were off to the Black Hills for a couple of nights.

Summer was ending, and Julie soon returned to ASU. The night before she left, she pinned a Dear John letter to my wall saying the sun had finally set on our relationship. I flew to San Diego, then hitchhiked back through Tempe, hoping to see her, only to be told to "keep hitchhiking." Later I learned she had dropped out of ASU and moved to Denver. Something had happened between us, but I never figured out what.

Years later, while attending an AGC convention in Lincoln, a friend and I went out for a drink and met two women who worked at the Nebraska State Penitentiary, a nurse and a guard. The guard recognized Colleen from a summer camp years earlier. The nurse and I hit it off, and before long it was three in the morning.

When we returned to the Holiday Inn, there sat Colleen, five or six months pregnant with Katie, waiting for me in the lobby chair. Her eyes said everything before her mouth did. I had no good answers. The shame of that moment stayed with me a long time.

My relationship with Elizabeth, the nurse, lasted about thirteen years, even after I moved to California. She wanted me to divorce Colleen, which I told her I would never do. As she approached her mid-thirties, she became determined to have a child. She told me that if she hadn't given birth by thirty-eight, it would be my responsibility to "make it happen." That is when the relationship ended.

Elizabeth stayed in Lincoln, built a reliable professional name, later had two sons, and divorced their father. When she learned I was divorced, she reached out, wanting to reconnect. I don't think she ever completely got over me.

Colleen always believed I had a relationship with my secretary, Christy. That never happened. I never even came close. But the more she questioned me, the more I realized how little trust remained in our marriage, and that hurt me deeply. After leaving the Navy, I refused to be with any professional lady because I never wanted to catch something and bring it home to my wife.

Although Colleen often suspected that I was meeting women on trips, the truth is I wasn't. I met a few ladies along the road, some who later became Facebook friends, but nothing more. Everything stayed fine until I met **Alexandra in Kazakhstan**. I promised her a trip somewhere, one of those things a man should never promise when life is already complicated.

While working in Puerto Rico, I became good friends with a taxi driver named Suni. She later introduced me to her daughter Tracy, who loved sushi. After my divorce, Tracy visited me in Mexico for a while. Later, she joined me for the 2016 Sturgis Motorcycle Rally. That same week, we watched Maggie Malone throw the javelin in the Rio Olympics.

Then came Lysandra and Sylvie, two young Cuban women who eventually moved to the United States. I didn't become involved with Lysandra until after Colleen told me she would never have sex with me again. To me, that meant our marriage was over. She never had the courage to say the words "I want a divorce," but that was what she meant.

I knew what the Cuban gals wanted all along, but their beauty, charm, and fun attitudes kept me around. I took Lysandra to Cartagena and later to Quito, Ecuador, where we visited the monument at the equator. I told her I wasn't looking for anything permanent, so she brought Sylvie into the picture. The three of us later traveled together to Bogotá, then met again in Las Vegas and New Orleans after they had both come to the U.S. Their husbands even knew about our past friendship.

Then, in January 2017, I met **Laura Sánchez-Garcia**, and everything changed. That was the end of all my wandering. For the first time in years, I felt alive again, settled, calm, and at peace. Laura is happy-go-lucky, dancing her heart out in the family room every morning. When she found out I was drafting a book, she fired up the computer, and I started writing again. We have been together eight years now, and I have enjoyed every moment.

I never knew how difficult life had become living with a deeply depressed woman for forty years, until I experienced what real happiness felt like again.

35

Laura
Breath of Fresh Air

It has been at least eight years since I last wrote here, and so much has happened. Since my divorce, my life has changed in ways I could never have imagined. I bought a home in Mexico and later married Laura Sánchez García, whom I met at Liverpool in Playa del Carmen. We were married on March 30, 2020, right in the middle of the COVID-19 epidemic, and again on November 27, 2021, in Playa del Carmen, for the benefit of her family.

Laura became an American citizen on March 7, 2025. But in between those milestones, life tested me. On March 18, 2022, I suffered a major stroke that drastically altered the course of my life. It left the left side of my body paralyzed and confined me to a wheelchair. Neither my left arm nor leg work well enough to be of any real use, and I rely on a catheter and a morning caregiver who comes each day to help me bathe, dress, and stretch my limbs. Still, I consider myself fortunate, to be alive, to be married to Laura, and to have a reason to keep writing.

My relationship with Colleen had not been going well for years. By 2014, I had begun building a house in Mexico and traveling there frequently. During that time, I visited Cuba, where I met two women, Lisandra and Sylvie, who, looking back, clearly took advantage of me for my money. I met Lisandra on one of my early trips through Central America. On a flight from Costa Rica to Belize, I met two women, Stephanie from Australia and Shawnee from Lake Tahoe, Nevada, along with an American expatriate living in Costa Rica. Each of us was headed to Belize for our own reasons. The Australian women seemed like free spirits.

When I reflect on those years, I realize I was searching, not just for companionship but for a fresh start. I had already been through enough disappointment and loneliness to know that I did not want temporary affection. Colleen filed for divorce in January 2015, and by then, neither of us was happy. It was time for both of us to move on. I will revisit more about that chapter of my life later, but for now, what mattered was that I found peace in Mexico.

I purchased a house in Playa del Carmen in 2014, completed it in 2015, and began living there full-time that July. I flew back to Lincoln periodically but found myself increasingly drawn to Mexico — the warmth, the sea breeze, and the sense of simplicity it offered. My only concern was medical care. I knew that if anything serious ever happened, I might not get the treatment I would need. During that time, I dated women casually. Once, a woman named Tracy came to visit from Puerto Rico. That became complicated. Her mother was furious because I had dated her, too, on a previous trip. Eventually, I decided I wanted more stability. I needed someone who was compatible with me, someone who could care for me as I would for her.

That someone turned out to be Laura Sánchez García, who worked in the bedding department at the Liverpool department store in Playa del Carmen. It was January 2017, and I had just returned to Mexico after spending Christmas alone in Lincoln. My Cuban girlfriend had disappointed me deeply, she had lied, stood me up, and, like others before her, only wanted my money.

I was not looking for love. I had simply gone to Liverpool to replace a missing bedspread. My property manager had called while I was in Lincoln to say that my house had been broken into. The thieves stole my large-screen television, and in the process, used one of my bedspreads to wrap it as they carried it out. So, I walked into Liverpool looking for a replacement.

I had been divorced only recently and was through with my Cuban relationships. I was ready, though I did not know it, to find something genuine again. Liverpool was my usual store for household shopping, and each time I visited, I had noticed a blonde woman standing near the escalator on the second floor. She worked in the bedding department and always greeted people with a bright smile. I had seen her two or three times before but never thought of asking her out. She was simply part of the scenery, until that day.

Throughout my time in Mexico, I had avoided dating Mexican women. In my mind, I had pictured them all as short, dark-haired, and Mayan-looking. But Laura broke that stereotype entirely. She was beautiful, confident, and carried herself with a calm grace that immediately caught my attention. When she asked if she could help me, I explained my situation, the stolen bedspread, and showed her a photo of the pattern I wanted to replace. She searched diligently through the shelves, checking every label. When she could not find it, she promised to contact other Liverpool stores and have one shipped if possible. She asked me to come back in a few days.

When I returned, she greeted me warmly and told me the truth: the design had been discontinued. The only solution, she said, was to buy two new matching bedspreads for my twin beds. That is exactly what I did, and I left the store with two new covers, and an image of her that stayed in my mind long after I got home.

A few days later, I returned to the store with the excuse of buying new sheets for my primary bedroom. I did not really need them; I just wanted to see Laura again. But she was not there that day; it was her day off. I left disappointed, only to return later in the week. This time, she was there, smiling as always. I asked for king-size sheets, good ones, even though I already had plenty. I was not there for linens; I was there for her. After paying, I finally gathered the courage to ask her out. She smiled politely and said no.

But fate intervened. Her best friend, Sofía, who had been standing nearby, grabbed my phone, entered Laura's number, and told me to call her later that night. Laura said she would be home after eleven, so at 11:30 I called. To my surprise, she answered, and we agreed to meet that Saturday at Telcel, the local phone company, a neutral, safe place for a first meeting.

That Saturday everything changed. We spent the entire day together, first at my home in El Cielo, then later driving up to Cancún for lunch and shopping. Laura lived in a small upstairs apartment with her daughter, Fanny, who was nineteen at the time. Her son, Jonathan, was twenty-four and had recently returned to Playa from Mexico City, where he had been living with his father. Laura had left her husband after twenty-five years of marriage. He had fallen into addiction, draining their savings and neglecting the family. By the time she moved to Playa del Carmen, she was ready to rebuild her life, just as I was rebuilding mine.

She was cheerful, kind, and full of laughter, the kind of person who could brighten a room just by walking into it. Our first road trip together was to Mérida, with stops in small villages along the way. It was in one of those villages that I bought her the first piece of jewelry I ever gave her, a gold necklace with a small cross. Laura and I were in no hurry. It was not until Valentine's Day that we shared our first kiss, sitting in my Jeep before going out to dinner. That night, as I picked her up, she confided in me about a small scar from an emergency surgery during Jonathan's birth. She told me because she wanted to be honest, because she somehow knew that our connection was real.

After months, I asked her to move in with me. She hesitated, understandably. She had been hurt before and was afraid of losing her independence. Her apartment was modest, only $200 a month, but it represented her safety net. Still, love and trust grew between us, and eventually, she said yes.

As we settled into life together, Laura's family became part of mine. Fanny, Jonathan, Beto, and their baby son Nico all applied for tourist visas to the United States. Only Laura was approved, perhaps because of her age and stability. That marked a new chapter for both of us, a shared life between two countries, between two worlds.

36

My Stroke

It was about seven o'clock in the morning on March 18, 2022. I had spent the night sleeping in my lift chair, something I often did when I was not feeling my best. When I got up, I went to the kitchen to pour a glass of orange juice for myself. My sugar level had been dropping, and I knew I needed something sweet to bring it back up. After drinking the juice, I began to feel strange, something was not right. Within minutes, by 7:10 a.m., I knew exactly what was happening. I was having a stroke. I did not hesitate; I called the paramedics right away and told them to get there as fast as possible.

After calling the paramedics, I called Laura and Christian so they could come up and be with me, for I knew something was seriously wrong. I even told 911 that I thought I was having a stroke. When the paramedics arrived, they asked if I could stand up and walk, and I thought I could. But as soon as I tried, I immediately collapsed. They caught me before I hit the ground, lifted me onto the gurney, and rolled me out to the ambulance. Foolish me, I did not realize then how critical every minute was, that the faster you reach the hospital and get the IV, the better your chances of recovery. I made the ambulance wait so Laura could get into the ambulance with them, causing a ten-minute delay that would have had an influence as to whether I lived or died. In either case, I wanted Laura to be with me.

When I got to the hospital, everything happened fast. The staff moved me quickly from the ambulance to the emergency room, taking scans of my head while setting up the IV. They started pumping clot-busting medication or TPA into me right away. I could see the urgency on their faces and hear the commotion around me, machines humming, nurses giving orders, doctors rushing from one side to another. Through it all, I stayed wide awake and completely alert, aware of every sound, every movement, and every word being spoken. As my family began arriving, I could sense their worry, but all I could do was hope that the medicine would start working before it was too late.

After the emergency room, they moved me into the intensive care unit to keep a close eye on me, until I was stable enough to transfer me to a regular room. The doctors and nurses monitored my blood pressure, heart rate, and brain activity around the clock. Those first nights were long and full of uncertainty, but I began to feel a little more stable each day. Once my condition leveled out, they transferred me to a regular hospital room, where the reality of what had happened started to sink in.

Once I was in intensive care, my mother showed up, even though I had asked everyone not to tell her because I knew she would worry drastically. Someone must have been heading to Lincoln, and my mother, being who she is, hopped in the car and came along. She spent the next six to eight weeks in Lincoln supporting Laura and helping her through a tough time. Every day, she came to visit me at the hospital, sitting by my side as I began my rehabilitation at Bryan West Hospital. Originally, I had been taken to Bryan East, but once my condition stabilized, they transferred me to Bryan West for the next phase of my recovery.

After I started my physical therapy, it was extremely difficult. My body resisted every command, and it took all the strength I had just to move an inch. The therapists pushed me daily, and though progress was slow, I refused to give up. When I finally returned home, I began making modifications so that it would be easier to get around the house. The Veteran's Administration was incredibly supportive, helping me with a handicap ramp and even covering the extra medical expenses that my insurance would not pay. Their assistance made all the difference in helping me adjust to my new reality.

As time went on, I grew stronger every day. Each sunrise felt like another small victory, another day without having another stroke. I continued to make improvements around the house to make life easier. One of the best things I ever did was a special bar built by Rivers Metal. I told Roger exactly how I wanted it to be made, and he had his son, who works at Rivers Metal, build it for me. The bar stands right next to my lift chair, and it has been a real lifesaver. It allows me to pull myself up safely and transfer into my wheelchair without anyone having to help. I even had another one installed in the garage so I could get into my Jeep Wagoneer on my own.

Although I had the financial capability to make life as easy as possible after being paralyzed, I still had to plan and organize everything carefully. I set up my home office surrounding my lift chair. On the left, I mounted my desktop computer; on the right side, I keep two iPads and two telephones. Everything I used to do, I can now do again without needing to move far. I was taught how to use my iPad and iPhone hands-free by utilizing Siri, giving voice commands for everything. That technology has truly given me back a sense of independence and control over my daily life.

The realization that I would never walk again hit me harder than anything. I was 100 percent paralyzed on my left side, confined to a wheelchair, and forced to reimagine what the rest of my life would look like. But I was not ready to give up. I fought too many battles in my life, personal, professional, and physical, to surrender to this one.

After my stroke, my grandson Christian moved in full-time. He became my Uber, my para, my aid. Everything I needed, Christian was there to help. To take me to the doctor's appointment and after about a month a trip to the office. Although Christian has other issues in his life, he has been a lifesaver to me. I do not know what I would do without him.

Traveling is out of my plans as they once were, although I made it to Mexico, to my home there on a couple occasions until exceedingly difficult to get on and off the airplane, so I limit my trips. Laura has free reign to travel wherever she likes. She goes to Mexico several times a year and has traveled to Italy with her daughter as well as Paris and England. I travel through her eyes and voice.

There are issues that do not appear immediately after you stroke. In my case there was a swallowing problem, speech problem, and the worst of them all is urinary tract infection otherwise called UTI. I have had my share of them and on occasions I have had to spend time in the hospital, which is the last thing one ever wants to do, for care there is not as good as the care you get at home. I wish they could examine you in just a new home with the proper prescription.

I do the best I can with what I have available to me — my wife, my grandson the folks at the office, they all help me get through every day with whatever needs done. I am thankful to everyone for the help.

37

REFLECTING

IT HAS BEEN MORE THAN FIFTY YEARS since I first set out on the open road, chasing adventure across miles of landscapes and moments that would come to define my life. Looking back now, I would not change a single thing. Along the way, I picked up passengers like Mark Pallard, Connie Steinhauser from Canada, and Colleen Kindig from Hastings, Nebraska, each one leaving a mark on my journey. Together, Colleen and I built a life that included four wonderful children, countless memories, and a spirit of discovery that never faded.

I still remember Julie Hellman and the Black Hills trip that almost did not happen because the phone was not properly hung up, followed by hitchhiking across the United States just to see her one more time before returning to Nebraska to devote myself completely to the woman I truly loved, Colleen. Every mile, every stop, and every face along the way became part of the story that shaped who I am today.

There were the many short trips to Pismo Beach with my children, simple getaways that carried the same excitement as the longer journeys, like the drive to San Felipe, Mexico, where we took all the kids so we could ride our four-wheeler across the sand dunes and enjoy fish tacos for Thanksgiving. Those were the moments that made life feel alive when the laughter of my children filled the air and the ocean breeze carried a sense of endless possibility.

Then there was that unforgettable trip to the northwestern United States, the one where we drove all the way to Vancouver, Canada, for a single salmon. We were not really chasing the fish as much as the experience itself. It was never about catching the biggest salmon; it was about being able to say we had gone salmon fishing in Canada. The drive, the conversations, and the quiet moments along the water are what stayed with me most.

There were the side trips too, the quick getaways to Las Vegas, the family adventures to Disneyland, and the unforgettable train rides to San Francisco. I still remember those long trips from Hastings, Nebraska, all the way to Fresno, California, with four children in tow. Life felt full then, noisy, chaotic, and beautiful all at once. Those were the years when time moved slower, and every day carried its own little story.

Then came the years of business and building, the companies, the long hours, the triumphs, and the losses. From the dust and noise of demolition to the quiet weight of ownership and responsibility, I learned that every dream carries its own price. I built things that endured and others that did not, but what mattered most were the people beside me, the workers, the friends, and the partners who shared the ride. Together, we built more than buildings; we built trust, pride, and the satisfaction of hard, honest work.

And then came the devastating news, Colleen was leaving me, for reasons that I felt wrong, yet in time I came to see them as justifiable. In that moment, everything else, the children, the years together, the countless trips, flashed before my eyes in a single instant. It was the kind of heartbreak that makes a man grow quiet and reflective, forcing him to measure the weight of love and loss.

When I least expected it, a new breath of life entered my world. After my divorce from Colleen, I met Laura and her children. Life had shifted, but adventure was still calling. Together we traveled to Panama, Cuba, Mexico City, Las Vegas, and my beloved Barcelona, where my earliest memories had taken root. It felt as though the circle had closed, returning me to where my story began, but this time with older eyes, a gentler heart, and deep gratitude for every mile.

Through the years, my journeys took me far beyond the familiar borders of home. Europe became my second classroom, Spain, France, Italy, Germany, and Greece, all places where I found not only history and beauty but pieces of myself. Riding a motorcycle along the coast of Andalusia, walking the cobbled streets of Paris, and standing before the ancient ruins of Athens filled me with a sense of wonder that never left. Each trip reminded me that the world is vast, but somehow it always leads us back to who we truly are.

And then came Asia, another chapter entirely. From the busy streets of Bangkok to the temples of Cambodia and the towers of Singapore, I found both chaos and serenity. In Hong Kong and Tokyo, I witnessed the balance of tradition and progress, a lesson that mirrored my own life, the old and the new existing side by side. Traveling across those continents was not just sightseeing; it was soul-searching. Each place taught me something different — patience, humility, and the importance of stillness in a world that never stops moving.

Years later came a different kind of journey, the long road to recovery after my stroke on March 18, 2022. That experience assessed every ounce of strength I had left. Learning to move, to speak, and to live again were the hardest roads I have ever traveled, yet each challenge reminded me of what I still possessed: love, memories, and a life worth holding onto. There is a certain kind of wisdom that only pain can teach, and I learned that gratitude and endurance go hand in hand.

Now, as I grow older and my health weakens, I find myself with a new purpose. I must finish the book I have been working on for fifteen years, for I can sense that my last adventure, my final road trip, is slowly coming into view. There is no fear in that thought, only reflection and peace. When I look back upon it all, the roads, the oceans, the laughter, and even the pain, I know I have lived a life filled with purpose, movement, and love. For that, I am deeply grateful.

This year, I lost my good friend and fishing partner, Hugh. We fished together in Alaska and Cabo San Lucas alongside his wife Betty, who has also since left us. Then their Dana, who battles cancer, and whose wife, who suddenly passed last year after having suffered a stroke. Each of these losses has reminded me of the fragility of time and the strength of friendship. I have learned that the greatest gift in life is not what we achieve, but who we share it with.

I remember my little brother Bobby, so different from the rest of us, yet loved just the same. My father, Robert, is gone now. He simply decided it was time to go, leaving my mother to stand on her own and become the strong, resilient woman she always was. Her courage carried us through years of struggle, and her quiet strength is something I still draw upon today.

As I sit here today, I know the road behind me is far longer than the one ahead, but every turn, every mile, and every companion along the way has shaped a story worth telling, and that, more than anything, is the legacy I wish to leave behind. For in the end, it is not the destinations that matter most, but the hearts that travel beside us.

38

Obituary of John Lecher Zapata

John Lecher Zapata, age [___], of Lincoln, Nebraska, passed away peacefully on [date]. He was born in Puerto de Santa María, Cádiz, Spain, on March 1, 1954, and immigrated with his family to the United States in early 1962, where they made their home in Nebraska.

John's early years were filled with adventure, traveling across Europe and Asia. From his youth in Spain to journeys abroad and later throughout the United States, he developed a lifelong curiosity, independence, and resilience. He attended Chadron Public Schools and, after serving his country in the United States Navy, graduated from the University of Nebraska at Kearney.

A natural entrepreneur, John founded and operated several successful businesses, including Midwest Demolition, Cadiz Equipment, and Central Nebraska Housing Corp. His career spanned decades and reflected his vision, determination, and tireless work ethic.

More than his professional accomplishments, John cherished his family above all else. He was the devoted father of:

- Michael Lecher of Lincoln, Nebraska
- Katie Lecher-Cederberg and her husband, Chris, of Lincoln, Nebraska
- Samantha Lecher-Sorenson and her husband, Jake, of Lincoln, Nebraska
- Megan Lecher-Talbott and her husband, Adam, of Lincoln, Nebraska
- Stephanie "Fannie" Sanchez-Gomez and her husband, Beto, of Playa del Carmen, Mexico
- Johnathon Sanchez-Villa Gomez and his wife, Jenny, of Playa del Carmen, Mexico

John delighted in being a grandfather to twelve grandchildren: Christian Lecher, Madison Cederberg, Avery Cederberg, Ruby Cederberg, Tanner Gossard, Reed Talbott, Nora Talbott, Judah Talbott, Bryson Sorenson, Nicholas Sanchez-Villa Gomez, and Giovanni Sanchez-Villa Gomez. Each of them brought him immense joy and pride, and he loved spending time with them.

He was a loving husband to Laura Lecher Zapata, whom he married on March 30, 2020, and remained close to the mother of his children, Colleen Kindig Lecher, throughout his life.

Outside of work and family, John enjoyed many hobbies that reflected his creativity and curiosity. He had a great passion for building intricate dioramas and collecting metal toy soldier pursuits that showcased both his love of history and his eye for detail. He also loved news and kept up with the news and enjoyed sharing stories from his travels. John love to travel and once drove his 2009 Jeep Sahara from Amsterdam to the border of China. John's favorite band was Creedence Clearwater Revival, and their songs often accompanied his road trips and quiet evenings at home. Above all, he was a devoted fan of the Nebraska Cornhuskers and missed very few games throughout his lifetime.

John is survived by his wife, Laura Zapata; the mother of his children, Colleen Lecher; his twelve grandchildren; his sisters, Millie Wild of Chadron, Nebraska, and Maria Semiar of Denver, Colorado; his mother, Milagros Lecher of Chadron, Nebraska; and many beloved cousins who still reside in Spain.

He was preceded in death by his brother, Robert John Lecher of Denver, Colorado, and his father, Robert Wayne Lecher of Chadron, Nebraska.

A memorial service will be held at [location] on [date]. In lieu of flowers, the family requests that donations be made to a youth club of your choice.

John's life was one of perseverance, adventure, and love. He will be deeply missed and forever remembered by all who knew him.

www.ingramcontent.com/pod-product-compliance
Lightning Source LLC
Chambersburg PA
CBHW042047280426
43673CB00076B/264